THE GALLUP ORGANIZATION

JASON DOMINICAK
Partner

1000 Town Center
Suite 2450
Southfield, MI 48075 USA

Direct: (248) 936-4155
Mobile: (248) 514-1590
Fax: (248) 727-0047
jason_dominicak@gallup.com

12

THE ELEMENTS OF
GREAT MANAGING

12

THE ELEMENTS OF
GREAT MANAGING

by

Rodd Wagner and
James K. Harter, Ph.D.

Gallup Press
New York

Gallup Press
1251 Avenue of the Americas
23rd Floor
New York, NY 10020

Manufactured in the United States of America

First edition 2006

10 9 8 7 6 5 4 3 2 1

Library of Congress Control Number: 2006932004
ISBN - 10: 1-59562-998-X
ISBN - 13: 978-1-59562-998-2

To my parents, Robert and Sherrie Wagner
- RGW

To RaLinda, Joey, and Sam
- JKH

TABLE OF CONTENTS

INTRODUCTION:

The Value of Employee Engagement

"**P**EANUT" WAS AN IMPROBABLE NICKNAME for the veteran union member who worked on the loading dock. Under the Big Dogs baseball hat and blue sweatshirt was an imposing man who bore a passing resemblance to onetime NBA power forward Karl Malone.

His manager, Lou, asked if he would agree to be interviewed for a study of what makes a good work life. Forget it, he said. He didn't really like the larger company, and he wasn't going to be part of any effort to sugarcoat things.

"They're not going to ask you about the company," said his manager. "They're going to ask about things right here. They're going to ask about me, about our team. Would you do it as a personal favor to me?"

"That's different," Peanut relented. He had plenty of good things to say about his manager, his team, and work on the dock itself. And, he told his manager, "For you, I'll do it."

After a few minutes of questions from the interviewer, Peanut loosened up and began talking effusively about Lou and the improvements he'd brought to the facility. Once Peanut started talking about his supervisor, he just kept going.

"Lou cares about everybody's situation," he said. "He has an understanding. He can take control of a situation. We've never seen the changes happen in our environment like they're happening now. You've got a guy who will look out for you. You call him with a problem; he'll help you work through it."

Each time the interviewer asked a question, Peanut ran with it, telling stories about Lou listening to the ideas of the men on the dock, praising good work, marshaling or fine-tuning the right equipment, picking up someone whose broken car left him stranded, or giving advice about personal matters.

"A good supervisor," the dockworker said, "is not only a person who comes to work to hand out orders from the top but also somebody who will work with people. Not every situation is about authority and writing people up, punishment for things that you might have messed up. It's also about somebody who looks out for you, cares about what's going on, will show the concern to pull you up if you've got a problem, and will ask you, 'Is there anything I can help you with?' You want those kinds of people in your corner. We've seen quite a few people come and go. Lou is the best we've seen. He has made a difference — a big difference."

As it turned out, Peanut had some sage insights into what makes a great manager, insights that match discoveries emerging from the world's largest database of employee opinion and business performance. Those results show that in rallying the troops, front-line managers matter more than senior leaders. Hardworking supervisors who care can motivate even the most cynical employees. Great managers like Lou drive better bottom-line results not only while improving the lives of their employees, but precisely because they improve those lives.

Identifying the mechanisms through which employee engagement is increased and translated into profits required a tremendous amount of research. More than a decade ago, The Gallup Organization took a broad view of how companies were managing their people and determined that most organizations were shooting in the dark. The typical business commissioned an excruciatingly long survey of employee opinion, hoping that somewhere among 100 or 200 questions, it would stumble upon the concepts that mattered. When the results returned, they were too cumbersome to feed back to the troops, where no one would have known what to do with them anyway. Executives assumed there was a general level of "satisfaction" that pretty much applied throughout the company, and that they — the senior team — were the main drivers of their employees' feelings about the company. All these assumptions were wrong.

Gallup assembled a select group of its social scientists to examine the 1 million employee interviews then in its database, the hundreds of questions that had been asked over the preceding decades, and every variable on business-unit performance that organizations had supplied with their employee rosters. These data were analyzed to find which survey questions — and therefore which aspects of work — were most powerful in explaining workers' productive motivations on the job. Ultimately, 12 elements of work life emerged as the core of the unwritten social contract between employee and employer. Through their answers to the dozen most important questions and their daily actions that affected performance, the million workers were saying, "If you do these things for us, we will do what the company needs of us."

The 12 Elements of Great Managing that emerged from the research are as follows.

1. I know what is expected of me at work.

2. I have the materials and equipment I need to do my work right.

3. At work, I have the opportunity to do what I do best every day.

4. In the last seven days, I have received recognition or praise for doing good work.

5. My supervisor, or someone at work, seems to care about me as a person.

6. There is someone at work who encourages my development.

7. At work, my opinions seem to count.

8. The mission or purpose of my company makes me feel my job is important.

9. My associates or fellow employees are committed to doing quality work.

10. I have a best friend at work.

11. In the last six months, someone at work has talked to me about my progress.

12. This last year, I have had opportunities at work to learn and grow.*

Behind each of these is a fundamental truth about human nature on the job. The correlations between each element and better performance not only draw a roadmap to superior managing; they also reveal fascinating insights into how the human mind — molded by thousands of years of foraging, hunting, and cooperating within a close-knit and stable tribe — reacts in a relatively new, artificial world of cubicles, project timelines, corporate ambiguity, and constantly changing workgroup membership. People neither were created to fit corporate strategies nor have evolved to do so. Rather than contest these facts, the most successful managers harness the drive, virtuosity, and spirit that come with employing humans, even as they understand the inevitable chinks in their armor.

The 12 crucial statements were disseminated widely in the bestselling *First, Break All the Rules*, published in 1999. Much of its success stemmed from challenging the prevailing ideas in ways that helped executives better understand what Peanut already knew, such as why he would do things for Lou that he wouldn't do even for the company's chief executive. "Leaders on snorting steeds . . . are important. But great managers are the bedrock of great organizations," Tom Peters wrote in touting the discoveries. "Great managers are an organization's glue.

---

* Each of the Q¹²® statements above represents millions of dollars of investment by Gallup researchers, and as such they are proprietary. They cannot be reprinted or reproduced in any manner without the written consent of The Gallup Organization. Copyright © 1993-1998 The Gallup Organization, Washington, D.C. All rights reserved.

They create and hold together the scores of folks who power high-performing companies."[1]

Many executives struggle to formulate a strategy for increasing profits through their employees. Often they resort to the simple arithmetic of fewer employees = lower costs, without considering the wide range in productivity that depends on each person's engagement. "I don't think enough investors have asked the more important question: Can companies be even more successful by focusing on optimizing each employee's contribution, rather than simply looking for ways to reduce the cost of employing them?" wrote a columnist for *The Wall Street Journal*. "Perhaps we, as investors, need to be more conscious of how those people who clean our hotel rooms, cook our meals, and deal our cards are treated and paid, rather than simply looking to see whether the expense can be cut further. Staff motivation, although difficult to quantify, should be part of the investment analysis."[2]

Staff motivation is quantified and its effect on profitability is perpetually being analyzed from Gallup's files. Lou's and Peanut's answers to the 12 statements above are just two of the now 10 million sets of responses in the digital vault. The 12 Elements today are measured in 41 languages and 114 countries, in industries as varied as electrical utilities, retail stores, restaurants, hotels, hospitals, paper mills, government agencies, banks, newspapers, and dozens of others. Each time Gallup conducts a census of employee opinion within a business, it also requests every available datum of performance: customer surveys, resignations, accidents, productivity, sick days, creativity, sales, and profitability. When analyzed together, the 12 Elements and the business metrics show how much of a company's health is affected by the engagement of its people.

Company performance starts with the most basic act: showing up for work. Engaged employees average 27 percent less absenteeism than those who are actively disengaged. In a typical 10,000-person company, absenteeism from disengagement costs the business about 5,000 lost days per year, worth $600,000 in salary paid where no work was performed.[3] Managers who maintain higher levels of engagement in their teams spare their companies the cost of what are sometimes euphemistically called "mental health days."

People resign for many reasons. Some of them, such as a return to college or a spouse being recruited out of town, don't reflect on the quality of work life. Even perfectly managed employees don't always plan to stay with the same company forever. But quitting often has everything to do with the job. In a free market economy, walking out for good is the employee's trump card against disengaging conditions, and an expensive consequence for the company. It is not unusual, for example, for some retailers to endure 100 percent annual turnover. Executives in such industries often chalk up the comings, goings, and perpetual new-recruit training as an unavoidable cost of hiring low-wage, college-aged people whose lives have not stabilized. Yet within the churn lies a hidden cost of poor managing: business units with a surplus of disengaged employees suffer 31 percent more turnover than those with a critical mass of engaged associates.[4]

Seeing the revolving door in other industries, leaders of low-turnover companies often breathe a sigh of relief, not realizing that while the movement of people in and out of jobs is slower, the effect of engagement on resignations in their fields is even greater. Within these more settled organizations, business units with many actively disengaged workers experience 51 percent more turnover than do those with many engaged employees.[5] Moreover, the cost of losing one person is often higher in low-turnover businesses. While it will cost 25 to 80 percent of an entry-level or front-line employee's annual wage to replace him, replacing an engineer, a salesperson, a nurse, or other specialist ranges from 75 to 400 percent of her yearly pay.[6] Disengagement-driven turnover costs most sizable businesses millions every year.

One of the unfortunate facts of life is that some employees steal. Retailers call it "shrink," an overly cute term for outright theft. It has a pernicious effect on profitability, because the company must sell five, ten or more identical items just to cover the cost of the one item stolen. It would be nice if all parents impressed upon their children a sense of right and wrong that would prevent them from stealing. As it turns out, some employees are susceptible to temptation, and that temptation is magnified by a feeling of detachment from the team. Workgroups with an inordinately high number of disengaged workers lose 51 percent more of their inventory to "shrink" than do those on the other end of the spectrum.[7]

Life on the job can be risky. Utility workers risk electrocution. Loading dock workers risk having their toes smashed under a forklift. Nurses risk getting stuck with a needle contaminated by blood-borne disease. In practice, all the safety glasses, steel-toed boots, latex gloves, and hard hats cannot substitute for constant vigilance and good team-work, both of which collapse when employees care little about their jobs. The chance of a disengaged worker having an accident on a given day are substantially higher than those of his engaged colleague. The workgroups whose engagement puts them in the bottom quartile of the Gallup database average 62 percent more accidents than the workgroups in the top quartile.[8]

To the outsider, the most obvious connection between employee engagement and the way a business operates is its customer service. Anyone who's been the victim of a surly flight attendant, a disgruntled waiter, or a slovenly cable installer knows how a customer's experience cannot be separated from the work experience of those who serve him. Anyone who's had the good fortune to encounter an enthusiastic employee knows how she can make even the boisterous claims in the company's advertising come to life. Although much of a customer's experience is outside the control of associates, being in the higher reaches of team engagement equates to 12 percent higher customer scores than those in the bottom tier.[9] No amount of legislating, demanding, or incentives can command the force of a deep emotional commitment to one's team.

These various effects combine to create an appreciable competitive advantage for a charged-up team. When the database of nearly 1 million teams is sorted from most- to least-engaged and split down the middle, teams in the more engaged half are more than twice as likely to succeed as their counterparts on the other side of the divide. When the teams are split into four equally sized groups, teams in the top quartile are three times as likely to succeed as those in the bottom quartile, averaging 18 percent higher productivity and 12 percent higher profitability.[10]

The same pattern that occurs at the individual and workgroup level emerges when an entire company achieves high engagement. Among the publicly traded companies in the database, the more engaged organizations outperformed the earnings-per-share of their competitors by 18 percent, and, over time, progressed at a faster rate than their industry peers.[11] In the companies that are better places to work, millions of small actions — statistically insignificant in isolation — created higher customer scores, reduced absenteeism, led to fewer accidents, boosted productivity, and increased creativity, accumulating to make a more profitable enterprise. In a contrast group of less engaged companies, managerial neglect diminished team spirit, and took a sizable chunk of profitability with it.

Worker commitment is by no means the sole cause of success. Depending on the company's circumstances, it may not even be the most important. Introducing an incredible new product, finding new production methods, managing currency or commodity risks, perfecting an efficient operating model, and many other variables quite separate from personnel strategy can have dramatic effects on the business's fortunes. But the evidence is clear that the creation and maintenance of high employee engagement, as one of the few determinants of profitability largely within a company's control, is one of the most crucial imperatives of any successful organization. It introduces a powerful edge impossible to replicate through any other channel. Because of the financial consequences of worker commitment, no executive can fully discharge his fiduciary responsibility to the shareholders while ignoring it. Regardless of her technical abilities in the function she supervises, no manager wholly fulfills her responsibilities unless she diligently attends to the engagement of her team.

Each chapter that follows describes one of the 12 Elements in detail. Wrapped around an explanation of the element is the story of a manager who epitomizes that aspect. The explanations draw not only on the 10-fold increase in data since the publication of *First, Break All the Rules*, but also on a wealth of insights from brain-imaging studies, genetics, psychology, behavioral game theory, and other scientific disciplines. When combined, these discoveries shout that one of the dumbest things companies do is try to make their "human resources" more productive while fighting what makes them human. They also demonstrate that great managing is not some amorphous, "difficult to quantify" concept.

The data give a clear image of what is most important for inspiring people to do what the company needs of them.

The managers profiled here were chosen from among thousands whose employee engagement levels were reviewed by the authors and then subjected to a careful vetting process. Even so, while each exemplifies success on that element, none of them is a textbook example of how to approach the challenge. There are no cookie-cutter answers to such complex team issues. Each requires a manager's judgment, his unique talents and strengths, and his dedication to prevailing.

Readers should not assume the companies represented by these managers are universally engaged. Some are close. Some aren't. Almost any large company has at least a handful of great managers who ought to be singled out. The 12 supervisors whose stories are told in this book are representative of those who can properly be called great managers. Those we profile are not a pantheon of the dozen absolute best, freaks of managerial nature the likes of which you may never meet in your own company. Rather, they are the gentle but determined souls you will find half the time in a great company, and one out of ten times in a poor one. They are managers like Lou who improve the lives of employees like Peanut, and change the course of their companies in the process.

"It all begins with management," said Peanut. "People started opening their eyes a little more. We opened our eyes, and now we see things we didn't see before."

THE FIRST ELEMENT:
Knowing What's Expected

S OMETHING WAS WRONG WITH WINEGARDNER & HAMMONS' HOTEL
south of the Dallas airport. The facility was not maintaining its expected pricing levels. Inspections showed myriad deficiencies. And
it was running more than a million dollars behind its revenue budget.

Yet for all the evidence that something was amiss, the cause wasn't
apparent. By all accounts, it was a good hotel. The manager there was
well-regarded, some say even "loved," by the staff. The building was only
four years old and as close to the action as one could hope, given the
Texas-sized distances around Dallas/Fort Worth International Airport.
What's more, it was a Marriott, a premier "flag," as those in the industry
call the outward brand of a hotel.

Winegardner & Hammons, Inc., the Cincinnati-based firm that
manages the hotel and 30 others around the country, decided it needed
a manager who specialized in getting employees to meet expectations.
The company found her just 27 miles away, running the Holiday Inn
Fort Worth North, another WHI property at the time, and summoned
her in August 2003 to find out what was wrong and fix it.

Nancy Sorrells was recruited to the task by Kent Bruggeman, then
senior vice president of human resources and a former general manager

himself. On a visit to the Holiday Inn, he attended a staff meeting that left him so impressed he was "almost in tears." "Every supervisor knew their goal in every numeric category and knew how they were going to get there," said Bruggeman. He needed the same clarity of expectations at the Dallas/Forth Worth Airport Marriott South.

"The hotel you are going to is sneaky-broke," Sorrells recalled Bruggeman telling her. "You walk around, and you won't see anything wrong, and there's no reason it should be broken. I don't know what the problem is, but it's going to take you more than a day or two to fix it."

Intensely driven, Sorrells conceded she was too optimistic about how quickly she could effect a turnaround. Instead, she found herself surrounded by skeptics. The greeting she received was less than warm. One employee cracked to another after first meeting the 5' 3" Sorrells that he thought she would be taller. Many of them looked down on her because she'd come from a Holiday Inn, a lesser flag in the hospitality pecking order.

"It was pretty scary for her," said Julie Faver, the hotel's revenue director. "She had people second-guessing her. Not knowing the direction, they felt uneasy. Obviously, they had a new manager and there was a lot of turmoil, and a lot of people didn't have a guest-service, 'I-can-do-this' type of attitude."

Sorrells began working through the hotel person by person, looking for those she could persuade to share her vision. Needing better support, she recruited like-minded managers from outside to help her. And she began removing what she felt were counterproductive ideas.

"We had too many incentives for people to do routine things," she said. The hotel had fallen into the trap of paying people for following a process instead of for reaching the right outcomes. The payments covered employees from the front desk to the shuttle drivers to waiters. In combination, those payments constituted a "secondary compensation system" that distracted people from the right goals, said Bruggeman.

In place of small process-based rewards, Sorrells pointed to WHI's standing offer of outcome-based rewards — bonuses to the supervisors for the hotel's financial performance. No one bit. "People were throwing it back at me, saying, 'Are you kidding? We never make budget!'"

These changes did anything but endear her to the team. "They're thinking, 'Here comes the Wicked Witch of the West taking away my stuff,'" said the manager.

Whether it was the new manager's style — Sorrells admitted she's better at correction than recognition — an entrenched culture of mediocrity, or both, Sorrells had only a few key allies during her first autumn at the Marriott property. It was professionally and personally isolating. "A month in, I'd walk up to people, and they'd stop talking," said Sorrells. "I was thinking, 'Don't you understand I'm here to help?'" Sorrells' plan wasn't working.

At the low point, one of the veteran department heads confronted her. "I'd like to follow you," he said, "but I don't know where you're going."

★

In struggling to organize her team around the right goals, the hotel manager faced the most basic, but sometimes most difficult, challenge of a supervisor: determining how to combine individual efforts for the greatest cumulative result. In his classic explanation of free market economics, *The Wealth of Nations*, Adam Smith describes how separating the simple industry of pin-making into several distinct jobs dramatically boosts production "in consequence of a proper division and combination of their different operations." If "one man draws out the wire, another straights it, a third cuts it, a fourth points it, a fifth grinds it at the top for receiving the head" and so forth, the team makes more than 200 times as many pins than if each man worked "separately and independently."[1] Yet for such a plain idea, finding the best way to orchestrate the work within a team has perplexed managers through the centuries.

Because so much of an enterprise's efficiency depends on the seamless combination of personal responsibilities, the First Element of Great Managing is job clarity. When Gallup researchers went in search of questions most predictive of performance, one of the most straightforward turned out to be one of the most powerful: "I know what is expected of me at work." Groups that have high scores on this item are more productive, more profitable, even more creative. Substantial gains on the First Element alone often correlate with productivity gains of five to ten percent, thousands more happy customers and 10 to 20 percent fewer on-the-job accidents.

One electric utility solicits cost-reduction ideas from its employees, much like the suggestion boxes at many businesses. Of those recommendations implemented, the average idea adopted from its less engaged workers saves the company $4,000. The average idea from the most committed employees saves $11,000. Clearly the more engaged people put more brainpower into helping their business. Of the 12 Elements, knowing what's expected plays the largest role in generating money-saving strategies at the utility.

For a manager trying to achieve positive answers from her team, the First Element is the easiest of the 12 — but it's still not that easy. On average, only about half of the employees in the international database "strongly agree" with the statement.[2] The numbers are not impressively high even in stereotypically well-defined roles such as security personnel, sales, truck drivers, registered nurses, or production staff, where the figure ranges from just over half to almost two-thirds. The number drops to a third for those in scientific, technical, and computer-related jobs. And it's amazingly common to find individuals making large salaries who will confide, "I really don't know what I'm supposed to be doing here."

The greatest pitfall of this element is that managers assume the simplicity of the statement means the issue requires only a basic solution: "If people don't know what's expected, I'll just tell them." This is analogous to American tourists who, not knowing the local language, speak English more slowly and loudly. And it's just as ineffective.

"Knowing what's expected" is more than a job description. It's a detailed understanding of how what one person is supposed to do fits in with what everyone else is supposed to do, and how those expectations change when circumstances change. A good team, some say, is a lot like a great jazz band in which each player listens to the other instruments as he plays his own. The better they pay attention to the rest of the band and work their way into the music, the better the result.[3]

A contrasting example emerged several years ago when a group of managers from one Fortune 500 enterprise was beginning several days of training together. "As we go around the room," said the facilitator,

"I'd like you to introduce yourself, tell us your job, and tell us how doing your job well increases the profits of your company." There were 25 managers in the room. Only five could make a credible connection between their jobs and the profits of the business. Had they been a jazz group as poorly organized, it would have sounded like the first day of fourth-grade band, with a lot of cacophonous honking and flipping through the printed music.

Successful businesses become fat and complacent, creating enough layers of management and distance from the front lines that the First Element suffers among middle managers. Executives in particular must constantly ask themselves whether each man and woman in the organizational hierarchy has an essential and well-integrated set of responsibilities that advance the company. Unfortunately, such questions are usually asked only during cost-cutting initiatives, as they were one year later for the managers in that training session. After years of dubious value to the business, many were finally given pink slips.

In 1776, Smith learned about teamwork watching pin-makers. Today, some of the most fascinating insights about collaboration come from the decks of aircraft carriers, from professional basketball teams, and out of operating rooms.

Few environments epitomize clarity of expectations like the flight deck of a nuclear-powered U.S. Navy aircraft carrier. Something about the persistent risk of death helps to focus the mind, and leads to a unique kind of teamwork from which less risky businesses could take a lesson. The dozen largest American carriers are more than 1,000 feet long, weigh at least 73,000 metric tons, carry 5,000 sailors, and launch and land 80 or more airplanes ranging from helicopters and early-warning radar planes to jet fighters. For all their size, the flight decks are, in fact, too confined for regular takeoffs. Only through the combination of the forward speed of the ship itself, the full power of a jet fighter's engines and a steam catapult hooked to the plane does it get airborne. A fighter goes from 0 to 150 miles-per-hour and flying in two seconds.[4] Or, if something fails, it spills into the ocean as the pilot tries to eject.

Returning to the ship is no better. A jet fighter can't land normally in the allotted 300 feet of deck space. Instead, the pilot must make a "controlled crash," dropping a tail hook over one of four cables strung across the runway to stop the airplane. To avoid dropping into the water if the tail hook doesn't catch a cable, he has to hit the throttle during the landing, ready to take off again and come around for another try. Since the mid-1950s, the landing decks of carriers have been angled 10 degrees to the port side of the ship to make such escapes safer, but that only complicates the pilot's job, requiring he constantly correct his descent as the carrier moves to his right.[5]

"So you want to understand an aircraft carrier?" said one officer. "Well, just imagine that it's a busy day, and you shrink San Francisco Airport to only one short runway and one ramp and gate. Make planes take off and land at the same time, at half the present time interval, rock the runway from side to side, and require that everyone who leaves in the morning returns that same day. Make the equipment so close to the edge of the envelope that it's fragile. Then turn off the radar to avoid detection, impose strict controls on radios, fuel the aircraft in place with their engines running, put an enemy in the air, and scatter live bombs and rockets around. Now wet the whole thing down with saltwater and oil, and man it with 20-year-olds, half of whom have never seen an airplane close up. Oh, and by the way, try not to kill anyone."[6]

The dangers are as innumerable as they are unsavory. One Navy training video shows a catapult operator approaching a screaming EA-6B Prowler (a radar-jamming aircraft) with its engines at full power, ready to launch. A sailor gets too close to one of the jet intakes and is sucked into the engine.[7] Propellers on a cargo plane are tough to see in daylight and invisible at night. The exhaust of a jet can burn a man or blow him overboard. If one of the arresting cables snaps, it will whip across the deck, slicing through whatever or whomever is in its path. Every man on deck is at risk from an out-of-control plane coming in. Live bombs and missiles multiply the danger.

For all the hazards, accidents on flight decks are surprisingly rare. Social scientists consider the deck of an aircraft carrier a "high reliability organization" (HRO) because so many things can go wrong — but almost never do. "If it performs some hazardous activity repeatedly without incident, it is highly reliable," wrote a trio of researchers who singled out aircraft carriers for particular attention. "HROs are expected to perform at high tempo for sustained periods of time and maintain the ability to do so repeatedly."[8] Many of the reasons HROs perform so well revolve around each person understanding what is expected of him, and understanding how what he does complements the work of the rest of the team.

The need to avoid role confusion in a fast-moving and hazardous setting led the Navy at least 70 years ago to create a system of colored shirts on the flight deck. Today seven colors are worn on deck: Purple by those who handle aviation fuel. Blue for handling planes and operating aircraft elevators. Red for weapons. Brown for air wing plane captains. White for landing signal officers and safety observers. Green for the men working the catapults and arresting gear.[9] And yellow jerseys for aircraft directors, the most coveted position for enlisted personnel and those who bear ultimate responsibility for what happens on "the most dangerous four-and-a-half acres of flight line in the world."[10]

Following the aircraft director's instruction, the men use headsets and hand signals to coordinate each team member's work into the whole. The visual vocabulary includes more than 100 signals. The most astonishing feature of teams on carrier decks is not that every sailor does his job well, but that under pressure the entire crew works as one entity, each member making adjustments based on what he knows the others will do or communicating efficiently to make sure things stay synchronized. "The crew members act as a team, each watching what others are doing and all of them communicating constantly through telephones, radios, hand signals, and written details. This constant flow of information helps flag mistakes before they've caused any damage," said one account.[11]

The men on a carrier analogize this harmony to a ballet or a symphony. Sociologists give the phenomenon various names: "heedful interrelating," "collaborative elasticity," "distributive cognition," or "collective mind." Boiled down, all these terms refer to the difference between each employee knowing his job by itself and everyone knowing how to do his job in concert with others so the team accomplishes the larger goal. This comprehensive view of knowing what's expected is what creates real teamwork. This is the First Element in action.

There is a temptation in managing to assume that with the right level of talent in each of the players, superior team performance is sure to follow. Of course talent matters, enough so that it figures heavily into one of the 12 Elements and has a tangential relationship to four others. But the evidence from disparate fields suggests talent alone won't cut it, even in the kinds of endeavors usually associated with star performances and individual stats.

Consider what can be learned from professional basketball. Like the supervisor of any run-of-the-mill workgroup, basketball coaches must juggle issues of directing the work itself, retaining talent, praising, developing, and motivating. In addition to being more entertaining to watch than a marketing department meeting or an executive strategy session, a National Basketball Association game is held to the clock and better scored than a traditional business endeavor. Viewed through a business statistician's eyes, the NBA is a perfect laboratory to study not just teamwork in basketball, but teamwork itself.

Having read the research on aircraft carriers and wanting to extend its discoveries, three management professors dove into the NBA statistics to see whether, above and beyond individual talent, playing together over time improved a team's performance. The professors analyzed data from 23 NBA teams from 1980 to 1994. Sure enough, the greater the stability of a team's roster — fewer trades moving players on and off the team — the better they played.

When players first join a team, they learn how to run various plays because the tactics are sketched out on the coach's easel. The general strategy, how plays should be set up and how to position players against the opposing team can be contemplated and explained in practice. The researchers call this "explicit knowledge." But as any basketball fan knows, drawing Xs and Os is one thing, making it happen on the court is another, requiring more than every player knowing his job in isolation. A better team record also depends on players learning hundreds of nuances and patterns in their teammates' play. Basketball, as one sports commentator put it, is a "chemistry sport."[12] This "tacit knowledge," the keen awareness of each others' styles, "cannot be taught by reading manuals or listening to lectures; it must be learned through experience," wrote the researchers.[13] "It is only through actually playing together — through cumulative playing experience — that each member of the team accumulates the stock of tacit knowledge about the game play of other members of the team that enables such synchronicity."[14]

In 2005, professors Robert S. Huckman and Gary P. Pisano pushed the idea a step further by investigating the effect a surgical team had on the success of cardiac physicians. The skill of a heart surgeon was customarily considered fully "portable," based on his abilities alone and therefore equally effective wherever he operated. The professors decided to test this assumption after they discovered the state of Pennsylvania kept records on every coronary artery bypass graft performed there during 1994 and 1995. The data covered 38,577 procedures performed by 203 surgeons operating at 43 hospitals. Given that cardiac surgeons often split their time among two or more hospitals, would their success be different at hospitals where they spent less time? Would they, like the basketball players, do better with a familiar team on a familiar "court?"

Scoring the performance of doctors is somewhat complicated, but it can be done. It requires a statistic called "risk-adjusted mortality." Risk-adjusted mortality takes into consideration age, gender, hypertension, heart attacks, kidney failure and other variables that come with particular patients. Combining these factors with the patient's outcome allows a head-to-head comparison of health care providers. "This outcome . . . is characterized by enough variation across doctors and hospitals to make it a meaningful dimension for performance evaluation," wrote the professors.[15] This is a researcher's way of saying that, all other things being equal, you could live or die, depending on how the doctor and the larger operating team do their jobs. "Meaningful dimension" indeed!

While the math employed for the analysis is daunting, the conclusions are easy to understand. The same doctors perform better at the hospitals where they do more surgeries than at the facilities where they do occasional work. "We find a substantial degree of firm specificity in surgeon performance," wrote the professors. "More precisely, higher volume in a prior period for a given surgeon at a particular hospital is correlated with significantly lower risk-adjusted mortality for that surgeon-hospital pair. That volume, however, does not significantly improve the surgeon's performance at *other* hospitals, thus suggesting that surgeon performance is not fully portable across organizations."[16] The doctor can't take all of the lower risk-adjusted mortality with him to a facility where he works part-time because, according to the data, coronary artery bypass grafts are also a chemistry sport.

How could this be? For the same kinds of reasons that landing a plane on a carrier takes more than the pilot and winning a basketball game takes more than a star forward. Teamwork matters. "The beneficial effects of accumulated tacit knowledge within one organization may not be fully transferable to another," wrote the Harvard pair. A surgeon at her primary hospital "might learn that the surgical nurses at the hospital generally do not speak up about possible problems during an operation, but that, if they do raise an alarm, it signals a very serious problem," the researchers suggested. "The surgeon might also become familiar with the various practice habits of the anesthesiologist with whom she operates or she might gain a sense of which residents she can call upon for quick and reliable information about one of her recovering patients. One can imagine that such familiarity helps the surgeon perform better." Across town at a hospital where she works only occasionally, the lack of that orchestration could handicap her performance.[17]

The study of cardiac teams corresponds with risk-adjusted mortality statistics that Gallup researchers analyzed across a large group of hospitals. A significant predictor of whether a patient lived or died in one of the 152 facilities was the engagement level of the employees who cared for the man or woman. The facilities were separated into four groups based on the First Element responses of the employees. Risk-adjusted "avoidable complications" were 12 percent higher and risk-adjusted "avoidable deaths" 21 percent higher in the units staffed by the least engaged quartile, as compared with the most engaged quartile.[18]

No one was undergoing heart surgery at the Marriott Hotel south of the Dallas airport. They weren't playing basketball, nor was anyone going to land a jet fighter in the parking lot. But Nancy Sorrells needed the kind of clear expectations and teamwork that make all of those endeavors more successful. Running a good hotel is also a chemistry sport.

★

Sorrells decided she needed to reassess her communication with her management team. "I took that on myself. If they don't know where I'm going, then I have not made it clear."

She called a meeting of all 14 department supervisors. In that session, she held firm on the need to improve the finances and her authority to oversee the transition. "We're on a life raft," she told them. "As long as I'm the one yelling 'stroke,' we're going to have to move in this direction."

The manager wrapped her conversations with employees around the five aspects of the hotel's mission: creating a great experience for hotel guests, a great work experience for employees, the profitability of the hotel, product quality inside the hotel, and growth of the company. If a product or process wasn't going to affect one of those goals, it probably didn't matter. Some employees resisted, and they either found other jobs or were let go. For example, "we had one person in housekeeping who should not have been dealing with people, never mind supervising people," said Sorrells.

For all the intensity of her command, Sorrells' staff noticed that she became a little more approachable during this time as they worked harder to meet the higher expectations. "In the beginning, she was very aggressive and very up front: 'There's no nonsense, and here's how we're doing it,'" said Shannon Small, sales administrative assistant. "A lot of people put up their guard: 'This is my property, and this is my hotel, and this is where I work.'"

Eventually, both sides relaxed. "It took people a little while to warm up to her," said Brandon Overby, guest service supervisor. Small added, "We all kind of opened our minds, and Nancy did too. It was obvious to me that, 'Okay, you open your mind a little bit as to how to see it, and I'll open mine on how I see it. Let's work together.' And it all came around."

As they got to know her, Sorrells' staff realized she was exceptionally hardworking and dedicated to the mission she espoused. She listened to Spanish language tapes to better communicate with the largely Hispanic housekeeping and maintenance staffs. "She's got little kids, but she came in at 6 a.m. for a couple months straight because she wanted to know why the restaurant scores were going down," said Overby. And despite the many challenges, Sorrells kept her cool. She was firm, but always fair and never loud.

After Sorrells and her team made peace, there was still a lot of work to be done, most of it in the details. Light bulbs burn out. Tables get nicked. Chairs start to wobble. The tile in the foyer cracks. "You have to be picky. If you're not picky, the little flaws start becoming acceptable," said Mike Cosse, assistant general manager.

"We started off with just the basics: being here on time, coming in, getting the basic stuff done," said Terry Hogg, maintenance supervisor. "Then in our next staff meetings, we'd bring up some other expectations. The same goals were always set, but the expectations grew month by month."

Employees at the DFW Marriott South can run through a litany of details expected of the group: Walk around the desk to hand the guest his keys in a more personal fashion. Don't point a guest to the elevators; escort her there. Don't leave the water running when cleaning the shower or leave power running in an empty room. When something is torn or scuffed, write a maintenance report. Pick up trash in and around the hotel. Keys to the management offices are to be checked out at the front desk in the morning and checked back when leaving — no exceptions.

Such attention to detail helped the hotel improve one of its basic inspection scores from a 59 out of 100 one month after Sorrells arrived to a score of 95 nine months later. The placard over the stairway from the managers' office reminds all who pass under it that "You only get what you inspect, not what you expect."

It's more difficult to delineate the expectations for creating an exceptional guest experience. That, too, depended on expanding the goal from executing a process to achieving an outcome. Sorrells worked to expand employees' definitions of their jobs. For example, employees at the registration desk should be thinking not only of issuing room keys and swiping credit cards, but also of doing whatever is needed for that particular guest. "My job is to accommodate guests, to treat them as if they were me," said Bryana Nealy, a guest services representative. "And it's not just what you do; it's how you do it."

Supervisors rotate assignments to do what's called "marble duty": spending several hours during the front lobby's busiest times looking for opportunities to help guests. (By common consent and mutual enforcement, if someone misses his duty, he picks up the next three shifts.) They offer coffee to people waiting up front, give directions, help with luggage, or jump in if many guests arrive all at once.

Asked when they really shine as a team, those who work at the Marriott talk about "distressed passengers." Because of its proximity to the airport, the hotel is one of the places airlines send passengers who are stuck in Dallas, grounded by bad weather. Those who checked their luggage may not have toiletries, pajamas, or extra clothes.

"Just imagine [the arrival of] 175 people that you didn't expect," said Faver. "They come at the same time because they come by bus. They all check in at the same time. They all tend to get hungry at the same time too." Instead of staying in their respective areas, the staff needs to double up first at the front desk, then at the restaurant, then in providing packets of essential supplies like toothbrushes and combs as the wave of guests settles in.

At other times, the emergency will involve only a few guests or even just one, such as the company CEO who was about to get an award in front of 2,000 people. He forgot to pack a tie, and his wife was in a panic trying to help him. When it became apparent there was no way to get to a store and back in time, "I just took off my tie and gave it to her," said Overby. "The executive sent back the tie with a glowing letter of appreciation. "When you read one of these letters, it just gives you chills," he said.

"I knew the hotel was turning around when people started coming to me to brag and when guest comment cards started mentioning people's names," says Sorrells.

Sorrells is something of a perfectionist, and that might not have gone over as well with the employees had her meticulousness not extended behind the scenes. "We're paying more attention to the quality of the food, the cleanliness of the break area, the cleanliness of the employee restrooms, and adding amenities in our restrooms for the associates — rugs and flowers and different things of that nature — to show the associates that we care about them also," said Hogg. "We're not just asking them to go out and please the guests. We put the same amount of time and effort into the back-of-the-house restrooms as we put into the front-of-the-house restrooms."

As the employees took greater pride in meeting higher standards and as they got to know Sorrells, employee engagement at the hotel took a jump, going from 25th place among WHI's 31 hotels to 6th place. Overall engagement at the hotel went higher than that of 90 percent of all other workgroups in the Gallup database and almost that high on the First Element.

The financial picture also brightened. After the increase in engagement, the hotel was able to maintain an average rate of about $125 a night. "We've raised our rate, and we've held steady," said Small, the sales director. "When I first came on, we sold out maybe twice. During 2004, I'd have to go back and look at the books, because we had a lot of sell-outs." When Sorrells took over, the hotel was nearly $1.5 million behind budget on revenue; sales since improved so that the hotel was $500,000 ahead of budget.

Although Sorrells is demanding, she is deeply committed to the success of her team. She tears up when talking about their accomplishments, such as Faver being named WHI's "Revenue Manager of the Year." "I want them to have that feeling," said Sorrells. "Revenue Manager of the Year! That is so cool!"

"She really does have the best interests of the customers and the employees at heart," said Overby.

Shortly after the improvements at her hotel, Sorrells herself received some unexpected recognition at Marriott's global manager conference. "I basically had the popcorn out because I was just watching the show," she said. "Suddenly, I realized they were talking about my hotel." She was summoned onstage to receive a "Global Leadership Award" for the many employee-engagement-driven accomplishments of the DFW Marriott South.

She also noticed something different over the holidays, as dozens of Christmas cards arrived at her home. "Now she gets Christmas cards from everyone," says Overby. "We joke with her. She once told me, 'I didn't get any cards that first year.' I told her, 'No one liked you then.'"

The Second Element:
Materials and Equipment

IGHT AND DAY, EVERY DAY OF THE YEAR, over 100,000 kilograms of molten glass glow so hot and bright in the furnace in Rio Claro, Brazil, that it cannot be seen with the naked eye or approached too closely without the observer being burned. Through the dark lenses of a special face shield, one can briefly glimpse through a small porthole what looks like lava in a man-made volcano.

At the rate of several tons an hour, raw materials including dolomite, aluminum, kaolin, and sodium carbonate — are fed into the top of the furnace while an equal amount of 1,600-degrees-Celsius liquid glass flows out of the tank into an orange-hot river that flows above the "forming stations" nearby. In fractions of a second, the glass runs through thousands of small holes and is transformed from hot to cool, from turbulent to delicate, and wound onto large spools of the final product: fiberglass.

"I have been here for 15 years and I am still amazed at the process we have," said worker Jose Duil Dos Santos, speaking in Portuguese. "You just don't see it every day."

Given the extremes inside Owens Corning's fiberglass facility 172 kilometers from São Paulo, it's not surprising there is a tremendous emphasis on the materials and equipment needed to make the job safe, comfortable, and productive. But the spirit of employee participation and the practice of refining tools inside "Fiberglass," as the local residents call the plant, is a model for teams working under less demanding conditions.

Despite the many other products it sells, which now make up the majority of its revenue, Owens Corning is a company created by the invention and production of fiberglass. In 1932, Owens-Illinois researcher Dale Kleist accidentally pointed a jet of compressed air at a stream of molten glass. It sprayed and stretched the material into thin fibers, a fortuitous breakthrough. Corning Incorporated was pursuing a similar line of research. In 1938, the companies combined their efforts to form Owens Corning Fiberglas Corporation, most famous in the United States for its trademarked pink building insulation. The Brazil subsidiary, Owens Corning Fiberglas A.S. Limitada, still carries the fiberglass designation that the parent company removed in 1996.

The Rio Claro facility has been making fiberglass since 1971. The basic process has not changed much because the chemistry and physics of creating the filaments remains the same. Gravity, a stream of air, and the already hardened portion of the filament pull a thin strand from each of 2,400 small holes under the channel of hot, liquid glass. A spray of water cools the filaments and a roller wet with chemicals changes them from fragile glass to flexible fiberglass.

While the essence of the process hasn't changed, many of the details have improved, often through the suggestions of employees. "The one who knows what he needs is the one doing the job," said Enio Wetten, a 27-year veteran of the plant and the unassuming manager at the heart of the operation. Wetten supervises a group of 10 managers and 70 employees who maintain the facility around the clock. "Everything here depends on the furnace," he said. Other parts of the plant, such as the machinery that weaves filaments into fiberglass cloth, can stop for events as important as a machinery problem or as innocuous as the lunch break. But the furnace is too difficult to restart if it stops, so it runs continuously.

As with any business unit, the suggestions for improvements in Rio Claro cover a wide spectrum, from those that can be accommodated easily, such as larger safety glasses, to major capital improvements that can be years in the making, if at all. All are covered by the Second Element of Great Managing: ensuring employees have the materials and equipment they need to do their work well. The importance of this element is often best illustrated by its converse. When employees lack the means to do their work well, frustration with their inability quickly follows, as does anger with the company for placing the worker in such a difficult spot.

Properly supplying its employees works in the company's favor in two ways. From a purely functional perspective, having the right tools makes a job safer, easier, and more productive. "The first thing we think is safety," says Wetten. "We always ask ourselves, 'What are the risks?' We work with high temperatures. We work with high flammables, such as gasoline. We work with oxygen. The equipment we have should be the best we can get."

Equally important, the employee's perception that the company backs him up with the equipment he wants and needs serves as a powerful psychological motivator. "This is a company focused on its people, which makes me feel confident about my job," says Dos Santos.

Consider the case of the gloves worn by the "slivers," employees at Rio Claro who fix interruptions to the flow of filaments through the forming stations onto the spools one floor below. Without gloves, the employees risk their hands being punctured by small shards breaking off the fibers speeding down. With gloves, they have more difficulty feeling the filaments, which are only 10 to 15 microns wide, about the width of a human hair.

"The first gloves we had weren't comfortable and the safety department provided gloves that we like," said Rogerio Nodari, a sliver at the plant. "I have a need to feel the strings and to feel safe. It's little things like this that make a huge difference for us." Dos Santos, who is experimenting with a new type of glove, agreed. "The gloves allow you to do your work better, not being worried about injuring your hands."

Slivers carry a small red metal tool that resembles a comb, which they use to separate the fibers while rethreading the machinery. Having one just the right size with the right spacing between the teeth makes the job easier. "We are always experimenting with different combs," said Wetten.

A similar balance was needed in the wand used to blow air over the holes when rethreading, said forming specialist operator Valdemir Pistarino. A small one they tried didn't have enough force to clear extra molten glass from the holes. A large one had too much force. One in between worked just right. It was further improved by fitting it with a circular shield above the handle to block heat from the glass above "It has evolved into a tight process of collaboration between the employees and the managers," said the operator.

Asked about other pieces of equipment that make his job easier, Dos Santos stands up and grabs the leg of his pants, showing the reinforcing at the knee. "We do a lot of kneeling in this job," he says. "The extra padding here makes it more comfortable."

Workers are required to carefully monitor the temperature inside the furnace. This was once done with an optical thermometer that had to be aimed, like a telescope, through a small doorway in the furnace at various locations inside. It was not dangerous, but the heat is intense and quickly becomes uncomfortable. Managers at the plant found an infrared thermometer that allows the readings to be taken faster. "We take good care of the people so they take good care of the furnace," said Wetten.

Just as small refinements to the team's everyday materials and equipment can dramatically improve their safety and comfort, modest changes to the process multiply over time. One of the ways the Rio Claro employees demonstrate their engagement is by looking for ways to increase the plant's production. "The greatest percentage of ideas is related to production improvement," says Wetten. "Normally it's a small modification that makes a big difference in the production. We run 24 hours a day, 30 days a month, 12 months a year, so a small improvement can make a big difference at the end of the year."

Dos Santos adds, "We all know if the company prospers, it's better for us."

The kinds of lessons learned in Rio Claro apparently were lost on legendary advertising executive Jay Chiat in 1994. It was during that year he hatched a scheme that provides the perfect cautionary tale of what happens when a leader seeks to crusade against the psychological needs behind the Second Element.

Possessed of an idea that people could be more productive and creative if they would shed themselves of their traditional offices, and having too little space to supply regular digs anyway, Chiat turned his troops loose in Los Angeles and New York campus-style offices designed, as *The New York Times* put it, "to keep the firm in a state of creative unrest."[1] It was a grand experiment in what was called the "virtual office." Assigned desks, cubicles, and computers were taken away. Instead, each employee was given a small locker in which to keep a limited number of personal effects, and was expected to work somewhere — anywhere in or out of the building — just not in one place and not with equipment he could keep for any period of time.

If he wanted, a worker could sleep in and then work from home. He could spend his entire day at a client's offices. Or he could go to the advertising company's headquarters and choose from working temporarily in a conference room, at a couch in an open area, sitting in a domed "Tilt-o-Whirl" car, working at the snack bar, or on the outdoor deck, typing at a computer console or at a work station that could be rolled around the common space. "Indeed," said *The Times*, "as they go about their business, half the staff seems to be out there treading the airwaves somewhere between New York and Television Land in the great ethereal beyond."[2]

The concept was greeted with enthusiasm by the press. More than for famous ad campaigns such as the Energizer Bunny, Chiat "may be remembered best for creating a new way to work," wrote one columnist.[3]

"Barely four months after moving in," wrote another, "Chiat and his staff seem, on the whole, to be happily at home inside this dream."[4]

The idea bombed.

Soon after the experiment began, it began to go awry. Employees hid computers in their lockers or squirreled supplies in hiding spots. Others converted their car trunks into filing cabinets, flitting in and out of the building to retrieve their papers. "Nesting" — staying in one spot — was not allowed, but still occurred. "Jay would walk around, and he'd give you this look and say, "Did you sit here yesterday?" And he'd make you get up and move," said one worker.[5]

"For a brief, swirling period . . . the ad agency became engulfed in petty turf wars, kindergarten-variety subterfuge, incessant griping, management bullying, employee insurrections, internal chaos, and plummeting productivity," wrote commentator Warren Berger in *Wired* magazine. "Worst of all, there was no damn place to sit."

Lacking an office or even a filing cabinet in which to keep her materials, Associate Media Director Monika Miller pulled a child's red wagon loaded with her work as she looked for a place to land. "Everyone thought it was so cute," she said. "I'd be trudging down the hall, and they'd laugh and say, 'Oh look, here she comes with that little red wagon.' It was like a bad dream."[6]

Chiat thought he had a logical and innovative solution. "I must have talked to 100 people at the agency about it. I'd say, 'Explain to me what's wrong with this idea.' And they'd say, 'We need private space.' So I'd say, 'Why?' And they'd say, 'So we can think.' And I'd say, 'You will be able to think because you'll have private space — it just won't be personal space.' And they couldn't dispute the logic of that." (A different version came from an executive of the agency: "Jay didn't listen to anybody, he just did it.")[7]

The key was in a hint of doubt one of those columnists inserted into his otherwise glowing report. "Eliminating private space may be in keeping with current technology, but it may well be an affront to human nature," he wrote. Indeed it was. An October 2005 Gallup survey of workers in the United States found that while being able to see the outdoors, having an office with walls (instead of a cubicle), and freedom from too much noise all help to explain engagement, none of these matters as much as having "a personal work space."[8] And so Chiat's advertising agency learned a rule that every utopian social planner eventually learns: Human nature always defeats a big idea about how to change human nature. "My fault," the agency head told *Wired*, "was not recognizing that emotional reasons were the reality."

Chiat raised interesting ideas about making people more productive. Some employees are, in fact, more comfortable in a fluid, minimalist workspace, bouncing from one spot to another. Most are not. For all the freedom he seemed to be encouraging — come in when and if you want, choose a different or novel work area each day — he restricted options that are important to many workers: places with their names on them, storage for their papers, places to put their stuff, computers they can call their own. The hard-wired human principle he violated was dictating Second Element terms to his entire agency and, as to one of the most innate psychological motivations, telling them essentially to "get over it."

The paperless office, another affront to human nature, was as much a chimera as the virtual office, for the same reason books sell far more often in hard copy rather than as less expensive, lighter, easily searched e-books: People like paper. People like tangible possessions. They like rubber-band balls, photos of the big fish they caught, today's *Wall Street Journal*, a computer memory stick, a cell phone, and a hundred other tchotchkes, widgets, and devices arranged in their personal space. Their stuff includes practical tools needed to get the job done. But some of it is just emotionally motivating. In either case, they cling to it, and feeling properly equipped increases their productivity.

"Artifacts come with being human," wrote MIT psychology professor Steven Pinker in his book, *How the Mind Works*. "We make tools, and as we evolved our tools made us. One-year-old babies are fascinated by what objects can do for them. They tinker obsessively with sticks for pushing, cloth and string for pulling, and supports for holding things up."[9] Pinker's definition of an artifact — "an object suitable for attaining some end that a person intends to be used for attaining that end"[10] — is as relevant to the workplace as it is to evolutionary psychology. A sharp-edged rock allowed early man to hunt successfully, to cut hides for clothing or dig roots from the ground. His rudimentary materials and equipment were the difference between life and death. The use of artifacts to attain a purpose is a fundamental human characteristic, so managers must accept the occasional irrationality of the drive when *homo sapiens* is dropped into the very recently introduced (in evolutionary terms) cubicle village.

Although it tanked in theaters, the 1999 movie *Office Space* became a cult favorite because it parodied the very strong reactions just below the surface when employees are patronized, dictated to, and put-upon. A character named Milton Waddams is so disregarded that he is reduced to begging not to have his office moved yet again and to have his red Swingline stapler left alone.

"I don't care if they lay me off either," Milton says while talking on the phone in one scene, "because I told, I told Bill that if they move my desk one more time, then, then I'm, I'm quitting, I'm going to quit. . . . Because they've moved my desk four times already this year, and I used to be over by the window, and I could see the squirrels, and they were merry, but then, they switched from the Swingline to the Boston stapler, but I kept my Swingline stapler because it didn't bind up as much, and I kept the staples for the Swingline stapler. And it's not okay, because if they take my stapler then I'll set the building on fire."

Pathetic? Absolutely. But the instinct rang true with so many viewers that Swingline, which did not have a red model like the one in the movie (the movie prop had been given a custom paint job), introduced a red stapler to meet thousands of inquiries from cubicle-dwellers who wanted one of their own.[11] "Much of the humor hints at a much more serious fact: Modern work is genuinely dreadful and alienating," wrote one *Office Space* buyer in a review on Amazon.com. "Perhaps many office workers love their job, but I hate mine, and I assume that I am merely one of millions."[12]

Job stress changes a person from the minute she awakens. In 2004, four researchers recruited 219 people around the town of Trier, Germany, and asked them to swab their cheeks upon waking and several times more during the first hour they were up. These samples were then analyzed for their level of cortisol, a hormone that boosts blood pressure and blood-sugar levels while suppressing the immune system. The mere experience of waking up, seeing light, and thinking about the day ahead triggers the body to increase cortisol, so it wasn't shocking to find that subjects had more of the hormone 30 minutes into their day than when they first opened their eyes.

What popped out was that cortisol levels shot up much faster on weekday mornings than on the weekends. Moreover, weekday cortisol readings were higher yet among those who said they had more work than they could handle or who agreed with statements such as "I worry that I will not be able to fulfill my tasks."[13] So when a temp worker in *Office Space* says of a grumpy coworker, "Uh-oh. Sounds like somebody's got a case of the Mondays," she was onto something.

When three of the characters in the movie take the unreliable office copier into a field and smash it to pieces with baseball bats, they too were just reflecting emotions that the research bears out. Of the 12 Elements, whether a person has the materials and equipment needed to do his work well is the strongest indicator of job stress. The data show there are few things more frustrating than to want to make a difference at work, and to then be held back by inadequate resources. The Second Element is a prerequisite to any higher connection with the mission of the company, a topic we discuss in Chapter 8. "The literature on workplace hassles and frustration suggest that such performance obstacles can erode the meaningfulness of even the most inspiring of jobs," wrote researchers Michael G. Pratt and Blake E. Ashforth.[14]

Nearly one-third of workers in the United States say stress on the job caused them to behave poorly with family or friends in the prior month. The figure is unacceptably high in other countries as well. It's 39 percent in Brazil, 33 percent in Canada, and 25 percent in Japan, for example. The materials and equipment issue looms large over the problem of bringing work stress home. A full two-thirds of American workers who say they aren't adequately supplied also report bringing job stress home with them. Among those who say they have what they need to do their work, only one in four reports being grumpy at home.[15]

Behind the connection between equipment and stress lies an encouraging fact: People want to do their jobs well. They want to be productive. If they were motivated to get away with doing as little as possible, why would they care that a lack of information, support, tools, or other supplies reduced their output? Why would they quit their jobs more often when this aspect is lacking? Instead, most workers say in their direct responses and in their actions, "Give me what I need to produce, and I will produce."

When workers join organizations, they have a honeymoon period of about six months, on average, during which they are generally highly engaged in their work. People usually join an organization about which they are excited. They get a lot of early attention, and haven't yet had enough negative experiences to become disengaged. The sharpest drop in engagement comes after that first half-year. But the downward slope is not consistent across all 12 Elements. The drop is steepest on the Second Element, where the amount of positivity is cut roughly in half.[16] The average worker joins with high expectations, and when she is not supplied with the tools she needs to reach her high ideals, she becomes disenchanted. The best managers are adept at avoiding the transition from honeymoon to divorce.

Lou, the manager introduced at the beginning of this book, is in the second category. Among his obsessions is the working order of his men's forklifts. "It's got to be in tip-top shape," he said. "We have a company that sends a mechanic in here frequently. They are very good communicating with the guys. They know who drives what forklift and they will want to talk to that guy to find out just how is it running. Some guys like a hard pedal, some guys like a mushy pedal. He will adjust these things to make these guys comfortable. They're on these forklifts 8, 10, 12 hours a day, and given that a forklift has no suspension, the least we can do is make it operate the way the guy wants to make them happy."

Those workgroups for which materials and equipment are managed most effectively average higher customer engagement and higher productivity than their peers. They also have significantly better safety records, and their employees are less likely to flee to other organizations. For example, those managers with bottom quartile Second Element scores average 20 to 40 percent higher employee attrition than top quartile managers, representing millions of dollars in direct and indirect turnover costs.[17]

In the database, less than one-third of employees strongly agree they have the materials and equipment they need to do their work well. There is wide range on this item; the most engaged workgroups are nearly unanimous in their positive responses to the question, while the least engaged have no one who feels he is well equipped for the job. The most peculiar wrinkle in the data is that even in highly legislated environments, where nearly identical workgroups are given the same machines, cash registers, office supplies, and tools, the opinions of the employees vary widely.

The secret lies in the involvement, judgment and action of front-line managers. Less-engaged workgroups typically say they were supplied the standard toolkit in a standardized fashion: "Here's what you get. Make the best of it." The most engaged employees say their manager made what turned out to be relatively minor accommodations, aggressively petitioned for more expensive tools when the business case was strong, and was generally vigilant in looking for new ways to make his team more effective, without the employees having to harp.

"No one uses pencils anymore, but I use them all the time," said one editor. "I went to my manager and asked, 'Could I get a nice electric pencil sharpener?' And she said 'Sure.' It only cost $10, but it makes a big difference to me."

It's not unusual for a workgroup to have one or more Second Element issues that can be fixed only with the authority or money from corporate headquarters. In Rio Claro, the biggest issue that defies a local solution is the electrical supply. The thunderstorms of the Brazilian summer produce lightning. Lightning creates power outages. And outside of raw materials, the one thing the furnace needs to keep operating is power.

The fiberglass facility is wired to Rio Claro's municipal power grid. It lacks its own generating station or a separate line from the city's generators. "If someone hits a power pole in town, it can knock out our power," said Wetten.

Djalma Altarugio, a forming engineer at the plant, estimates that 80 percent of the fluctuations in production are due to power outages. "When we have a power failure, just one minute or two minutes or 30 seconds, the temperature of the glass that we control so carefully decreases," he said. Depending on the length of the power outage, it can take hours or days to return the furnace to full temperature, taking with it the plant's efficiency and production ratios. When properly running, the plant can convert over 90 percent of its raw materials into finished fiberglass. But when the power dies, efficiency drops with it. "It's a serious problem that we have in our plant," said Altarugio.

As bad as a power outage is for production, nothing better demonstrates the teamwork of the group. Everyone remembers well when the power went out and stayed out on Christmas Eve of 1998. Workers who were not at the plant knew there was a problem when their power went out at their homes. "The guys left their houses and their families, and they came to the plant to restart the operation," said Altarugio.

"Everyone who was in town immediately went to the plant because they knew how critical it was to keep that furnace working and they also knew how hard of a job it was for their peers to get it back up and running," said Wetten.

The Christmas Eve power outage was a particularly bad one. Electricity was not restored for three hours. The furnace had recently been rebuilt and improved, and the workers therefore were not completely familiar with its vulnerabilities. One of the pipes that carries molten glass cooled to the point that the glass hardened. It took three days to resume normal fiberglass-making, after which the company added special heaters to the points in the system most susceptible to rapid cooling. "We learned a lot in that experience," said Wetten.

Although they are rarely as long as the Christmas Eve outage, power interruptions continue to occur, requiring the employees to scramble into action. Wetten points to a graph of ratios that fluctuate above and below the conversion efficiency goal. There is a distinct seasonal nature to the graph — high through much of the year, but consistently lower in January and February, the middle of the Brazilian summer.

When the power stops, the first priority is to fire up a diesel generator at the back of the plant that supplies just enough electricity and heat to avoid catastrophic problems, but nowhere near the 10 megawatts the facility consumes at full power. "The furnace is held tight by the expansion of the heat inside," says Wetten. If it were cooled too much, would it contract or collapse? "Both!" he said.

Different procedures kick in as the outage continues, all designed to maintain the heat in the furnace and keep the glass fluid. Unless operators act quickly, a power outage that lasts longer than 10 or 15 minutes can cause serious damage to the furnace. Although with a fast and co-ordinated response, the plant can make it through an extended outage, there's only so much the workers can do. "After that," said the manager, "there's nothing we can do but cry."

When the power comes back on, a thousands blinking alarms demand attention. "This is where the commitment and the employee actions are so important," said Wetten. "You have the procedures, but every power failure is different."

In 2006, Owens Corning's headquarters in Toledo, Ohio, approved the construction of an on-site power substation to eliminate the interruptions. Like many managers who can't immediately fix a problem beyond their control, Wetten had to mix commiseration with determination to maintain the engagement levels of his employees while waiting for the substation.

"The key to overcoming the lack of certain equipment is to show my commitment to my people by being there with them during times of need, like the Christmas Eve power outage," he said. "This is how I gain their respect, not by being their boss."

"The high level of team commitment makes me confident about my work," said Pistarino. "People are committed to quality. It's not about giving orders or taking orders. It's about knowing what to do."

Wetten says his view of equipping employees is guided by a three-fold hierarchy of imperatives. At the top is employee safety, and so he is always looking for ways to protect his workers from the inherent dangers of the furnace, the hot or sharp glass, or the falls and falling objects that could occur in a multi-story industrial site. The second priority is avoiding damage to the facility — the kinds of complications they fight when the power goes out. "The impact of the failure of the furnace is serious for the company, but safety is unconditional," said the manager. For all the emphasis on production, it comes third. So, for example, requiring the slivers to wear gloves means they rethread a forming station slower than they would if they could feel the thin fibers with their bare hands. But working without gloves is not as safe.

Wetten also tells employees to trust their gut instincts to avoid an accident. "If you are not comfortable to do a job, you should not do it.

And you should talk to your boss," he said. "We are encouraging people to analyze everything they do to ensure it is safe."

In the past several years, the facility has added a small tool elevator to avoid the possibility of a worker falling or dropping a heavy tool as he climbs the stairs between levels. Heat shields have been added between the molten glass and where the workers stand to reduce their exposure the infrared rays. "There is a huge difference between having the shield and not having it," said Pistarino.

The emphasis on the right tools and safety has particular meaning for Pistarino. "I almost lost my foot in a prior job," he said. "If you don't request the equipment that is necessary, you are contributing to a lack of safety. Every time you see a problem, it's a potential accident and you should immediately communicate it to your manager."

Believing they had too large of a gap between the forming stations, where hot glass becomes fibers, and the winding stations one floor below, the employees and managers collaborated on the design for bright yellow metal grids that are now bolted into the concrete floors at each station. As a 35-year-old facility, Rio Claro may not have the latest technology, said Wetten, but they work hard to upgrade and improve what they have.

In other settings, managers frequently say they manage Second Element concerns partly by making individual accommodations to employees. They allow employees to pick from a variety of choices the cell phone that works best for them or modify the standard software in a laptop computer to meet the working style, talents, or work demands of each employee. Wetten does not have that luxury. "We work in shifts, so we have a lot of employees doing the same thing with the same tools," he says. "We try to have all the procedures well defined. We try to find a consensus. There is no way to try to adjust for each person."

Instead, a group of operators assembles once a month to discuss concerns and ideas about how to make the plant work better. "They are responsible to receive information from other operators, to check conditions in the plant and find improvements or make suggestions to avoid incidents in our area," said Altarugio. "It was based on a report from this team that we decided to install the grills between the forming and winding levels."

"We give ideas and the company responds," said Nodari.

"This is a company focused on its people," said Dos Santos, "which makes me feel confident about my job. Most important is knowing I am going to return to my family at the end of the shift without a scratch."

Through the power outages and the collaboration on better ways to work, the team at Rio Claro has built a strong level of employee engagement. They have learned that while they may not be able to rely on the power, they can rely on each other, particularly in an emergency. "The employees are very committed to the plant," said Altarugio. "In my opinion, it is the best feature of our plant." Because an outage can compromise the team's ability to reach its production goals for the entire month, and because they have a high degree of ownership for those goals, said Wetten, they display a strong professional ethic during the outages.

"I love what I do every day because I always have a challenge. You don't come to Owens Corning thinking about a lack of equipment, because it's all here," says Pistarino. That feeling helps fuel their commitment to each other.

"*O time veste a camisa!*" he says, employing a Brazilian soccer metaphor for a unified and proud team. Translated literally, it means, "The team wears the jersey!"

THE THIRD ELEMENT:

The Opportunity to Do What I Do Best

STRYKER'S NEW SYSTEM FOR HIP REPLACEMENT SURGERY was an important step forward.

The technology was unthinkable a generation ago. Called a "navigation" system, it was designed to use electronic devices anchored to a patient's pelvis and thigh bone combined with sensors locked onto the operating instruments to help the surgeon place the new joint in just the right spot. The positioning of the new artificial joint into the hip could be seen on a computer screen, eliminating less precise estimations by the doctor.

Getting the joint perfectly aligned gives a patient much better range of movement in activities as simple as sitting or walking up stairs. With conventional surgery, the acetabular shell — the cup into which the new ball of the thigh bone fits — might not be aligned as well, reducing movement and even creating a risk that the hip could dislocate. Addressing the problem was exactly the kind of innovation upon which Stryker is built, a profitable product in high demand, incorporating medical and technological advances that improve the lives of its client's patients. Hopes and expectations were high.

Soon after field testing began in 2004, Stryker's hip navigation systems were being returned to the company with complaints from orthopedic surgeons, said Dr. Amir Sarvestani, a project manager in the company's research and development facility in Freiburg, Germany. "Just a few days after we shipped the product to customers, unexpected problems were identified. We couldn't believe what we saw when our instrumentation came back."

"Pieces were broken and beaten up, and the electronics were frequently not functioning like they should have been," said engineer Dieter Teschke. "We said, 'What's happened to this instrumentation?'" No one anticipated what the devices would endure in a hip replacement surgery.

The responsibility for fixing the problem fell to team leader Klaus Welte, vice president and plant manager in Freiburg. His team would need to meticulously rethink each component and strengthen it against the stresses that were being applied through repeated, high-impact use in operating rooms. He also needed to assemble his team in the same way as the product, each employee well fitted to his role and working flawlessly together with the rest. The failure of any one component, or any team member, could cause the product and the entire group to fall short of their goals.

The facility in Freiburg was known as Leibinger before its acquisition by the larger Stryker Corporation in 1998. Leibinger specialized in software that used three-dimensional X-ray or magnetic images of a patient's brain, helping a neurosurgeon plan the operation he needed to perform. After becoming part of Stryker, the Freiburg division extended its work into the development of the actual surgical tools guided by the same navigation technology.

"We developed a system that consists of a pointer, a wand that the surgeon holds in his hand, that he can use during the operation," said Welte. "Through the pointer we were able to create a link between the actual patient during surgery and the image that was created of the patient beforehand."

The next logical extension of the Freiburg team's work was into orthopedic surgeries, which make up a much larger part of Stryker's business. Hip and knee replacements are far more common than brain surgery, particularly as advances in health care allow more people to live longer. The company figured if the same combination of software, tracking, and imaging could be incorporated into bone operations, it could substantially improve hip and knee surgeries while creating another source of revenue. "Stryker believes that our image-guided systems are integral to the future of total joint replacement surgery," the company said in its 2003 annual report. "For this reason, [in addition to a knee navigation system] we are also developing a hip navigation platform that will support less invasive hip replacement with smaller incisions and more accurate placement."

But as the Freiburg engineers were about to find out, instrument design for orthopedic replacements differs from neurosurgery in one crucial aspect: sheer force. The brain is composed of soft tissue, and the instruments used for surgery on it are relatively delicate. "Our company came from a history of neurosurgeries," said Teschke. "Before this we made micro-instrumentation and micro-implants for brain and head surgeries. The difference between those customers and the orthopedic customers? They're worlds apart."

As anyone who has ever seen one can attest, a hip replacement surgery, while at some stages done with a light touch, necessitates a certain amount of bone cutting, grinding, reaming, and pounding on the instrumentation with a hammer. "It looks brutal," said Jürgen Pross, another member of the Freiburg team. "Actually, it looks like working in a garage, fixing a car."

Further complicating the design specifications, the surgical tools have to be sterile. Between surgeries they are placed in an autoclave, a sort of medical pressure cooker in which 270-degrees-Fahrenheit steam at high pressure kills any bacteria that could endanger the patient. Not only did the metal in the instruments have to maintain its integrity through repeated cycles of being struck and heated, the precision electronics had to continue to function perfectly.

While Stryker had been successfully manufacturing electronics to be "autoclavable" for years, the addition of the impact stress created another level of complexity: The electronics could be affected by the pounding during surgery or the heat of the autoclave. As for which stress was causing the electronic problems, "actually that was sometimes not so easy to answer," said Pross. "We didn't know at that time." In addition, the repeated heating and cooling made some of the buttons on the side of the instruments stick or caused the infrared sensors to rise from their flush positions in the metal housing.

"If you look at the situation as a curve, the curve was going down into a deep valley," said Sarvestani. "The trust in the reliability of a new product is of utmost importance to our customers and to our sales force." The issues had to be resolved before going to market.

The reputation of the Freiburg group was on the line. Because of the urgency of fixing the problems, a team of Stryker engineers in Kalamazoo, Michigan, was asked to give advice and double-check the design. While the assistance was appreciated, it added to the pressure. "We knew that we had only one chance to fix this problem and that if we would fail, it would have big impact on the organization here," said Pross.

The challenge for Welte was assembling and directing a team of the right people who could put the hip replacement system back on track. To succeed would require both a clear view of what had to be accomplished and a deep understanding of each team members' abilities.

Matching a person to the right job, or a job to the right person, is one of the most complicated responsibilities any manager will face. As a consequence, no other element of managing has as much depth as the Third.

The Third Element emerged from the ability of a straightforward statement to predict the performance of a given worker and entire teams: "At work, I have the opportunity to do what I do best every day." With a front-row seat on their own thoughts and feelings, workers have no trouble assessing this element in their own work lives. But the simplicity of the statement belies the complexity within it. The reasons why this element is so powerful go to the heart of the most recent discoveries about human nature and touch on debates about individuality that stretch back for centuries.

For the manager, the problem begins with a simple question: Who would excel in this assignment? But the more a manager delves into that question, the more it spins off additional puzzles. What makes someone succeed where others fail? Is it something innate, something she learned, or is she just trying harder? Can excellence in a certain role be learned? How fast and how much can people change? Can a job candidate be molded to fit the needs of the position, or is what you see during that first interview what you get? These dilemmas not only get to the heart of human nature; they also stir up a swirl of history, politics, legal constraints, and wishful thinking around philosophies that are often deeply held — and wrong.

The most insidious notion about human potential in circulation is that an employee can do anything if he puts his mind to it, can envision it, tries hard enough or cares enough. "You can do anything you wish to do, have anything you wish to have, be anything you wish to be," wrote early 20th Century motivational author Robert Collier.[1] This belief was restated by Henry Ford, sung by Carole King, brought to life in "My Fair Lady," sold on DVDs by Wayne Dyer, and is boilerplate language for high school graduation speeches every spring. Standing at the center of the Herodian Amphitheater, surrounded by a full orchestra that had just finished playing one of his songs, John Yanni Christopher philosophizes in the CD that launched his career: "Everything great that has ever happened to humanity has begun as a single thought in someone's mind. And if any one of us is capable of such a great thought, then all of us have the same capability, because we're all the same." The audience applauds loudly.[2]

Although he may not realize it, Yanni's opinion of human potential has its roots in a psychological approach called behaviorism, which held sway in the field of psychology from the early to mid 1900s. Its chief proponents argued that an individual's personality is simply the sum of adaptations he made to match his environment. Under this theory, people are infinitely malleable, each a collection of Pavlovian drooling responses to the world's dinner bells. "Give me a dozen healthy infants, well formed, and my own specified world to bring them up in and I'll guarantee to take any one at random and train him to become any type of specialist I might select — doctor, lawyer, merchant-chief, and yes, even beggar-man and thief, regardless of his talents, penchants, tendencies, abilities, vocations, and race of his ancestors," wrote American psychologist John B. Watson.[3]

The idea of every person having identical potential has tremendous appeal, particularly in how it refutes more foolish or destructive ideas of human capacity. "We are all the same" is so much more appealing than the ancient idea that a man's astrological sign pre-determined his personality, the divine right of kings, or the assorted beliefs in racial superiority that fostered tragedies from slavery to Nazism. It seems to correspond with the "self-evident" truth in the United States' Declaration of Independence "that all men are created equal."

More frequently than one might imagine, companies hesitate to put too much emphasis on any one person's abilities or accomplishments for fear others will feel hurt or left out. "There's a lot of 'Harrison Bergeron' thinking around here," one personnel executive confided privately, referring to the 1961 short story by Kurt Vonnegut that begins, "The year was 2081, and everyone was finally equal." The story describes a future in which government "handicappers" snuff out all forms of exceptional performance. "Nobody was any smarter than anyone else," it says. "Nobody was better looking than anybody else. Nobody was stronger or quicker than anybody else."[4] In other words, Yanni's world.

Meaningful differences present opportunities not just to advance business interests, but also to improve the careers and lives of employees matched to more personally fulfilling jobs. The current evidence points to the conclusion that individuals are not born the same and not infinitely capable. Instead, the research says any given person is a unique combination of talents who will succeed to the degree these essential traits are employed. This does not make as catchy a bumper sticker as "You Can Do Anything," but it's a clearer picture of the challenge.

Many of the most recent insights about range in mental capabilities are taken for granted in physical endeavors. Basketball players must practice for years to refine their games, condition their bodies to perform, and train their reflexes to hit a three-point jump shot. But none of this is sufficient by itself to make it into the National Basketball Association, where the average player is over 6-foot-7 [5], compared with the average American man's height of 5-foot-9½ [6]. Does anyone doubt that, in addition to years of coaching and practice, Houston Rockets' star Yao Ming owes much of his success to being 7 feet, 6 inches tall?

"You can't coach height," says the old bromide. Pro basketball players are first born, then made.

A growing accumulation of evidence indicates that in their functioning, brains are just as variable as bodies. There are even tantalizing hints of anatomical differences in the brains of those with extraordinary mental abilities. The most famous example is that of Albert Einstein. After the physicist died in 1955, his brain was removed, measured and preserved. In 1999, three scientists from McMaster University in Canada compared Einstein's brain to the university's collection of "normal brains" donated for research.

Einstein described his scientific thinking as not using words, but rather "associative play" of "more or less clear images" of a "visual and muscular type." Because of Einstein's abilities and his own description of his thinking, the professors paid special attention to his left and right posterior parietal regions, responsible for "visuospatial cognition, mathematical ideation and imagery of movement." Einstein's brain had unique attributes not seen in any of those in the McMaster collection "nor in any specimen documented in the published collections of postmortem brains," the professors wrote in the British medical journal *The Lancet*. "Einstein's exceptional intellect in these cognitive domains and his self-described mode of scientific thinking may be related to the atypical anatomy in his inferior parietal lobes."

Extrapolating to the population in general, the scientists hypothesized, "variation in specific cognitive functions may be associated with the structure of the brain regions mediating those functions."[7] The implications are incredible: Because of real physical differences in the brain, a person might be to accounting what Yao Ming is to basketball, to marketing what Roger Maris was to baseball or to corporate creativity what Pelé was to soccer, an employee's brain structure giving him an advantage over others in the same way physical stature gives an edge to the champion athlete. "This innate geometry and cabling can have real consequences for thinking, feeling and behavior," wrote Steven Pinker in his 2002 book, *The Blank Slate: The Modern Denial of Human Nature*.[8]

Einstein was far outside the usual range of cognitive functioning. What about "normal" people, those with whom we work or those we consider hiring? Do they come pre-wired for excellence in a particular discipline? Brain imaging and post-mortem examinations have not progressed to the point at which they can answer this question, but other methods strongly suggest the answer is yes.

By studying twins reared apart, researchers "are finding that genetics, in addition to familial interests, educational, social and other environmental pressures, have a considerable impact on how we choose what we do — and how happy we are with that choice," wrote Dr. Nancy L. Segal, professor of developmental psychology and director of the Twins Studies Center at California State University at Fullerton. "Twins reared apart, one University of Minnesota study showed, chose jobs that were similar in terms of complexity level, motor skills and physical demands. In other studies, twins have been shown to have similar tendencies when it comes to 'enterprising,' 'conventional' and 'artistic' undertakings; they also share basic interests, be they science, the pastry arts or public speaking."[9] The results of such studies strongly implicate genetics as a decisive influence on intellect, personality, job interests, and even personal idiosyncrasies.

The role of nature in molding an employee is becoming more difficult to refute. "The slate cannot be blank if different genes can make it more or less smart, articulate, adventurous, shy, happy, conscientious, neurotic, open, introverted, giggly, spatially challenged, or likely to dip buttered toast in coffee," wrote Pinker.[10] But for executives, managers, and personnel strategists, the issue is much simpler. Companies don't hire toddlers; they hire adults whose formative years are past. By the time an applicant shows up at an organization's door, the die is cast. Massive studies based on tens of thousands of hires and their subsequent performance show that the right combination of personality traits, talents, and abilities predispose some people to succeed in a job where others fail.[11] Most hiring managers seem to have an intuitive grasp of this truth; majorities say they value personality characteristics over an applicant's education and background.[12] Yet most of these decision-makers do not use anything scientific to examine job candidates' inherent tendencies.[13]

Gallup brought its research to bear in 2001, in the culmination of decades of investigation led by former chairman Donald O. Clifton. Dr. Clifton was concerned that traditional psychology spent far more energy on mental abnormalities than it did trying to understand the factors that create superior levels of performance. In 1969, a group of Gallup scientists began looking for a series of questions that could differentiate the various ways of naturally thinking, feeling, and acting that make someone uniquely successful.

At the time, the literature on the mind was rich with descriptions of mental disease. Yet there was little outside of standardized mathematical, verbal, and logic tests to help a normally functioning person understand the most praiseworthy aspects of her personality. As evidence of this neglect, the field even lacked a standardized language of positive mental attributes. Like-minded scientists such as Martin Seligman were conducting research in a similar vein. Today, the nascent positive psychology movement publishes books, holds an annual conference and appears to be broadening traditional psychology into topics such as hope, resiliency, purpose, engagement, and well-being.

The Clifton StrengthsFinder has since been administered to 2 million people around the world in 18 languages. Its 34 distinct talent themes include "Ideation," a gravitating toward novel ways of thinking; "Input," the ability to digest large amounts of information; and "Achiever," an inner drive that leads one to ever-higher levels of accomplishment. These themes are relatively consistent — they don't change much over time in a person — giving further evidence each individual is not a lump of clay being dramatically reshaped by events around him, but has a durable personality. He has his weaknesses; he has his talents. And the better a manager can help him recognize and utilize his innate talents, the more effective he will be.

"Having the conversation about gifts is a fabulous conversation to have with someone, but it takes time and it takes presence," said one hospital manager who uses a talent-based approach. "I pose a couple of questions: 'So what are your gifts? Where are you most happy?' Then, 'Let's look at what you're doing today — let's map that out. Tell me about your day. Tell me about where you're using those gifts every single day. And if you aren't, what about this position over here?' It's actually having the conversation and breaking it down and talking about it in a very positive, passionate way rather than the old historical way, which is 'You're not meeting your job expectations.'"

Those who reach the highest levels in their professions often talk about an irresistible urge that impelled them toward their "calling in life" or "the thing I was born to do." In his essay "Why I Write," George Orwell describes this kind of need to be true to his nature: "From a very early age, perhaps five or six, I knew that when I grew up I should be a writer. Between the ages of about seventeen and twenty-four I tried to abandon this idea, but I did so with the consciousness that I was outraging my true nature and that sooner or later I would have to settle down and write books."[14]

Claremont Graduate University Professor Mihaly Csikszentmihalyi, another important influence in the field of positive psychology, calls this marriage of personality and pursuit an "autotelic experience" or "flow." At work, these optimal situations are those in which the employee enjoys the work itself rather than enduring the job just to earn the pay or to gain the chance to be promoted to a better, more fulfilling job.[15]

When employees talk about what they do best, they rarely frame the discussion in terms of a job description. Certainly people can form attachments to their professions to the point that being a salesperson, professor, or nurse becomes part of their self-image. Their talents, however, being more an instinctive part of them than any specific job, are transferable from one position to another, even across industries. A salesperson with exceptionally persuasive talents in "Woo" might have found equal fulfillment and success as a political lobbyist or a talk show host. A college professor with powerful "Communication" talents might have just as easily found his calling as a consultant. In fact, some people who have switched careers several times remark that the only thing that makes their life's work cohesive is the reemergence of their talents in each occupation. It is likewise not unusual to find two people in ostensibly identical roles who, by virtue of "doing what they do best," perform in quite different fashions — one a banker who loves the business because he gets to work closely with people in his town; another a natural capitalist who can't imagine not being involved in the constant movement of stocks, interest rates, and precious metals prices.

To get the most from her team, a manager must help each employee mold his job around the way he works most naturally, maximizing the frequency of optimal experiences in which he loses himself in the work, is internally motivated, and finds himself naturally gifted. She must also realize that as long as he accomplishes the goals for which he is responsible, without any harm along the way, how he gets there does not matter. Acknowledging one's greatest natural talents and weaknesses does not mean accepting a narrow set of career possibilities. Rather, it means each employee will succeed in a relatively unique way, applying his own style to the accomplishment.

Imagine that a large group has plans to meet for lunch at the top of a mountain. There are three routes to the top. The first option is a slow, winding path, none of it very steep, but it requires several miles of walking. The second alternative is steeper and goes through the woods; it requires more stamina and the ability to use a map and compass to avoid getting lost. The third route is almost straight up, climbing the rock face of the mountain; it requires technical climbing skills, but is the shortest of the three possibilities. If each person in the group chooses his or her own route, and if each makes it safely to the top in time for lunch, none of the routes can be said to be better than the other two. The same phenomenon occurs in business. As British business executive and author Sir John Harvey-Jones once said, "I have worked with leaders whose style is so totally different to my own that I have found it incomprehensible that they achieve results, but nevertheless they do."[16] The 12 managers profiled in this book are prime examples. No two share exactly the same talents, and several differ dramatically. Each succeeded in his or her own way, but they all got there by taking advantage of their natural talents rather than by trying to be someone each is not.

A personnel strategy based on talents creates concrete financial advantages. Several years ago, Gallup analyzed the responses of 2,000 managers to open-ended questions about their management approaches. Of particular interest was whether the supervisor believed it was better to devote more of his energy to "fixing" people's weaknesses or to further improving an area of strength. When the interview responses were compared with performance data for their teams, it turned out the managers of the best workgroups were more likely to spend a disproportionate amount of time with their high producers, match talents to tasks and emphasize individual strengths over seniority in making personnel decisions. On average, a workgroup led by a strengths advocate was almost twice as likely to create above-average results as one led by a manager biased toward patching up problems.[17]

A recent study found organizations focused on maximizing the natural talents of their employees increased engagement levels by an average of 33 percent per year, equating to an average net gain of $5.4 million in productivity per organization over enterprises using more traditional methods.[18] Another recent study found that sales representatives who received feedback on their strengths sold 11 percent more than those who did not receive such feedback.[19] The Third Element is powerful in explaining not only productivity, but also the future profitability of teams within companies. Business units in the top quartile of Gallup's database on the "do what I do best" statement exceed the profits of those in the bottom quartile by an average of 10 to 15 percent.[20] A recent analysis of multiple studies reveals managers whose talents are aligned with their job demands achieve, on average, 15 percent more in sales and 20 percent more in profit, have 24 percent fewer unscheduled absences, and deal with 13 percent lower employee turnover than the average.[21]

For all the evidence that this approach is good for business, only about one in three employees can strongly agree that they "have the opportunity to do what they do best every day." The amount of money left on the table is staggering. Businesses agonize over marketing plans, inventory strategies, labor models, and new product introductions in search of one or two more points of profit. Few of them realize part of the answer is so close to home.

There was very little ambiguity in what the Stryker team needed to accomplish. "We have a very well-defined process," said manager Klaus Welte. "The key performance targets are defined for the product, and we continually refine them over time. That gives the team a pretty clear direction on where they should be going and what are the right questions to ask." The difficulty was not in understanding what had to be done, but in actually designing a hip replacement system that could simultaneously maintain its electronic circuitry while enduring the mechanical stresses of the operations and the heat and pressure of sterilizations.

"Nobody had ever achieved meeting all these three requirements at the same time," said Sarvestani. "It's very simple to meet one requirement, for instance to make it very robust to withstand the impact. The challenge was to look at all the requirements at the same time and to make sure that we have good coverage of all of them."

In their favor, the employees began with a good understanding of themselves and of each other's talents. "We do one-on-ones with our employees very often, every two or three months at least," said Welte. "In those, we really ask them, 'What do you do best?' and, 'What do you like about your job?' We try to help people understand themselves. What they describe they do best is really what gets exactly to the role we want them in." On the Third Element, the Stryker team ranks in the top 15 percent of workgroups in the global engagement database.

Welte assembled a team of the best people at Freiburg in operations, computer-aided design, engineering, and research. He looked to Sarvestani for "structured analysis," thorough communications and follow-through. Having more friends in the building than anyone else on the team, Pross provided the "social glue." That, combined with a high degree of responsibility — "He would never stop until everything is complete," said Welte — made him central to keep the project moving. Teschke is a natural organizer and always well-grounded in the facts. "He takes the speed out if the team gets ahead of itself," said Welte. Michael Porbadnik is particularly talented at understanding how a design will stand up to the manufacturing process.

When the team is designing systems rather than fixing problems, Welte also relies on Jose-Luis Moctezuma. He's a kind of in-house visionary whose ideas, such as a gravity sensor in the overhead "locator" that tracks the positions of all the other components, at first seem unorthodox, and later turn out "not only useful, but imperative," said Welte. And, "he knows as much or even more about orthopedic surgery than many orthopedic surgeons." In the natural conflict of perspectives, Moctezuma eager to jump forward and Teschke cautious to not move too fast, the team found the optimal path.

Asked about his own greatest talents, Welte said, "I analyze things and see their properties and work to put them together in an ideal combination." He enjoys doing this both with the devices Stryker creates and with the members of a team. "If you combine technology, you see a much more rapid result," he said. "With people, it takes longer to see the result."

Once he had these first key players in place, Welte looked for holes in the team's abilities. "After we have a team assembled and the team starts its work, we analyze what they are doing and we see what's missing," he said. "We are looking for the missing piece of the puzzle. At the same time, I have a mental picture of each person and what he contributes, what he does best. To find that missing piece, we look through our list of people and ask "Who is the person that has the best ability to fit into that puzzle and fulfill the specific role that we need at this time."

"Creating an effective team," said Welte "requires more than just filling all the job descriptions with someone who has the right talent and experience. By no means can you substitute one engineer for another. There are really very, very specific things that they are good at." And how well the team members' abilities combine is as important as the abilities themselves.

"It usually takes about six months or more to find out exactly about a person," said Welte. "Sometimes it's also quite surprising because it's not always what you saw in their résumé. There have been several cases in the past where we hired somebody and then ended up after, let's say, a year or so reassigning him to a totally or a significantly different task." As an example, Welte mentions an engineer hired as a research and development manager who turned out to be somewhat risk-adverse, but intensely drawn to performance metrics. His cautiousness handicapped him at the beginning of projects, when numerous possibilities need to be explored without inhibition, but made him well suited for the later stages, when it is crucial to make sure everything is right.

With the high pressure and external stress of finding a solution for the hip navigation system, it was important to get the interpersonal nuances right.

The newly formed team took over a meeting room as their central gathering point for the project, where they would spend about half their time together for the next six months. They called it the war room, "a very, very unpleasant room," Welte recalled. "Everybody felt the situation so intensely that we had the feeling that we were right in the middle of a war fighting against these problems," said Pross.

There were no simple solutions. Each aspect of the instruments had to be analyzed separately, and about 10 problems had to be rectified. "The only way to get out of that situation was to work hard," said Teschke. Examining the broken predecessors, the engineers found where the electronic connections were breaking from the surgeon's blows. Three months were spent determining the right glue for the capacitors that had been a weak link. A different welding technique was used to encapsulate the electronics within the shaft of the probe. After testing various metals for the buttons, the team found one that would not expand with repeated sessions in the autoclave.

Things started to click. "There was the point where we as a team really started in a systematic way to dig down to the problems and work on systematic solutions," said Pross. "That really raised the confidence in everybody that we were on the way to a good way of solving the problems. From every perspective, the knowledge came into play. The test plans got much better than before. The design was really reviewed in each and every aspect. And the more we progressed in a systematic fashion, the more the team was confident that we were close to a solution."

Sarvestani was impressed with how the various talents of the team members combined into an effective and collegial group that made all their major decisions by consensus. "It was true teamwork," he said. "We had some people who were very strong in mechanics, and others who were stronger in electronics, others who were strong in processes, others who were strong in how to validate designs. That was all brought together into one master plan."

Because of the number of problems to be solved, the team didn't want to attempt solving them simultaneously and assembling the full set of untested solutions in one prototype. Instead, they solved the issues one by one, beginning with the most crucial and working their way down to the relatively minor. This meant the group didn't get to see a fully assembled prototype until they had tackled the full list of solutions. "The most encouraging situation was when we did the pre-pilot test," said Sarvestani. "We assembled all the components and for the first time we could see that the entire design, after all the changes and improvements we did, was working."

As the initial introduction painfully made clear, it was one thing to make a working instrument, but quite another thing to make one that looked and worked the same after many surgeries and sterilizations. To guarantee that reliability, the team hired a group of local students and procured a robot (one of Porbadnik's ideas) to put the prototypes through the same conditions as in a hospital. The robot moved instruments into and out of the autoclave around the clock, through 600 heating and cooling cycles. Working in continuous shifts every day of the week, the students loaded freshly autoclaved devices into "impaction machines" that mimicked the pounding they would take in an operating room. "The whole building was shaking," said Teschke.

Even with continuous testing, the re-design of the hip navigation system took four weeks longer than upper management had hoped. But the devices came through with flying colors. The LEDs lit up after autoclaving. None of the buttons or moveable parts stuck after repeated heating and cooling. There were no cracks in the housing after the instruments took a pounding. Through a long list of criteria, the work passed its inspections. "We had 100 percent success — 100 percent of the instruments passed our test criteria," said Teschke. "From a quality standpoint, this project brought our whole hardware electronic team to another quality standard. It was fantastic what we learned in this short timeframe."

There was no celebration when the improved hip navigation system was shipped to orthopedic surgeons around the world. The team was simply too nervous and didn't want to claim victory until the device proved itself in larger numbers and actual operating conditions. The nature of design work is that the number tested is usually far less than the number manufactured. "That makes it very difficult to conclude from your own results how the product will perform later in the field, where the sample size is much bigger," said Sarvestani. "That was one of the reasons why we were always skeptical, even after it passed all the tests and we released it. None of us was really totally convinced." The team waited for news from the field.

Because of the sensors attached to the patient's bones and every instrument used in the operation, the Stryker hip navigation system shows a precise display, accurate to seven thousandths of a millimeter, of the bones, the instruments, and the components of the artificial hip. Coloring the instruments yellow when out of alignment, blue when on course and red if the doctor goes too far, the system shows the surgeon how much bone to remove and at what angle to make the cuts.

For all the effort they put into creating a system to give the surgeons instantaneous, detailed, and accurate feedback, the Freiburg team received silence — precisely the wonderful, reassuring silence the team hoped for. In the medical devices industry, when a product suffers problems, the reports and the devices come back, just as the first version of the hip navigation system did. Success is much quieter. They have a Bavarian saying about success: "Nicht gescholten ist Lob genug" — Not being scolded is praise enough. Or, as Americans would say, "No news is good news."

The lack of "scolding" was phenomenal. "We're now one-and-a-half years after we released the instruments," said Sarvestani. "For the first nine months we didn't have a single complaint. That is an incredibly low number for this type of instrument." The team's hard work allowed Stryker to make good on its promises to the market, and to trumpet in the annual report released in spring of 2005, "Stryker pioneered the emerging field of image-guided surgical navigation, and we remain the only company to develop fully integrated navigation hardware and software."

Team leader Welte is less effusive than his colleagues in his excitement, partly by nature. "I'm a person who is never really 100 percent happy with the way things are. I like constant improvement." Nonetheless, he said he is quite pleased with the way the team meshed together, got the product back on track, learned more about each other's talents and increased their capabilities in the process.

"That was a big victory for us."

The Fourth Element:
Recognition and Praise

O NE HUNDRED KILOMETERS SOUTH OF GDAŃSK, where Lech Wałęsa and the Solidarity trade union upended decades of Communist rule in Poland, Elżbieta Górska-Kołodziejczyk is working on a more modest revolution.

She wants to make her employees smile.

Górska is the manager of the warehouse in the formerly state-owned paper-making plant in the city of Kwidzyn. International Paper purchased a majority stake from the government 14 years ago, and dramatic changes to the business have occurred since then. In a facility where 4,500 people were once employed, only 1,600 are now needed. Where 200,000 metric tons of paper were produced each year, the enterprise now ships three times as much. As a state facility behind the Iron Curtain in 1980, it packaged paper in only five different wrappers. Today, as a private concern and with Poland now a member of the European Union, the paper leaves in 300 different patterns or brands, bound for stores across the continent.

But situated in the basement, with none of the natural light that surrounds the machinery on the main level, the warehouse posed a particularly difficult challenge. The obstacles had undone three previous managers, all men in a male-dominated facility. For reasons she does not know, Górska was asked "out of the blue" in 2002 to assume responsibility for the 24 people working three shifts supplying pallets, packaging, plastic wrap, and glue for the plant's operations. Suddenly the diminutive new manager, who once hoped for a career as a political leader, was given the chance she always wanted to improve people's lives, and it scared her.

"If I was afraid of anything in this job, that I could not handle it, it was the people," she explained in Polish. "I knew the specifics of the technical side of the work here. I was just really terrified with how to manage the people, to be responsible for them."

She had reason to be daunted. The work flow in the warehouse was poorly organized. Employees did not have a good sense of their individual responsibilities. There were no computers in the warehouse; everything had to be looked up in catalogs or tracked on paper. There was no team spirit and there was nowhere for team members to meet, formally or informally.

A general sense of malaise hung over the place. Employees there felt the rest of the plant looked down on them, both literally and figuratively, and that they were in "a dark forgotten place." On top of it all, being the only female middle manager didn't help Górska.

"When I inherited the team I had four men — big boys, healthy looking guys — who could not in any way accept the fact that a woman, and a tiny one — because I am not a very tall woman — was going to give them orders," she said. "And this was my biggest problem, the male chauvinism, as I would call it today. In the beginning they did not want to do what I told them. It was unpleasant. For a long time they were resisting. I tried to get through to them. I tried to convince them that if a man takes a broom, for example, he will not have an allergic reaction to it."

The team did seem to have an allergic reaction to Górska's initial attempts to introduce recognition and praise into the group. One autumn, production was curtailed while the machinery on the main floor was upgraded. The pace in the warehouse settled proportionately, leaving additional time on the employees' hands. Four members of the warehouse team took it upon themselves to put things in order. At their own initiative, they conducted an internal inventory check, packed up loose items, and better organized their work areas.

At one of the new team meetings that Górska initiated, she gave the four employees what she considered well-deserved praise for their efforts. But instead of the acknowledgement and smiles most managers would expect in that situation, they shyly hung their heads, saying they were just doing what was needed and no recognition was called for. After the meeting, word came back to Górska that her comments in the meeting disrupted the group, causing feelings of jealousy and perceptions that she was playing favorites. "I have to say that it hurt me," said the manager, "because this wasn't my intention."

The manager chalked up part of the reaction to "our Polish mentality: 'Sit quietly, let them give you what they are supposed to give.' We are a nation of solitaries and we just complain — *wrong, too little, not good*," she said. "If it rains — *not good*. If the sun shines — *not good*. Forty degrees — *not good*. Minus 20 degrees — *even worse*." Data from a Gallup World Poll suggest Górska's impression is correct. Among the residents of 33 countries asked the question, "Do you feel enthusiastic about your future?" only 36 percent of Poles responded "yes," the lowest percentage among the nations studied. The average among the countries surveyed was 77 percent.[1]

But it's typical for teams in any country unfamiliar with regular recognition and praise to react in an unexpected fashion when a manager tries to increase positive feedback. Because kind words are viewed as a rare commodity, they sometimes inspire more envy than gratitude and motivation. When introduced into the warehouse team, after decades with little praise, Górska's congratulations backfired. She needed to devise a strategy for a situation more complicated than it first appeared.

Górska's team needed many changes to reach their full potential. Leading the list was greater recognition and praise, the Fourth Element of Great Managing. No matter how much praise embarrassed them or caused internal strife, there was little chance the warehouse workers would give their best efforts without the power of that reinforcement.

In the perception of employees generally, praise is painfully absent from most companies and the workgroups within them. Less than one in three employees can give a strongly positive answer to the statement, "In the last seven days, I have received recognition or praise for doing good work." At any given company, it's not uncommon to find between one-fifth and one-third of the people disagreeing with the item, as if to say, "Not only have I not received any praise recently; my best efforts are routinely ignored."

Businesses could write off this issue as a collection of sad but irrelevant emotional deficits if reinforcement were not so important to motivation on the job. But it is. The effects on the company begin with intentions to quit: Employees who do not feel adequately recognized are twice as likely to say they will leave their company in the next year.[2] There are even larger consequences for outcomes short of quitting that reflect the energy the employee brings to work each day. Variation in the Fourth Element is responsible for 10- to 20-percent differences in productivity and revenue, and thousands of loyal customers to most large organizations.[3]

In one large health care organization, a difference of 10 percentage points on the recognition statement represented an average difference of 11 percent on patients' evaluations of their experience. In one investment firm, the difference between half of its investment advisors feeling recognized and one-third feeling that way represented an 11 percent difference in revenue — millions of dollars in play. A large, multi-company analysis puts the average benefit of such a shift in recognition at 6.5 percent greater productivity and 2 percent higher customer engagement, the latter being the most difficult and profitable metric to move, where each percentage point equates to hundreds of millions in sales for a Fortune 500 company.[4]

These linkages hold true, regardless of the type of industry or culture. Some industries, such as manufacturing, and some countries, such as France, are even more prone to low recognition. Such generalities can be misleading if they obscure the fact that one can find managers who charge up their teams with praise in any country and in any industry. However, such managers are the exception. Because of its power, ridiculously low cost and rarity, the Fourth Element is one of the greatest lost opportunities in the business world today.

A simple experiment helps illustrate how people gravitate toward positive reinforcement. Some years ago, it was conducted on a professor at a certain graduate school of business. Running a little late that day, the professor entered the classroom to find the students waiting, pens and notebooks ready as usual.

The professor liked to pace a bit while he lectured, slowly moving from left to right and back again as he explained the intricacies of production and operation management. And so he did on this day, moving quickly into the material to make up for lost time and beginning the slow game of Pong his students had come to expect.

Something strange happened over the course of the period. The longer he lectured, the more he favored the left side of the room. He didn't think about it. Mentally immersed in the course material he was teaching, he wasn't really conscious of this growing preference. But something did seem to be pulling him to one side. By the end of class, he was nearly pinned against the left wall, inexplicably unsettled by the idea of leaving a small region on one end of the court.

Finally, one of the students confessed. While waiting for the professor before the lecture, the student organized the rest of the class to use the instructor as guinea pig. The more the professor moved to the right, the more the students feigned boredom, looking at their watches or down at their notes. The more he moved to the left, the more they perked up, nodding in agreement, participating in the discussion and chuckling at his comments. The unseen force was positive feedback. The students anchored it on the left wall, and the professor huddled up to it like a chilled traveler next to a warm hearth.[5]

Only within the last ten years have scientists been able to determine what happened within the brain of the professor, or in the brain of anyone receiving immediate positive feedback, for that matter. In 1998, researchers in London recruited eight men between the ages of 36 and 46. Each subject was asked to play a video game, the object of which was to move a tank through a battlefield, collecting flags while shooting at and destroying enemy tanks. The enemy tanks could fire back and destroy the three "lives" of the subject's tank. If all the flags were collected, the player moved to the next level. The player knew in advance that for every level achieved, he would receive £7 (about $12). Ten minutes into the game, the researchers injected the player with a small amount of a trace chemical so they could monitor by positron emission tomography scan which areas of the brain were activated by the psychological reward of winning.

One part of the brain that lit up was the ventral striatum, two string-bean-sized areas in the lower-middle of each hemisphere. Neuroscientists believe the ventral striatum and the nearby nucleus accumbens together form a key center for processing rewards and that a neurotransmitter (a chemical that sends a signal from one part of the brain to another) called dopamine is what tickles them, giving a feeling of enjoyment and satisfaction. The readings from the video game players "suggests at least a twofold increase in levels of extracellular dopamine," a level "similar to that observed following intravenous injection of amphetamine or methylphenidate."[6]

Other studies have implicated dopamine hitting the ventral striatum as part of the mechanism behind enjoying good tastes and smells, receiving money and even seeing a pretty face.[7] The brain craves a surge of dopamine. People alter their behavior to get those delightful bursts. Some increase their exercise regimens so they can eat more of the foods they like without gaining weight. TV viewers switch news broadcasts to see an attractive anchorwoman's face. Gamblers pull the lever again and again and again trying to get the surge that comes with winning. "At a purely chemical level," said *Time* magazine, "every experience humans find enjoyable — whether listening to music, embracing a lover or savoring chocolate — amounts to little more than an explosion of dopamine in the nucleus accumbens, as exhilarating and ephemeral as a firecracker."[8]

Positive words specifically have been found to activate regions of the brain related to reward.[9] One employee interviewed by Gallup tried to put the effect into words: "For me, receiving praise and recognition kind of sets off a little explosion inside. It's kind of like, 'Oh, that was good, but you know what? I can do better.' It helps give you that drive to want to continue achieving, doing yourself one better." The effect of dopamine seems to be so gratifying that some people ruin their lives trying to artificially induce the buzz. Cocaine, heroin, nicotine, and alcohol are believed to get their addictive power in part by artificially increasing the level of the neurotransmitter in the brain.[10] (After prolonged exposure, those who use artificial stimulants suffer lower baseline dopamine levels and want the drugs just to feel normal levels of the neurotransmitter.)

While blessedly few people have a cocaine addiction, every normal employee has a dopamine habit. Managers shouldn't want it any other way. A lack of naturally produced dopamine causes patients with Parkinson's disease to struggle making decisions.[11] They have difficulty learning from situations that require trial and error because they don't have the proper emotional response to positive feedback. Without enough dopamine, their good choices are not reinforced well.[12] The chemical not only makes healthy employees feel good when they get praise; it also is crucial to memory and learning. It creates an internal reward system that makes employees want to repeat behavior that the company needs — if doing the right thing earns them recognition.

The thirst of this part of the brain for good news may explain why teams with a high quotient of recognition and praise perform better than those with relatively more correction or sniping. In one study, researchers observed 60 business teams, coding each interaction in meetings as positive (supportive, encouraging, or appreciative), negative (insulting, sarcastic, or cynical), focused on others, focused on the speaker, advocating, or inquiring. When the observations were later matched with performance data about each team, it was discovered that the high-performing teams had 5.6 times more positive than negative comments, were inquiring, and achieved a balance between comments about themselves and comment about others. (The first finding closely coincides with a 5-to-1 ratio found in successful marriages by another researcher.)[13] The low-performing teams had 2.8 negative comments for every positive comment, and 29 self-referencing comments for every "other-referencing" comment. The struggling teams were negative and self-advocating. They were in a narrow-thinking survival mentality, while the productive teams operated in a culture of openness and more expansive thinking. It was not that the best teams brooked no criticism. They did discuss problems, but they did so in a larger context of reassurance and appreciation. The authors of the study referred to this to as "grounded positivity."[14]

Some executives question the "extreme" wording of the Fourth Element statement, which asks about recognition "in the last seven days." They want to know why significant recognition such as a sales award or mention in an executive speech can't carry over for a month or more. It can, but it's not enough. The neurological research tracks dopamine levels moving in minutes, not months. All the evidence suggests the employee brain is perpetually watchful and eager for reinforcing signals, particularly an unexpected, spur-of-the-moment boost.[15]

Highly engaged employees do not see the seven-day qualifier as an obstacle. "One of the things I like about working for my boss is that he's a very, very positive-reinforcement-oriented guy," said one salesman. "I don't imagine I've ever had a conversation with him that he doesn't tell me I'm doing a good job. It's a small thing, but it motivates me."

There are at least two reasons why a culture of recognition is rare. First, some of the deepest human emotions are essentially selfish. We are better wired to receive praise than to give it. We feel our own hunger more than we empathize with others around us. "When things haven't gone well for you, call in a secretary or a staff man and chew him out," said U.S. President Lyndon B. Johnson. "You will sleep better and they will appreciate the attention."[16] Second, while the ventral striatum seems to be programmed to positive events, other parts of the brain are even more vigilant for negative news. Biologists believe this is a survival instinct. For our distant ancestors in the woods and ourselves on the highway, failing to see something good is disappointing; failing to see something bad could be fatal.

There is overwhelming evidence for this "negativity bias" in humans. For example, give someone a small possession and he will pay twice as much to keep it (not to lose it) as he would to get it in the first place.[17] To avoid losses, investors will forego much larger gains.[18] Citizens bemoan negative political campaigns, but they commonly vote not so much "for" a candidate as "against" his opponent.[19] Studies find that people spot angry faces much faster than they find happy expressions.[20] "A growing body of literature is documenting an attention bias toward negative information," wrote four American researchers in 2002. "Our attention is automatically drawn to negative information more strongly than it is automatically drawn to positive information."[21]

So it should not be surprising that the majority of managers and companies are quicker to swat down a problem than they are to praise exemplary performance. In a fast-paced business there are always problems. Without a conscious effort to maintain recognition, the negative events will continually jump in line before the positive ones.

If an employee anticipates she will be recognized for something, the disappointment of finding only silence causes a dip in dopamine levels. The drop in the neurotransmitter conditions the employee to avoid the thankless task. If the task must be done for the employee to earn her pay, she will likely reduce her effort to the minimum required. Shunning what gives no psychological reward is as basic for humans as it is for bears not to forage where there are no berries. "The worst thing about working here is not being recognized for doing things that help fellow employees," wrote one worker in this predicament. "Every Friday night that I work, my department gets out fairly early. The adjoining department still has stuff to do before closing. I stay and take time out of my Friday night to help out, and not one manager has recognized me for it." The employee said he was going to stop being so helpful.

Employees who don't get their dopamine fix in one place will look for it somewhere else. Who hasn't seen an employee create a mediocre spreadsheet for a company project and a thing of beauty for the office NCAA basketball tournament betting pool? Given that winning a game of solitaire on the computer also tickles the reward centers of the brain, companies should not be shocked when under-recognized workers steal away a little company time for a quick game or two — or ten.

There are several excuses managers and even top executives give for being parsimonious with praise. Some tell their employees up front, "If I don't say anything, you're doing a good job." This "no news is good news" idea is logical enough to work on machines like lawn mowers, where the motor is designed to keep running until the operator hits the kill switch, but it flies in the face of the neurobiology just described. Other managers dismiss their responsibilities with statements such as, "I'm just not very good at giving praise." While they get points for candor, the explanation for defaulting on such a managerial imperative doesn't cut it. Would the same leaders also dismiss themselves from financial results by saying, "I'm not very good with math"?

Managers who fail to deliberately use the power of positive feedback are not only handicapping their own managerial effectiveness, they also diminish the power of the salaries they are paying. Those who score the Fourth Element highest are two-and-a-half times more likely to agree that "from my most objective viewpoint, I am paid appropriately for the work I do" than those at the other end of the recognition scale.[22]

If that's not enough, managers who need one last reason to change their ways might consider a recent experiment in which subjects were given one week to write and deliver "a letter of gratitude in person to someone who had been especially kind to them but had never been properly thanked." The delivery of the letter was statistically linked to increases in happiness and decreases in depression for up to a month after the communication.

These positive changes happened to the person who *gave* the praise.[23]

One of the most effective ways of improving recognition of employees is to discover the forms of feedback that mean the most to them. To discover how to better manage her team, Elżbieta Górska-Kołodziejczyk began having individual meetings with the workers. "I started with listening to them, what they have to say, how they see it, how they want the work to be organized, what more they expect, what kind of work materials are they lacking," she said. "At the same time, I wrote down the problems and issues they wanted to be resolved. When we met again, I gave a report on what had been done. It also brought us closer." She disregarded comments that she was mothering her employees and followed her instincts.

Because of the extreme sensitivity to public praise, Górska found that one-on-one conversations were crucial to not only identifying the type of praise most important to each worker, but also to delivering it in a way that would not provoke jealousy. "All of them expressed the opinion that they would prefer I come to them individually when they were at the beginning of their shift and not to [praise them] at the meeting." She was resolute that she would continue giving them praise, but she was aware she had to be careful about when and where to dole it out.

"I don't spare the praise, but just how could I get through to them all, so that everyone would be happy? It was difficult."

"She says things such as, 'Girls, keep going. Good job. It was super!'" said Irena Krajewska, a five-month employee at the warehouse. "Elżbieta is happy when she sees everybody. She's like a colleague, without the formality." One sign of the feelings between the manager and her team: They address and refer to each other in the informal form of the Polish language, something only done when both parties agree they are on such friendly terms.

Asked how she acknowledges when an employee has done a good job, Górska reaches over and with one hand embraces the neck of two-year employee Ania Haffke, gives her a peck on the cheek, and flashes a big smile. "She's approachable, like a colleague," says Haffke. "She's also demanding. It's better not to say what she says when she's demanding. But she's not controlling every person every minute. She shows people their errors and mistakes without raising her voice. She shows you how to do things right."

The warehouse employees are still getting used to receiving recognition, even in private. They frequently act shy and dismiss their efforts as just part of their jobs. But Górska knows it means something to her team: They are learning that "their heads will not be cut off if they receive public praise" and her positive words are slowly having the intended effect. "Sometimes they are a little bit shy, but the face and eyes speak for the person," she said. Employees say they are more likely to help each other out and thank each other for assistance, and that a spirit of reciprocity is building where once there was little team cohesion.

In an effort to be responsive to the team's initial reaction of jealously and favoritism, Górska now makes sure that any praise she gives can be backed up with objective examples. She gives public praise only to the entire team, such as the time she wrote in the log book at the end of the weekend's entries, "Thank you everyone for making everything shining clean!"

The men on her team were the most difficult to persuade. "They were like cement at the beginning," she said. "Like cement." They resented that she was a woman and, as experienced as they were, that she would presume to give them orders. They took her instructions as personal whims rather than crucial safety guidelines. She felt they were trying to draw her into a conflict with some of their derogatory comments, and she refused to take the bait. "I would pretend I didn't hear or see anything. They were not executing my orders. I smiled and gave them other orders. I displayed zero anger."

In largely Catholic Poland, most people have a larger celebration on their saint's day than they do on their birthday. Górska keeps a calendar with the dates important to her employees and brings the mostly female team flowers she's grown at home or other small tokens of her affection on the significant occasions. And for the men? "I give them heart-shaped lollypops or a teddy bear. Maybe a pen. Something to surprise or amuse them. They are surprised." Slowly, following her instincts began making a difference. "A smile and good words open any door," she said.

Recently, she and one of the men on her team came to terms. "At the end of his last evaluation, we had an honest talk," she said. Although she hastens to add she is not a psychologist, Górska hypothesizes that in giving the employee special tasks, then showing him how well he performed, she boosted his confidence and made him more open to receiving both praise and direction from her. "He felt sorry he behaved like that. He said it was wrong. We are set up to have a beer together in the future."

The manager also tried to bolster the team's sense of worth, reminding them that without their efforts, the entire plant would come to a halt, and that they were just as important as any other part of the facility. She tried to instill in them the advice her father gave her to "avoid stupid people" and "go around the foolishness."

"Stand up straight," she told them. "Put your head up. Don't care if someone from production screams at you. Production is them *and* us."

The manager said it took two years of hard work, with 12-hour days when she first assumed the role, to change the culture in the warehouse. She introduced computers into the operation. She encouraged cross-training so team members could adjust to changing work demands. She petitioned for the funds to create a "social room" with a refrigerator, a microwave, cupboards, a table, and chairs, to make work life more enjoyable for her team. Those efforts drove employee engagement from the most disenchanted quartile in the Gallup database to the top quartile. The team progressed from a "disorganization" to a "real warehouse." The change attracted the attention of *Klip*, International Paper's in-house magazine for the Kwidzyn facility. They approached Górska and her team about doing an article.

Reluctant at first, the team decided they would agree to the article. When it appeared in the magazine, it became a crowning achievement of all their hard work. They felt acknowledged in a way they never anticipated. "Everyone took a copy. Everyone wanted to have it," she said. "They were proud. They were very happy that it turned out that way. There were a lot of discussions that it was worth to try, it was worth the work. Today, they look at themselves differently. They value themselves. They know that their work means a lot here."

Finishing Department Superintendent Włodzimierz Wódecki pulled Górska aside one day while he was looking over the improvements in the warehouse. "He told me that I had done a hell of a good job," she said. "This I do remember this, yes, I remember. This really gave me satisfaction. This was my compensation for all the hours spent here, for the work which I had done, for all my efforts and trouble." Her eyes well up when she thinks about all the years she hoped to make such a difference, and now finally it is happening.

"I must be crazy. I'm so positive about people," said Górska. "I know that some people tap their finger against their forehead behind my back, but it doesn't bother me at all. I have my private philosophy, and it keeps me alive."

Górska aspires to have her employees be increasingly cheerful at the paper mill, knowing that if they have a good day at work, they will have a better life at home. And in the future, "even if they don't work here, I hope they will remember me as a good mother — remember the times here, and they will be smiling."

The Fifth Element:

Someone at Work
Cares About Me as a Person

O NE MORNING — NO ONE RECALLS EXACTLY WHEN — they simply left the lights off in half of Qwest's Idaho Falls call center. Only the computer screens glowed in that half of the large semi-circular space, reminding the remaining employees of colleagues who had quit or were fired and not replaced.

At the soda machine, people were counting the years remaining on the building's lease. Surely the company would at least see the lease through. Or would it?

The center's results were poor, consistently near the bottom of the 11 such sites Qwest Communications International maintained around the United States. Attrition was high. Attendance was low. Customer satisfaction scores and revenue were poor. The telecommunications firm had stopped recruiting in the area, and the end seemed as near as the dark side across the room. "We were all pretty much figuring we were going to be gone at some point," said Donna Jenkins, a telephone representative.

"I would think of any reason not to go to work," said employee Chyanne Smith. "I would think, 'Somebody hit me with a truck. I do not want to go to work today.'" Doors were sometimes slammed. Employees occasionally overheard each other crying on the phone to their friends. Some petitioned for transfers to other Qwest call centers.

The union and local management were at odds. Employee grievances were at an all-time high. Workers were fearful and not motivated. Rumors of the problems spread to Qwest's Pocatello, Idaho, call center; refugees from Idaho Falls were willing to drive the 50 miles for better working conditions.

In April 2003, Qwest tapped 13-year company veteran Larry Walters with the daunting task of pulling the Idaho Falls operation back from the precipice. Walters accepted the assignment without hesitation and packed to make the move from Helena, Montana, to the troubled call center in Idaho. Honored by the opportunity, he required only a "two-minute conversation" to be drafted. "Within 48 hours, I was here, living out of a hotel," he said.

Things began to lighten up even before Walters arrived. Employees were happy to see a change — any change — coming. They were encouraged by the little they knew of Walters from his occasional visits to Idaho Falls. He always made sure people had coffee. He asked about their interests. He seemed genuinely curious about their lives.

But now he was more than an incidental visitor, and time was running out for the center. "I knew I could get it turned around, but could I get it turned around quick enough to have an impact on our customer service, and quick enough for Qwest?" Walters said.

Facing such a challenge, Walters could have invoked his authority and demanded improvements. "We need to improve our customer numbers!" he could have announced. "Get on those phones and sell more!" Many managers in similar predicaments have tried that kind of shortcut, as if they were Pharaoh Ramses in the movie *The Ten Commandments* when he declares, "So let it be written; so let it be done!" In the short run, giving orders sometimes works. But there are limits to how much can be accomplished through directives, financial incentives, fear of discipline, and intense scrutiny of people's work. All organizations inevitably depend on their employees' psychological commitment to their immediate manager and colleagues.

One of the crucial questions for a team leader trying to get the most from his people is whether they form a cohesive, cooperative, self-sacrificing, motivated crew — in short, a tribe. Such attitudes are the essence of the Fifth Element of Great Managing. It is measured by an employee's reaction to the statement, "My supervisor, or someone at work, seems to care about me as a person."

The fact that being a great manager requires a special ability to influence emotions makes many supervisors uncomfortable. American industrialist Henry Ford is reputed to have once remarked, "Why is it that I always get the whole person when what I really want is a pair of hands?" It would be easier if teams could restrict their need for bonding to home, church, and neighborhood, but they can't turn off the reflex that easily. Those who see the "cares about me" statement as more worthy of a discussion on *Oprah!* than in the vernacular of a results-driven manager need a deeper understanding of human motivation.

Given a decision that affects someone else, the mind has two fairly distinct ways of weighing the alternatives. One of the best illustrations of this difference is in two hypothetical scenarios published in the influential journal *Science*:

1. "A runaway trolley is headed for five people who will be killed if it proceeds on its present course. The only way to save them is to hit a switch that will turn the trolley onto an alternate set of tracks where it will kill one person instead of five. Ought you to turn the trolley in order to save five people at the expense of one?"

2. "As before, a trolley threatens to kill five people. You are standing next to a large stranger on a footbridge that spans the tracks, in between the oncoming trolley and the five people. In this scenario, the only way to save the five people is to push this stranger off the bridge, onto the tracks below. He will die if you do this, but his body will stop the trolley from reaching the others. Ought you to save the five others by pushing this stranger to his death?"[1]

Mathematically the two situations are the same: sacrificing one person to save five. Yet most people say yes to the first dilemma and no to the second. "When the victims are just statistics somewhere down the track, as in the first situation, the areas of the brain associated with social intelligence and emotion stay quiet and we seem to look at the problem rationally," wrote author Richard Conniff. "But our emotions kick in when the connection is personal."[2]

The trolley experiment is just one of many showing that people treat each other differently when they form a personal connection. Experiments conducted after the Holocaust found that subjects told to administer what they thought was a painful shock to a stranger were more willing to do so if a barrier separated them from the other person.[3] Something as simple as knowing the name of the person with whom one is playing a strategic game of dividing a pie makes the players more generous.[4] A mere "pair of hands" will be reassigned, neglected, laid off, or considered interchangeable much more easily than will a "whole person." Perhaps the HR executive who complained layoffs weren't happening fast enough — "I want to stand at the door and count crying faces go by," he said — would have been more humane if he knew them personally. Employees recognize the difference and give more effort in a group when they feel they are more than just a number.

The importance of the Fifth Element in the Qwest call center can be seen in a 2002 study conducted by four professors. They wanted to know whether people staffing phones at a different company would falsify their reports to boost their pay. Given the financial incentive to cheat, the business was faced with the issue of how closely to monitor its 16 call centers. Should they spend more money to audit the work, or could they trust their workers to do the right thing? One of the best predictors of an employee's trustworthiness was his perception of whether the company "cares about my personal well-being." "'Conscience' alone is not guiding the actions of the workers we observe in the experiment," the researchers concluded. Compared with those who feel their company is looking out for them, "a disproportionate number of the workers who view the employer as unfair and uncaring" will cheat when they think they can get away with it.[5]

For those workers who "feel like I'm just a number" but who can't imagine cheating, quitting their jobs provides an ethical alternative that is also expensive to the company. The correlation between not feeling cared about and resigning has been observed repeatedly in studies of individual companies in the Gallup database and in analyses where data from many organizations are combined.[6] In high-turnover companies, workgroups in the lowest quarter of the "someone at work cares about me" statement average 22 percent higher turnover than their top-quartile counterparts. In organizations where resignations are less common, the difference rises to 37 percent. While an employee managed by someone of a different race is more inclined to consider resigning than someone supervised by someone of his own race, a high degree of the Fifth Element corrects that racial gap.[7]

The question of why people have this need for someone taking a personal interest in them goes to the core of much larger issues about humanity itself. Those inclined toward a religious explanation see "caring" as a divine imperative. St. Paul told the Corinthians "the members should have the same care one for another, and whether one member suffer, all the members suffer with it."[8] The teachings of Buddha emphasize "thousands of people may live in a community but it is not one of real fellowship until they know each other and have sympathy for one another."[9] Every major religion has a similar principle.

Anthropologists see people today as the descendants of the most cooperative humans living across time. In the rugged past, people who didn't work together didn't just have a bad day at work — they died. "Society works not because we have consciously invented it, but because it is an ancient product of our evolved predispositions," wrote British science writer Matt Ridley. "It is literally in our nature. . . . We are, misanthropes notwithstanding, unable to live without each other. Even on a practical level, it is probably a million years since any human being was entirely and convincingly self-sufficient: able to live without trading his skills for those of his fellow humans. . . . One of the things that marks humanity out from other species, and accounts for our ecological success, is our collection of hyper-social instincts."[10]

Generations ago, the object of these "hyper-social instincts" was easy to find. In agrarian cultures, brothers, sisters, aunts, uncles, and cousins were only a few farms away. Nomadic clans dragged everyone along to follow the caribou, the seals, or whatever food source kept them on the move. Because they were closely related, members of the group looked alike. To further set themselves apart, they often used tribal symbols, such as the Scottish tartans one can find today worked into the tie or scarf of a Gordon, Stewart, or McDonnell descendant. The clans of the past had a wealth of shared experiences. They trusted each other because they had proven themselves, because betraying the tribe was unthinkable and dangerous, and because instincts that served their ancestors well biased them toward cooperation with each other. That they cared about one another was taken for granted.

Today's world-traveling corporate warrior with a two-page résumé needs to go back only several generations to find ancestors who may not have moved far from their birthplace, never changed jobs, worked for decades with the same people, and for whom working well together was a deadly serious business. In his book *The Children's Blizzard*, David Laskin tells the story of South Dakota pioneer farmers snowed in and at risk of starving because none of the wheat in their primitive homes had been milled into flour. Ukrainian immigrant Anna Kaufman "heard that some families were boiling their unmilled wheat kernels into a kind of mush, but she knew she could not keep her children alive on that diet. Without flour they would never survive the winter," he wrote. "Finally, when it was clear that the weather would not break, six Schweizer farmers decided to make the twenty-mile trip to the nearest mill together; Each farmer took a wagon loaded with grain sacks and a team of horses, and each team broke trail for half a mile or so until the animals were exhausted; then that team would drop to the rear and the next in line would break through the drifts for the next half mile. It was a long grueling trip, but the men returned with flour, and Anna was able to make bread for her family."[11]

Planes, trains, and automobiles; instantaneous communication; and the nature of employment itself have broken up the traditional tribe, but not tribal motivations. The encyclopedia definition of a tribe — a "group of people sharing customs, language, and territory" with "a leader (and) a religion teaching that all its people are descended from a common ancestor" — is eerily close to what outsiders notice in a large corporate headquarters. Reverence for company founders substitutes for that toward a common ancestor. While it does not have a religion, every business develops its orthodoxies and powerful legends. Every close-knit organization develops its own exclusive vocabulary, inside jokes, chants, symbols, and wardrobe that reign inside its security-badge-protected territories. The differences between an ancient clan and Thomas Watson's army of white-shirted IBM employees in the 1950s were more stylistic than organic. Because they are not computers, workers may be more motivated by the emotional need to support their comrades as by the cognitive appeal of an employee stock ownership plan.[12] Yet it's not unusual for companies to invest as much or more in the latter than in the former.

Tribes are more fluid today. A boy born two decades ago not only might not have had an extended family around him during his formative years; he might not even have had a father in the home. His "tribe" may have changed every few years as he migrated from a day-care center to elementary school, to his new school (if his mother moved), to his baseball team during the summer, and to his high school, college, and fraternity. One day he finds himself in his new workgroup, be it a store, bank branch, loading dock, newsroom, construction crew or law firm. Although his group memberships may have been transient throughout his life, certainly shakier than those of his ancestors, his nature still drives him to belong. He may display it as pride in his ethnic heritage, wearing the logo of his favorite sports team or calling himself whatever was the mascot of his university. But chances are high part that of his self-image is wrapped up in being a member of a group. As *The Wall Street Journal* described one businessman's dilemma, "the continuing tug of school and fraternity ties in the business world (is) bizarre but difficult to escape."[13]

Yet under the right conditions, productive new tribes form inside a company. People from disparate backgrounds, of different races, who attended various colleges and grew up with assorted customs, nonetheless become one unified troop. They enjoy the social benefits of belonging and feeling supported. The business reaps the rewards of greater teamwork.[14]

For Larry Walters or any other manager, this inclination means a large variation in his team's effort depended on the degree to which they felt a real part of the group, a cohesiveness sometimes called "social capital." "Social capital makes an organization, or any cooperative group, more than a collection of individuals intent on achieving their own private purposes," wrote authors Don Cohen and Laurence Prusak. "Social capital bridges the space between people. Its characteristic elements and indicators include high levels of trust, robust personal networks and vibrant communities, shared understandings, and a sense of equitable participation in a joint enterprise — all things that draw individuals together into a group. This kind of connection supports collaboration, commitment, ready access to knowledge and talents, and coherent organizational behavior."[15]

These benefits don't flow unless the members of the business units feel someone takes a personal interest in them, a fact that can come as a rude awakening to some managers. "When I first became a manager, I was 22 years old. I was very focused and I was very result-oriented," one manager said in an interview. "I used to give people tasks and I guess I was very rude about them. I'd say, 'See, I need you to do X-Y-Z,' and I would walk off. I had an older lady on my team in so many words tell me that I was a jerk. We had a decent rapport, so I sat down and I said, 'I want to listen. Why do you think I am a jerk?' And she told me, 'Haven't you ever heard of "Good morning," "How's your family?" or "How did your weekend go?"'" That left a lasting impression on me and will for the rest of my life."

To rejuvenate the Qwest call center in Idaho Falls, Larry Walters embarked on a fourfold strategy: embrace the front-line associates, emphasize results, talk straight with the union, and distance himself from some of the six "coaches." He feared that these managers who reported to him and supervised 10 or 12 telephone representatives were holdovers from the previous management days.

Larkin Beauchat was a coach who was hoping for something better. He was hanging on; "It was just a job" at that point, he said. But he was eager to rally behind a genuine leader. "That first day, Larry called us in and said, 'We're currently in last place. Out of 11 call centers, we're 11th.

We need to turn that around,'" Beauchat said. "He then said that managers' jobs were on the line and that over the next two to four months, each one of us was going to be evaluated on our performance, as well as by Larry's feeling of what's going on in the center."

"What struck me most was his willingness to jump in and try to change the mindset," said fellow coach Matt Tower.

The first meeting with the managers that morning, Walters recalls, revealed one of his toughest challenges "because most of the managers did not want to change. They took the attitude that 'We're doing it our way.'" Walters didn't mind rattling the recalcitrant coaches. In fact, if they were determined to dig in, he was going to use their conversion or dismissal to send a message to the call center reps who had been intimidated by some of the coaches. "When I went back to that hotel room, I was thrilled," Walters said, "because those coaches came out of that room scared, and the front line saw it, and the reps saw that something was going to change."

Walters struggled to get four of the coaches to work with him, to get them to stop managing by intimidation, to learn more about the phone system, and to understand the reps' frustrations. One by one, they failed the test. "I just couldn't get them to turn around. They would say the right things to my face, but they wouldn't walk the walk — turn around and do it the right way," Walters said. Beauchat and Tower welcomed and survived the change. The other four coaches did not.

Walters' meetings with the union were described by both sides as straightforward, candid discussions that set the foundation for an excellent working relationship. Kathy Berger, an employee at the Idaho Falls call center and secretary-treasurer of Local 7621 of the Communications Workers of America, describes Walters in language uncommonly effusive for a union steward. "He is so my hero," she said. "He is absolutely everything to me." Walters earned that praise, Berger said, by being consistent and direct. He meets with Berger every Tuesday at 10 a.m., almost without fail, to discuss any issues. He never shades the truth, she said, and he seems to understand that by increasing union membership and giving members more fulfilling jobs, the health of the center does as much for the union as it does for Qwest.

"We just hit it off and agreed to work together to make things better," Berger said. "There was no more of the (local managers) having secrets and not letting anybody on the union side know. His attitude was, 'You have a problem? Come to me, and let's talk about it. I'm going to tell you what I'm hearing; you tell me.' I don't think I've ever seen a better union-company relationship than in our center, and Larry is just totally, I mean totally, to be credited." Berger said that she knew things were going to be different when she and Walters were working their way through a grievance that one of the employees filed. After they were done, Walters suggested, "The next time you have a grievance, let's try this: Come talk to me before it gets to the grievance procedure, and let's see what we can do."

When the next disagreement occurred, Berger took him up on the offer. Walters understood the employee's concern. They reached an agreement, and the grievance was avoided. As a result, grievance filings a year after Walters assumed responsibility were about half of what they were when morale was at its lowest, even though employment at the center grew six-fold.

When Walters arrived at the call center, he was surprised not to find the site's results posted prominently. He set about to fire up the team to get out of the basement of Qwest center standings. "As far as decorations on the walls, it looked fine, but there were no results on the walls! Within the first week after I arrived, results were posted on the walls. How do we rank for our sales, for our customer service, for our attrition? How do we rank against the other centers? I wanted to start building that sense of pride in our center and what we do." He egged them on. "I was actually showing people, 'Do you realize we're last in sales right now? Does that bother you?'"

The focus on results might have landed flat but for Walters' secret weapons — a genuine concern for his employees combined with a theatrical, self-deprecating motivational style. Walters' employees can run through a litany of costumes and stunts he's used to put the team in a great mood. He puts on in-line skates and rolls through the center singing and playing the guitar. (His associates hasten to mention he doesn't know how to play the guitar.) One day, Walters bought hamburgers for everyone at the nearby Sonic Drive-In and talked the restaurant into loaning him a Sonic milkshake costume that he could wear while passing out the burgers. Lisa Roberts, whom Walters recruited from Pocatello to be a coach, recalls first meeting him in a "Captain Bendo" costume. She's since bought him a full-sized SpongeBob SquarePants outfit.

But the costume that seems most memorable was a take-off from an agreement by Qwest to offer MSN Internet service. Walters got his hands on an MSN butterfly costume and floated through the office pumping up the troops. "Have you ever seen Larry? He's — what? — six-one, six-two, maybe 120 pounds soaking wet. He had an MSN butterfly thing with the hood covering everything except his face, and he would walk around the office in that. We'd have to put customers on hold, we'd be laughing so hard," Berger said.

"It helps people feel like he's a real person," said Roberts. "It's not like, 'I'm over the whole center, and you should be scared to talk to me.'"

Inside the butterfly, milkshake, or Captain Bendo costume is a manager who wants to know each of his employees and see them succeed. "I love these people, and I'm not just kidding," Walters said. "I know their names. I know their spouses' names. I make fun of them when their football team loses. The first thing out of my mouth in the morning isn't, 'How are your numbers?' Instead, it's, 'How was your son's Little League game last night? Who won?' It really brought the faith back that we're here as one team."

Idaho Falls center employees recite two mantras Larry taught them: "For the love" and "You're all rock stars." Standing on a desk in the middle of the building, he tells them he loves them and that he believes they can accomplish great things — messages they didn't hear before he arrived. "Larry changed my entire attitude about Qwest," Smith said. "Two years ago, I would have had nothing good to say about Qwest. Now people ask, 'Are you still there?' I say, 'Yes, and I plan to retire from there.' I'm proud to come to work, and I'm proud to say I'm a Qwest employee."

Changing the management ranks, focusing on results, building a partnership with the union, embracing his employees, and leavening it all with numerous costume changes had just the right effect. The numbers posted each day got better. Customer satisfaction scores bumped up 5 percent. Revenue per call jumped 16 percent. Sales productivity skyrocketed 68 percent. Qwest leadership, seeing the turnaround, decided to begin hiring more people in Idaho Falls. The lights went back on throughout the building, which was abuzz with activity. In March 2004, Gallup administered a survey of the 12 Elements at the Idaho Falls call center. Employees who described their workplace in harsh terms just a year before scored their work life above the 70th percentile of Gallup's North American database — an unusually high level for such a large and unionized group.

One afternoon, Paula Kruger, executive vice president of Qwest's consumer markets group, was in town visiting with Walters and discussing changes to the center. Gesturing to the building next door, Walters said, half joking, "In two years, I want that building."

"Why wait two years?" she replied. "You're doing all the right things. Let's get to work on it." Key to the business case for hiring more people was Walters' success in motivating his team. It didn't make sense to hire more people if they were going to founder. But Walters' people were having too much fun, were too attached to him, and were succeeding too much to make that an issue. In April 2004, Qwest announced the expansion that would make the call center the largest in the company. Qwest officials and state dignitaries came to Idaho Falls for a large press conference. Walters bought dozens of permanent markers and asked the workers to sign their autographs on dozens of blow-up guitars he bought for his "rock stars." "I cried when they announced the expansion," Walters said. "There were about 150 employees at that announcement. They went berserk. They clapped and cheered and freaked out, and I started crying. Some of the managers cried."

Among those in attendance was Idaho Governor Dirk Kempthorne, who leaned over to Walters and remarked, "I have never, ever seen such an incredible ovation. You should look into politics because these people love you, and they love what you've done." Down to just 65 people when it was in a single, half-darkened building, the Qwest Idaho Falls call center soon employed more than 400 people in two buildings. Walters was promoted to site director over the team leaders who are each responsible for the employees in one of those buildings. The call center, which was last in sales for the company before Walters arrived, exceeded its January 2004 sales objectives and became first in sales.

Balloons float from the cubicles. Large baseballs, "applause" signs, and a pirate flag hang from the ceiling. Telephone reps smile as they carefully stack the emptied cans of Mountain Dew, Coke, and Red Bull that keep them charging forward. It's now a fun place to work. And those who have been there long enough to know what the center went through find themselves grateful to Larry Walters for showing them, in his unique way, how to be rock stars.

"To be on the bottom and now to be number one — it's truly breathtaking to me," said Roberts. "It seems easy now, but we've seen the other side."

THE SIXTH ELEMENT:
Someone at Work
Encourages My Development

A S A TEENAGER IN LETHBRIDGE, ALBERTA, Pete Wamsteeker was looking more for a job than a role model when he found both. A man who attended the same church owned a local feed business. He approached the 15-year-old about working for him.

In his first real manager, the boy found someone who handled adversity with grace, who followed good values, and who invested a lot of time in other people. "There was no value judgment" of other people in the owner, Wamsteeker said. "Often you'll hear people say 'That guy's a clown.' I never ever saw that with him. Everybody was important. It was all about serving people well and, 'You have to respect people for who they are.'"

Over the next few years, the businessman challenged his young employee. "I was a 15- or 16-year-old kid and he would say things like, 'What are your plans?' 'What are you doing?' 'Why would you go to college?'" Some would say it was in a Socratic way, but he would challenge me about what I learned and why I did the things I would do."

As the end of high school approached, Wamsteeker applied to and was accepted at several colleges. The manager kept pressing the young man about his intention to leave a stable job in his hometown.

"It got to be the summer between my senior year in high school and my freshman year in college," said Wamsteeker. "He pulled me into his office and he said, 'Now I really want you to consider whether you want to go to college. You could stay here and I'll pay you this kind of money and you really don't need college. You're suited for this business.' He was going on and on and I felt like, 'Enough already! No more!'"

The businessman kept testing the then 18-year-old's resolve, asking what he was going to do with his education and whether he realized the sacrifices he would have to make to attend school. "Man, that's going to be expensive! Do you know how much college costs these days?" asked the manager.

"I'm perfectly aware of how much it costs," Wamsteeker said.

"What does it cost?"

Wamsteeker quoted the cost of tuition at one of the schools he wanted to attend. The feed business owner pulled out his checkbook and wrote a check to contribute to Wamsteeker's tuition.

"He ripped it out and he said, 'You'll come to work for me next summer? I think you're the kind of guy who has a place in this business long-term. I'm awful proud of your resolve.'"

The feed business owner supported Wamsteeker during his college years and, more for the reasons behind his generosity than through the money itself, made a lifelong impression on the kid he hired in the hallway at church. "It's very reinforcing," Wamsteeker said. "He grew up with the right values. He's done the right things and, you know, you have to be proud of that. You have to listen to him because he knows what he's doing. He's got kind of a proof of character. This guy modeled values for me in everything that resonated with me. I was always afraid of letting him down."

Just before Wamsteeker graduated from college, his employer sold the business to Cargill, the Minneapolis-based food and agricultural conglomerate. In the process of negotiating the sale, the manager arranged for Wamsteeker to keep a job with the business. Two decades later, Wamsteeker is an accomplished Cargill manager applying the principles he first learned as a teenager.

When Odysseus departed on the long journey that would take him to the Trojan Wars, he left behind his wife Penelope, his son Telemachus, and all his property. The poet Homer wrote that matters were left to "an old friend of Odysseus, to whom the King had entrusted his whole household when he sailed, with orders to . . . keep everything intact."[1] It's assumed that among his duties, the trusted friend was to advise, counsel, and nurture Odysseus's young son. The special counselor was said to have "regulated the whole course of the life of Telemachus in order to raise him to the highest pitch of glory."[2]

The advisor became symbolic of a basic human need, an idea that reverberates through the halls of business today. His name was Mentor.

The notion of a personal guide is an ancient idea that perpetually reemerges in forms such as the relationships between master craftsman and apprentice, doctoral candidate and thesis supervisor, or resident physician and intern. Musicians learn by watching better musicians. Surgical students look over the shoulders of experienced surgeons. There is something about working closely with someone who supervises the less experienced person's progress that cannot be accomplished as well in any other way. From this fact stems the Sixth Element of Great Managing, measured by the statement, "There is someone at work who encourages my development."

Although mentors have existed through the ages, the neurological mechanism behind the power of example was discovered only in the early 1990s, and only then by accident. A group of researchers led by Dr. Giacomo Rizzolatti, a neuroscientist at the University of Parma in Italy, placed small electrodes in the brains of monkeys near the regions of the brain responsible for planning and carrying out movements. If the monkey picked up something, an electronic monitor connected to the wires in the animal's brain would sound — "brrrrrip, brrrrrip, brrrrrip" — to register the firing of those neurons.

Then something happened, something so unusual the researchers thought it had to be a mistake. If the monkey saw one of the scientists doing something — eating an ice cream cone, picking up a peanut or raisin, grabbing a banana — the monitor registered the firing of brain cells as if the monkey had done it, when all the animal did was watch. "It took us several years to believe what we were seeing," Rizzolatti told *The New York Times*. The structure behind the phenomenon was discovered to be what they called "mirror neurons," cells scattered throughout key regions of the brain that mimic everything the monkey sees another do.[3]

Subsequent research found a far more complicated set of mirror neurons in people. This "human see; human do" circuitry is believed to be why a yawn can be contagious, why even a newborn will stick out her tongue if she sees someone else do it, and why American boys sometimes mimic the idiosyncrasies of their favorite baseball players at bat. "It explains much about how we learn to smile, talk, walk, dance, or play tennis," said a 2006 cover article in *Scientific American Mind* magazine. "At a deeper level, it suggests a biological dynamic for our understanding of others, the complex exchange of ideas we call culture, and psychosocial dysfunctions ranging from lack of empathy to autism."[4]

The discovery of mirror neurons, as one researcher said, "completely changes the way we think about how the brain works." "Mirror neurons will do for psychology what DNA did for biology," said another.[5] The implication is that that humans don't just passively observe other people in action, but in their minds "do" whatever they see. When a soccer fan's favorite player scores a goal in the World Cup, part of the fan's brain has him, the fan, scoring the goal. The phenomenon helps to explain the power of television and movies to put viewers themselves into the action. Most important for business, the discoveries demonstrate that if a company wants its employees to quickly assimilate "best practices," there is no faster conduit to a protégé's brain than watching a good role model in action. "Mirror neurons," said Rizzolatti, "allow us to grasp the minds of others not through conceptual reasoning but through direct simulation."[6]

The Sixth Element requires this kind of guidance through personal interaction. It is fulfilled by a person more than the understanding that makes the First Element, the resources that support the Second or the opportunities that define the Third. While all of the elements require personal manager-to-employee or peer-to-peer interaction, the Sixth requires a higher degree of personal investment by the counselor in the education of his charge. For this reason, and the power of mirror neurons when one person serves as mentor for another, the Sixth is also a conduit to the other elements of managing.

It is difficult to get traction on any of the other elements without the Sixth. Consider the fairly large group — on average, four in ten — who feel neither their manager nor anyone else is looking out for their development. A mere 1 percent of those who have no mentor are able to achieve real engagement with their employer through the strength of the other 11 elements.[7] Conversely, two-thirds of employees who report having someone at work who encourages their development are classified as "engaged," while one-third are "not engaged" and less than one percent are "actively disengaged." These statistics indicate that regardless of whether a company's Web site or personnel department promises it, having a mentor is fundamental, part of the unwritten social contract workers anticipate when they are hired.

Unfortunately, in their eagerness to force the issue universally, many companies create formal "mentoring" programs that try to assign the two people to each other or impose connections that, to be effective, must form naturally. As one Internet commentator complained, "What has been historically an informal, unofficial, voluntary, mutually agreeable, and self-selected interaction between two people has become a program — an institutionalized stratagem for trying to force what probably can only come about naturally — and a staple, if not a commodity, in the bag of tricks toted from client to client by many a consultant."[8]

A worker's manager is usually first in line to fulfill this role, but she is not alone. Doctors are often managed by administrators who are not physicians, but look for advice to the chief of surgery or to an approachable, more experienced doctor. Junior reporters may have their writing honed by editors, but they learn how to track down stories by following more senior reporters. Musicians follow the conductor, but they learn a substantial amount from those who play the same instrument.

Business writer Don Cohen once noticed that a few of the familiar brown United Parcel Service delivery trucks were always parked around 2 p.m. near a park in Massachusetts he often passed. The drivers sat on the nearby benches eating their lunch and talking. Curious, Cohen finally stopped one day to ask if this was just a way to avoid eating alone.

"Yes, they got together to have some company at lunch, but 'We talk about everything and anything,' including a lot about work," wrote Cohen. "Drivers who had worked in town longest could tell newer drivers how to find unmarked streets and addresses and when particular customers were likely to be available to sign for a delivery. The veterans shared other special knowledge too: which customers wanted packages left in the garage or around the side of a house; when school let out and there were kids to watch for on the street and buses slowing traffic." The drivers also told the author that they frequently exchanged packages to even out the workload, to help someone get home early or to correct a mistake at the sorting center.[9] Such gatherings may seem a small thing, but given that much of exceptional performance is in the details, and the importance of emulation to human learning, they can be some of the most important venues for creating a results-driven culture.

Despite its importance at any point in a career, the frequency of Sixth Element connections steadily declines with age and tenure in the organization. More than half of employees aged 18 to 24, and of those less than six months into a new job, indicate that someone at work encourages their development. But the percentage slips to just one in four for workers over 55 years of age, and to one in five for workers with 10 or more years at a particular company. Nothing in the data indicates having a mentor is any less important for senior managers or employees than for newcomers, yet it appears many companies do not look after the guidance of their longstanding, loyal employees as well as they do those who just arrived.[10]

Consistent with the biological imitation circuitry, the Sixth Element also has the strongest connection through levels of a company. Executives who have a mentor are more likely to be one, the effects cascading from CEO to front-line employee. The Sixth Element is the most sensitive among the 12 to this phenomenon of "manager see; manager do."[11] A supervisor who is himself engaged feels a general reciprocal desire toward his employer and a specific interest in seeing new talent contribute to the company's success.

The guidance of a newer, younger employee by a manager is the stereotypical example because it most closely approximates the relationship of Mentor and Telemachus. But in its broadest usage, as captured by the Sixth Element, a mentor is anyone who, in the eyes of the employee, ensures she successfully navigates the course. The important aspect is not which of many terms this protector goes by — friend, coach, advisor, sponsor, counselor, supporter — but whether the employee feels she is not abandoned inside the business. As one grateful employee said of her guide in a Gallup interview: "She has seen things in me that I couldn't quite see in myself, has encouraged me to excel, has invited me to be promoted, has supported me and buoyed me up in a time when I was thinking, 'Gosh, won't I drown doing this? Are you sure I can?' And she told me, 'You might founder a little, but you won't sink. We won't let you.'"

Similar results using quantitative methods have been made dozens of times in assorted settings. For example, first-year M.B.A. students assisted by second-year students who were assigned to help them navigate the program said the guidance helped them fit in at the graduate school, and that the more help they received from the more experienced students, the more it reduced their stress.[12] Repeated failures of training manuals or computerized "knowledge management" systems have demonstrated that information, from hard facts to the most unofficial but helpful advice, travels much more effectively through these kinds of very personal channels. "We experience work as a human, social activity that engages the same social needs and responses as the other parts of our lives: the need for connection and cooperation, support and trust, a sense of belonging, fairness and recognition," wrote Cohen and co-author Laurence Prusak. "But analysts still often see organizations as machines (for producing goods, services, or knowledge) or as an assemblage of self-focused individuals — free agents or 'companies of one' — who somehow manage to coordinate their individual aims long enough to accomplish a task."[13]

In the early 1980s, Boston University Professor Kathy E. Kram interviewed young managers at a public utility in the northeastern United States about their careers. Her key question: "Is there anyone among those that you have mentioned today that you feel has taken a personal interest in you and your development?" In follow-up interviews, she asked these managers about their sponsors.

From those interviews, the professor identified a number of benefits the young managers received. "Through career functions, including sponsorship, coaching, protection, exposure and visibility, and challenging work assignments, a young manager is assisted in learning the ropes of organizational life and in preparing for advancement opportunities," she wrote. Equally important, the protégés received "psychosocial" support — a role model, a feeling of acceptance and confirmation they were doing well, counseling, and friendship. People need role models whose accomplishments seem within reach.[14] Patient and approachable mentors can bring seemingly impossible goals down to earth and give those they advise a shot of confidence.

Many highly accomplished people can recall a time early in their careers when such a shot in the arm made all the difference. "In fact," wrote "Dilbert" cartoonist and business cynic Scott Adams, "the most influential people in my life are probably not even aware of the things they've taught me." Adams described how he suffered one rejection after another before Sarah Gillespie, an editor at United Media, called to offer him a contract. "At first, I didn't believe her. I asked if I'd have to change my style, get a partner — or learn how to draw. But she believed that I was already good enough to be a nationally syndicated cartoonist," he wrote. "Her confidence in me completely changed my frame of reference: It altered how I thought about my own abilities. This may sound bizarre, but from the minute I got off the phone with her, I could draw better. You can see a marked improvement in the quality of the cartoons I drew after that conversation."[15]

The benefits of being a protégé are clear, and are sometimes emphasized so much that they overshadow the benefits of being a mentor. However, the fulfillment of encouraging another's development comes through in several of Kram's interviews. "I can tell you that the biggest satisfaction that I get is seeing someone that you have some faith in really go beyond where you expect and really see them get recognized," said one supervisor. "To see them do an excellent job and see them get recognized for it is probably the most gratifying thing, like seeing your son graduate from college, like seeing your mother get a degree when she's 45 years old — it's that kind of pride that you take. You know you had faith in these people, you've helped them along, but you haven't told them what to do . . . it's like raising children . . . when you see those people get promoted and you're really pleased. And you say, 'You know, I've had something to do with that.'" [16]

Pete Wamsteeker needed everything he learned about being a mentor when he was asked to leave Canada to reinvigorate Cargill's U.S. pork business in mid-2002. Decades-long trends had changed the nature of the industry and unsettled the company's place within it.

Founded in 1865, Cargill is one of the world's largest privately held companies. The uninitiated may associate the enterprise with some of the more quaint aspects of its history, such as the Saturday night "barn dance" it sponsored generations ago on a high-powered Minneapolis AM radio station, or the "pretty print" material used for feed bags so farmers' wives could make them into tablecloths or clothing. Back then, the business model was not much more complicated than farmers raising hogs and Cargill selling feed. Traditional concerns — weather in the American Midwest and matching mill capacities with demand — loomed large.

Pork production today is more scientific, more concentrated in the hands of large companies raising hundreds of thousands of pigs and, in some cases, done by enterprises that have their own milling facilities to make feed. "The pork marketplace has consolidated out of the hands of what you and I would term the classic American farmer into the hands of a much more businesslike person who is really about operating a manufacturing facility," said trading specialist Mark Hulsebus. The challenge for Wamsteeker was to improve Cargill's position within an industry that needs less of what the company traditionally delivered.

From a business perspective, a pig is just an organic version of the most basic accounting equation: revenue – expenses = profit. When everything is working well, it costs about $100 to get a pig from birth to market and the animal will sell for about $120, giving the producer a $20 margin. But factors outside the producer's control, many of them moving with global financial markets, can reduce, eliminate or even invert the profit. If poultry farmers raise an abundance of chickens, it depresses the price of both chicken and pork. Pig feed is primarily made of corn, for carbohydrates, and soybeans, for protein. Higher oil prices are creating greater demand for corn because it can be made into the alternative fuel ethanol. The price a driver pays at the pump is connected to the price of the bacon he had for breakfast.

What is at first a simple formula quickly becomes complicated. Over time, making the right decisions about where and when to buy grain, to whom to sell the hogs, and how to improve efficiency in between can mean the difference between a pork producer thriving and going out of business. An industrial-scale pork business may not need bags of Cargill feed, but having the right expertise is imperative. Could Wamsteeker form a team of consultants and specialists who could bring together what Cargill knew about pork biology, feed, and financial markets to fulfill the needs of the country's largest pork operations?

The answer turned as much on Wamsteeker's coaching abilities and the interpersonal abilities of his staff as much as they did on the technical knowledge of the company. "Hog producers are survivors," said Mike Astrauskas, one of 10 "pork consultants" in the workgroup. "We've gone from thousands of them down to 50 companies owning 50 percent of the pork now. They don't tell everybody everything. When you build a relationship, they understand you're trying to help their business, then they let you know what you need to know, on a need-to-know basis."

Luke Wells had been with Cargill only a few years when he transferred to Wamsteeker's newly formed group, headquartered in West Branch, Iowa. "The first time you meet him you know something is different about this guy," said Wells. "You spend any time with Pete and you'll pick up very quickly that his passion is about developing people and developing teams."

Several years ago, Wells and Wamsteeker were at a "tailgating" gathering before an Iowa State University football game in the large hospitality tent of one of their biggest customers. The customer had earlier asked Wells to research some information for him. "We went up to him in the middle of this group with a whole bunch of people around and gave him the information he was looking for," said Wells. "I was nervous. It was really early on in my time with Pete and, quite frankly, I was in a new job and doing things that I didn't even know if I could do."

After the conversation with the customer, Wamsteeker pulled his employee aside. "I sensed you were a bit nervous there," he said. The manager tried to calm Wells' fears and build up his belief in himself. "I want you to be like a prize fighter," he said. "I want you to get out and fight a bit on your own. I don't mind if you maybe get knocked down a few times. But you've got to have the confidence I'm never going to let you get knocked out."

A large part of encouraging someone's development is helping him to find the kind of job that matches his talents. In this way, the Sixth Element and the Third are closely related. For several of the members of Wamsteeker's new team, finding that match was one of the most important ways in which the manager could be a mentor.

The company struggled to find the right position for another promising although arguably misplaced employee, Patrick Duerksen. "He's a very quiet guy. He's very deliberative. He's often misunderstood because he is quiet and a little hard to get to know," said Wamsteeker. Several different options — working in electronic ventures, becoming a business manager, a turn at sales — didn't seem to produce the right fit. "After getting to know Patrick, I was convinced that there would be a right fit created for him by focusing him on what he is good at," said the manager.

One of the crucial aspects of raising pork is "productivity." It covers such variables as the number of piglets a sow produces, the optimal conditions for rapid growth of the hogs, and the best processes along the way. Improving those factors reduces expenses and increases profits. Wamsteeker put Duerksen in that role and things soon clicked. "We developed this specialist role around productivity, and I would say in Cargill's pork business globally he's probably one of the most requested guys in that capacity," said his manager. "He's really flourished. It's very rewarding."

Duerksen attributes part of his success to Wamsteeker being his advocate, advertising his talents inside the company. "Pete takes the time to question and understand what you are doing," he said. "A poor manager would only look at what's on the surface and wouldn't question any deeper than that."

Hulsebus grew up on a farm in southeast Iowa and got a degree in animal science from Iowa State University, but at Cargill he gravitated toward the mathematics of food production. "I am relatively analytical and I'm very good at math and have an affinity for numbers," he said. "A lot of people will ask something and I'll tell them, 'It's just numbers.'"

Hulsebus struggled when he tried to be a sales leader. "I could just sense he wanted to get a passion around being involved with trading and helping to coach people, but he didn't want to supervise people," said Wamsteeker. When Hulsebus was made a trading specialist, was teamed up with Duerksen and another specialist, and when the three of them were challenged to come up with innovative ways of helping pork producers, some incredible things happened, said Wamsteeker. Using proprietary software and processes with names such as "PigPlan," "SowPlan," and "MarketFlex," the Cargill team helps producers forecast their cash flow and income under various alternatives to find the one that maximizes their profit. "Too often people get caught up in the emotion of the moment and forget that they really are working on margin per head," said Hulsebus.

Astrauskas likes to tell people that when he was hired seven years ago, "They gave me a laptop, an American Express card, and a plane ticket, and said, 'So there you go. Go do it!'" Virtually no training was in place. New college graduates today go through a yearlong education process in which they learn pig physiology, nutrition, and the production business. But all that education doesn't help unless someone coaches the new consultant and prepares him before having him face a tough clientele. "Pete's pretty good at that. He just doesn't throw those kids in," said Astrauskas. "He let's them win. They build confidence. They build understanding. Most of the producers we're calling on are professional people who can easily sense it when a consultant does not understand the intricacies of the business, and they will not do business with people who do not understand the business. They're not a bunch of weaklings out here. They're successful, hard-core-survivor business people."

Wamsteeker's means of accomplishing the Sixth Element revolves around a host of questions, not unlike the interrogations he took from the feed business owner in Lethbridge. "I really, truly, want to learn all I can about you," he tells them. "I can't effectively serve you unless I really know what makes you tick." Later, when the person is gone, he writes notes to which he can refer when coaching the person. The manager says he does this in part because "I can't invest superficially" and because he deeply enjoys seeing his people succeed.

"At first I thought, what's he after?" said Astauskas. "But he really wanted to know. I mean he really wants to know. He's engaged with his employees."

"He asks the right question in a manner where it's not offending," said Wells. "He's earned the right to ask them."

The engagement of the pork team isn't limited to their manager's coaching. They also mention that Wamsteeker quickly follows up to eliminate technical problems, advocates for them with the company's leadership in Minneapolis, and — with almost three decades in the agriculture business — knows what he's talking about. "He gets it," said Astrauskas. "He's been around this business quite a while, but he really understands the people aspect." The team said their manager takes the same approach with his employees as he does with the business: Invest in the relationship, do the right thing, and the results will ultimately follow.

To ask Wamsteeker why he manages as he does is like asking him why he's 6-foot-4 or why he has blond hair. "I'm just wired that way. I view the world that way. I really want to do the right thing." And, of course, there's the desire not to disappoint his mentor, with whom he visits or plays golf when he returns to Lethbridge, and who inquires into Wamsteeker's family as much as the Cargill manager inquires into his team's relatives.

When Wamsteeker's team was surveyed on the 12 Elements during the summer of 2006, their answers put them in the top fifth of business units in the Gallup database. Their Sixth Element responses were in the top 10 percent.

His approach and philosophy makes Wamsteeker a somewhat unconventional manager within his company. The phrase "not a typical Cargill guy" is frequently repeated in interviews with his employees. "Pete's not the traditional Cargill guy, but I do feel that Pete is what will be successful as the new kind of Cargill leader," said Wells.

"For a lot of years I was viewed as soft, that I couldn't make the tough people decisions," said Wamsteeker, who points out he's quite willing to confront problems when needed. "In a self-satisfying way, that pendulum is swinging in business today, and particularly in our organization. Now senior leadership is saying, 'Wow, there's a lot of merit in that! We've got to really focus on people's strengths. We've got to coach. We've got to develop. We've got to see potential. We've got to really focus on engagement."

When it's all boiled down, Wamsteeker says, "I really want to do the right thing."

THE SEVENTH ELEMENT:

My Opinions Seem to Count

THE 10-YEAR-OLD GIRL CARRIED ALONG A SMALL STUFFED CAT as technologist Matt Fry escorted her to the large MRI machine. The patient knew the territory. She had a brain tumor removed three years before and was what the staff calls a "frequent flyer" of the Diagnostic Imaging unit at Toronto's Hospital for Sick Children.

Still, she had been sobbing in the staging area. Fry was ready to offer tissues and some of his tried-and-true reassurances, such as, "It's just a big camera."

"Can I borrow your tiger for just a second?" he said. She reluctantly surrendered it. Fry held it to the side of the MRI machine to ensure it contained no metal, and quickly returned it. The technologist invited the girl to climb onto the gurney. "Do you fall asleep sometimes?" he asked. She nodded. "I always fall asleep," he said, hoping to calm her fears by reminding her that he had been in the MRI many times.

Fry gently arranged her on the gurney and asked twice if she was warm enough as he engaged the motors that moved her into the center of the magnetic circle. He positioned the tiger on her stomach so she could see it through the mirror inside the "doughnut."

The technologist backed away to the control room and began the imaging session. "Remember, you will be able to hear me talk to you through the microphone," he told the girl. "She'll be fine," he remarked. "When I left her on the table she had a big smile on her face." Technology meets tigers and tears every day at the hospital nicknamed "Sick Kids." The unique challenges of treating seriously ill children mean it often takes a little more — more explanation, more reassurance, more time.

Time, however, is in short supply. The patients and staff who entered the hospital that day walked past *National Post* newspaper boxes bearing the lead headline, "PROVINCES SET NEW WAIT TIMES: Patients should receive new hip within 6 months, cardiac bypass in 2 weeks." In June 2005, the Supreme Court of Canada ruled long waits for medical care in Quebec violated that province's charter of rights, intensifying a national debate on the issue.

A few years ago, patients needing a non-emergency MRI (magnetic resonance imaging) appointment at Sick Kids had to wait an average of over nine months. Sometimes the delay was over a year. By increasing their hours of operation, refining their patient scheduling and — maybe most crucial — fostering an atmosphere of greater respect among the different professions who work in the imaging centers, Sick Kids was able to reduce its average wait time to four weeks. Ensuring that employees knew their opinions matter was the linchpin to the turnaround, the staff said.

The Hospital for Sick Children is one of the leading pediatric health care and research facilities in the world. It employs a staff of more than 5,000 employees, plus another 1,200 in its research institute. It handles almost 99,000 patient days, over 23,000 operating room hours, 47,500 visits to the emergency room, and more than 300,000 visits by patients who don't need to be admitted for a hospital stay. The government-run hospital spent C$538 million in its 2004/2005 fiscal year.[1]

Although the facility serves the Toronto area, treating relatively minor ailments such as earaches and stitching deep cuts, many of the children are among Canada's most seriously ill. A steady procession of heart-wrenching troubles comes through the door. Some are severe traumas, such as a teenaged boy hit by a truck and flown to the hospital. Some have congenital abnormalities, such as a heart on the wrong side of the chest, or require organ transplants. Others have cancer or are recovering from surgery to remove tumors.

At the beginning and throughout the process, it's crucial that the doctors look inside the bodies of their young charges. The Diagnostic Imaging department brings a number of different technologies to the task, from traditional X-rays to ultrasound to CT (computed tomography) scans and MRIs. The beauty of all the methods is they allow a detailed view without any incisions. It also means Diagnostic Imaging is under tremendous demand, becomes a bottleneck, and is therefore an area of continuous pressure. "You're not able to do that hip surgery, that oncology treatment, that cardiac surgery, or that ophthalmology work without first having a diagnostic imaging done," said Ellen Charkot, chief technologist and a 30-year employee of the hospital.

Diagnostic imaging requires the combined efforts of at least four types of professional: nurses, technologists, anesthetists, and radiologists. The coordination of the "techs" and nurses seems to make the greatest difference in increasing patient flow without sacrificing the quality of the images.

Strategies for maximizing production through a bottleneck are well established and taught at most business schools. But those solutions assume a higher degree of control over the "inputs" than children allow. With most adult patients, the process of obtaining scans can be speeded up by their understanding of what's required of them. An MRI session can last 30 to 60 minutes, maybe more. The patient must lie still for long stretches of time inside a sometimes claustrophobia-inducing space. An adult is less emotional, more tolerant of pain, and far less wiggly. Wiggling is the bane of a clear image.

How long does it take to get a good CT scan or MRI of a child? "It depends on the kid. It depends on the day," said tech Christine Billanti. Every patient is different. The decision many patients pose for the staff is complicated. One certain way to get a clear picture is to sedate the patient so she doesn't move while in the MRI or CT scan machine. But sedation takes a while to wear off. It ties up nurses in the recovery area and it slows down the process. It's better if the patient can remain still long enough without sedation. Going without sedation also carries risks. If the child moves, the procedure must be repeated. That slows down the process and, in the case of a CT scan, the child receives a double dose of the radiation that creates the image.

At Sick Kids, the difficulty of these decisions was made worse by disagreements and a lack of respect between the techs, who were concerned most with getting a crisp image, and the nurses, who were are primarily responsible for the medical care of the child during the procedure. Nurses were more likely to argue against sedation. Techs were more likely to favor it, in hopes of getting a good picture on the first try. "From the tech's perspective, it's a safety issue. Say a child tries (to lie still) and fails. They have already given a radiation dose because they've attempted to scan," said Catherine Pratt, clinical leader of the nurses in Diagnostic Imaging. On the other hand, "if they really are truly still, they can get a good (CT) scan in maybe three to four minutes. So the nurse is thinking, 'Why am I going to sedate a kid for two hours for a 10-minute process?'"

This led to a pervasive animosity between the two camps, the techs feeling the nurses "bulldozed" through the process and the nurses seeing the techs as "button-pushers." Neither felt the other side respected their expertise. Because of these disagreements, other forms of cooperation also broke down. Neither side was eager to jump in and help with shared responsibilities. The techs stayed in their control rooms next to the imaging machines, and the nurses stayed at the nursing station. Communication broke down, so the two groups were not properly coordinating when one patient would be done and the next should come in.

"What people had not realized," said Charkot, "is when you throw a diverse group of people together in one situation without looking at the dynamics, without planning how they'll work together, what happens — especially among professionals — is a little bit of a turf war, a little bit of territory guarding and really a misunderstanding of what the other person is doing." None of this helped reduce the wait times.

"How to put it nicely?" ponders nurse Marie Little as she watches a sedated patient undergo an MRI. "Have you ever seen the movie 'Babe,' where all the animals want to do someone else's role, where the duck wants to be the rooster and wake up the farmer in the morning? That's what it was like. The problem came from not knowing or respecting each other's roles."

Hospital Vice President Brendan Gibney hired three successive managers in the search for someone who could make a difference. The third time was the charm. In May of 2001, Susan Jewell had a nursing background and six years of management experience, but she had not worked in what's traditionally called radiology. Nonetheless, "she was a very vital type of person — very committed to the hospital," he said. "She had lots to learn, but she had the vitality, the interest, the dedication and the personality I thought would really work."

The new managing director of Diagnostic Imaging had her work cut out for her. She sensed her colleague and key partner, Radiologist-in-Chief Dr. Paul Babyn, didn't feel included in her hiring and didn't know what to expect. Many in the hospital didn't understand her department or its constraints. The hours of operation weren't long enough, but she was in no position to ask more of a staff that was fairly disengaged already; the best could simply quit and have their pick of jobs anywhere in Canada or the United States.

The patient wait times were unacceptable by any standard. "I met with Paul Babyn and asked him what he would like to see me focus on in the first year," said Jewell. "He said, 'I want you to reduce the MRI wait list.' And I said, 'How long have you been working on it?' He said, 'As long as I can remember.'" At that time, the average wait to get a CT scan with anesthesia was 27 weeks. For an MRI appointment, it was 41 weeks. "It was horrible," she said.

And then there was the tension between techs and nurses. "It was absolutely an entrenched culture that was impenetrable, according to them, a long-standing issue, and it couldn't be fixed," she said.

Managers faced with an operational bottleneck such as the imaging machines at Sick Kids Hospital are often tempted to design the optimal solution without worrying what team members think. A typical "production and operations management" manual gives plenty of advice on the steps to be timed and formulas to be calculated, but it tends to treat workers as cogs in the machine, whose rate of production can be improved by "behavioral modification in quality control" or through a "behavior-performance-reward-satisfaction sequence."[2] Although there is always a need for expertly designed systems that help maximize production, nearly every system depends to a huge degree on the motivation of the people who run it. That motivation, it turns out, requires workers strongly agree that "At work, my opinions seem to count." This is the Seventh Element of Great Managing.

To appreciate this element, managers need to understand how the history of management entrenched ideas of dictating to workers that conflict with the Seventh Element. To understand why they need to listen to their staff, managers need to know about Henry Noll.

By all accounts, Noll was a good worker. He would walk home after a 10-hour day at a brisk pace "about as fresh as he was when he came trotting down to work in the morning."[3] He was frugal — one of his coworkers said "a penny looks about the size of a cart wheel to him" — saving enough of the $1.15 per day he earned in 1899 to buy a small plot of land. Before and after his shift at Bethlehem Iron Company in Pennsylvania, he worked on constructing the walls of a small one-and-a-half-story clapboard house.[4] He was not a large man, only 135 pounds, but he was strong and athletic. He had worked three years at Bethlehem when he was discovered and eventually made famous by Frederick Winslow Taylor.

Although the son of a wealthy family, Taylor apprenticed in a machine shop. He was endlessly experimenting with improving processes, particularly with lathes, metallurgy and the tools used to cut the metal. Taylor was obsessed with output, how to help employees "do their work in the best way and in the quickest time."[5] In 1899, he turned his attention to the problem of 80,000 tons of "pig iron" sitting in a yard east of the iron mill and tried to apply to human productivity the scientific approach he previously used on mechanical workings.

A "pig" was a block of metal four inches wide, four inches tall and 32 inches long. It weighed about 92 pounds. More than 1.7 million of them were sitting in the Bethlehem yard. Taylor recruited a team of men to experiment with just how fast they could load a railcar with the iron.

Each pig had to be lifted, carried across wooden planks to the railcar and handed to another man stacking them in place. The usual rate of loading was 12½ tons per man in a 10-hour day. Challenged to load a car as fast as possible, ten men running up and down the planks with the iron could complete the task in fourteen minutes, a rate, if they sustained the unsustainable pace of 71 tons per man per day. Making adjustments for rest and delays, Taylor estimated a "first-class" worker could load 45 tons per day.[6]

Why would anyone work at a pace twice to three times what laborers had averaged? In his utopian view, Taylor assumed it was simply a matter of higher pay for harder work and persuading workers to leave the thinking to a group of methodical overseers using Taylor's methods. "The development of a science (of managing tasks) involves the establishment of many rules, laws, and formulae which replace the judgment of the individual workman and which can be effectively used only after having been systematically recorded, indexed, etc.," he wrote when summarizing his approach in *The Principles of Scientific Management*.[7]

Right from the beginning there were problems. Although Taylor recognized in his writing and speeches that workers avoided piecework out of a fear management would greet higher productivity with lower pay rates, that's precisely what happened at Bethlehem. When paid by the day, workers made about $1.15. Two of Taylor's lieutenants set the piece rate at 3.75 cents per ton, meaning a worker would have to move more than 30 tons to equal what he had been paid before for moving less than half that weight. A worker could earn $1.69 if he hit the supposedly attainable 45-ton mark, but that would mean lifting almost 1,000 pigs during his shift, almost 100 an hour. Ten men who agreed to try piecework changed their minds and went back to the day-rate crew. Taylor saw to it they were fired. Seven more men were recruited. Only five reported for work. One of them was Henry Noll.

The five men averaged 32 tons each that day, but two more dropped out. Noll's coworkers moved between 35 and 40 tons each. Noll did 45¾, earning $1.71. Very soon, only Noll remained. "Other men were recruited, some of whom could keep up with him," wrote Taylor biographer Robert Kanigel. "But most gave up after a few eighty- or ninety-cent days, or after earning more but deciding they couldn't endure such grueling work."[8] The last man standing, Noll became Taylor's poster child. The efficiency expert claimed his worker wasn't unusual, that many workers who weren't "soldiering" or failing to follow orders could equal his output. But the engineer certainly didn't think much of his ideal worker's intellect, as shown by Taylor's recollection of his directions to Noll on how he could earn higher pay.

"If you are a high-priced man," Taylor said, "you will do exactly as this man tells you tomorrow, from morning 'til night. When he tells you to pick up a pig and walk, you pick it up and you walk, and when he tells you to sit down and rest, you sit down. You do that right straight through the day. And what's more, no back talk. Now, a high-priced man does just what he's told to do, and no back talk. Do you understand that?"[9]

In some ways, Taylor succeeded in revolutionizing industry. Anyone who has struggled to organize a yard project among family members quickly realizes that having the right tools and a good plan can save hours of wasted effort and a spouse's anger. Incremental improvements to production lines have dramatically cut the cost and improved the quality of everything from cars to packaged foods to handheld electronics. Taylor called it a "scientific" approach; today it's sometimes called re-engineering. It is simply a methodical approach to working smarter. With today's computers and robots, predictable, repetitive, and heavy work can now be done by machines.

But Taylor also spawned "Taylorism," a pejorative used to describe his pessimistic view of employee abilities and the treatment of men as machines. "It would be possible to train an intelligent gorilla so as to become a more efficient pig-iron handler than any man can be," he wrote. "Yet . . . the science of handling pig iron is so great and amounts to so much that it is impossible for the man who is best suited to this type of work to understand the principles of this science, or even to work in accordance with these principles without the aid of a man better educated than he is."[10] Taylor's methods sparked congressional hearings, helped galvanize the labor movement he thought would be unnecessary with his approach and fostered bad management practices that continue today.

"Scientific management was degrading," wrote Kanigel. "In reducing work to instructions and rules, it took away your knowledge and skill. In standing over you with a stopwatch, peering at you, measuring you, rating you, it treated you like a side of beef. You weren't supposed to think. Whatever workmanly pride you might once have possessed must be sacrificed on the altar of efficiency, your role only to execute the will of other men paid to think for you. You were a drone, fit only for taking orders. Scientific management, then, worked people with scant regard not only for the limitations of their bodies but for the capacities of their minds."[11] And as if he had not insulted Noll enough in his conversations with him and his descriptions in print, Taylor went one further. Instead of using his real name, he called him simply "Schmidt."

Taylor's ghost haunts the way many companies still do business. One company had the same experts who designed its computer systems write protocols for interacting with customers. The inch-thick manuals described in Tayloresque detail and flow-charted steps how the employee should behave and how the customer should react, including a five-minute limit on the interaction itself. Call centers frequently keep a stop-watch on their telephone representatives. Banks keep scorecards on functional process steps that are as easily observed as they can be meaningless when delivered without emotion. A few companies even try to dictate to a company's workgroups which of the 12 Elements to work on each month of the year — the First Element in January, the Second in February, and so forth — making July particularly rich in irony as the month when company higher-ups command employees to work on how to make their opinions count.

Airlines, arguably among the worst offenders, routinely lock passengers in with a crew of Schmidts reading from a script and processing passengers like Bethlehem workers moving pig iron. The experience of one frequent flyer shows the direct connection between employee feelings of empowerment and the quality of customer service.

"Do you have any hot chocolate?" asked the passenger when the attendant and her beverage cart reached his aisle.

"Not even," she said with a contemptuous look.

"How about some orange juice?"

The flight attendant nodded and began pouring the juice. While she did, the passenger pressed the question. "I don't understand why this airline doesn't keep some packets of hot chocolate on board," he said. "They store easily. They're easier to make than the coffee you have to make fresh."

"We used to have some," said the attendant, handing the passenger his plastic cup of juice. "Maybe all the flight attendants drank it. Don't ask me. My opinion isn't worth a lot around here."[12]

Millions of these small interactions establish a company's reputation much more than their stated aspirations, which in this case included, "Always put customers first," and, "Always strive to improve."[13] When Gallup conducted an exploratory survey using a new customer engagement metric a few months later, it was no shock to find that the airline, Northwest, scored near the bottom of the heap. Nor was it startling to find that the stock performance of the airlines with higher customer engagement, such as Southwest, performed better after the tragedies of 9/11 than those without the same reserve of goodwill.[14]

The mechanism that connects this element with better business performance appears to be a greater sense of responsibility for or psychological ownership of those things over which one has a say. No matter how strong the external incentives, they never seem to measure up to the internal drive of advancing something that is at least partially one's own idea. Nearly half of employees who say their opinion counts at work also feel their current job brings out their most creative ideas. Among those who are neutral or negative on the Seventh Element, only 8 percent feel their creativity is well employed.

Lou, the manager of "Peanut" we introduced at the beginning of this book, went out of his way to listen to his skeptical team when he accepted the job as manager. "Once they realized I wasn't the type to say, 'This is the way we're going to do things now because I'm the boss,' they said, 'Hey, this guy really listens!'" His men approached him about rearranging the shipping area, wanting to put the more frequently shipped products closer to where trucks backed in for loading. "I allowed them to come in on weekends (when there were no trucks) and rearrange things the way they wanted it," said Lou. "So, this is their home. It worked very well." If Lou had ordered the shipping area be reorganized, is there doubt follow-through would have been half-hearted?

In this element as with all 12, many modest, discretionary actions by employees create meaningful differences in the enterprise's metrics. For example, when manufacturing plants in one large organization were ranked by their scores on the "opinions count" statement, those in the top quartile averaged one in three employees strongly agreeing, while plants in the bottom quartile averaged only one in seven. Accidents later that same year were more than twice as likely to occur in the bottom-quartile plants as they were in the top-quartile plants. On a larger scale, improving the proportion of employees with high Seventh Element scores from one in five to one in three has a substantial impact on customer experience, productivity, employee retention and safety, all of which create, on average, a 6-percent gain in profitability.[15]

Incorporating employee ideas pays back twice. First, the idea itself often is a good one. Second and equally powerful, that the idea comes from the employees themselves makes it much more likely they will be committed to its execution. Welcoming employee opinions also produces greater feelings of inclusion among workers. When the 12 elements are compared against a number of statements testing perceived racial or gender bias, the "opinions count" statement is most highly correlated with feelings that employees are always treated with respect, that the company treats its workforce fairly.[16]

More than a century after Taylor and Noll met, and less than 200 miles away, two professors took on the same problem of how to best increase productivity. Derek Jones and Takao Kato went to a small manufacturing facility in central New York to investigate whether inviting employees to share their opinions about process improvements created the hoped-for benefits.

The real name of the company was not revealed. In their paper, Jones and Kato called it "PARTS." PARTS was a subsidiary of a multi-national company. It made a range of small components used by large manufacturers. Its customers demanded high quality, so the 134 machine operators it employed had to be careful to not deviate from design specifications. Pieces outside those tolerances were rejected.[17]

The parallels to the problems Taylor sought to solve are intriguing. Like Taylor, Jones and Kato were studying a manufacturing environment. Like Taylor in his experiments with lathes and metal, the professors were investigating how man and machine (or woman and machine; 62 percent of PARTS operators were female) can combine for maximum production. Like Taylor, Jones and Kato were studying the productivity of low-wage workers. Only a third of PARTS operators had education beyond high school, and virtually none had a four-year college degree. The average wage was $7.64 an hour.

Beyond the advances in technology during the century that separates them, the major difference between the studies is that while Taylor wanted a mindless compliance with management's thinking, PARTS executives were inviting workers to strategize on the best ways to improve the work with which they were so familiar. For example, the 400-square-foot shipping area "was originally quite disorganized, and access to the shipping area was cumbersome at best," wrote Jones and Kato. "A team reorganized this shipping area and thereby created additional free space equaling 175 square feet. In turn, this allowed workers at all stations to access the shipping area quickly and smoothly." Operators developed a new labeling system for spare parts, reducing both the time needed for labeling and defects caused by using wrong parts. Employees developed a better exhaust system for the wire soldering station, revised manuals, and rearranged machine locations for better efficiency.[18]

PARTS provided a good environment for studying employee input because at the time of the research, only some of the employees were eligible to participate in the new operator-input "team" program. The professors interviewed 90 percent of the operators face-to-face, and were able to compare the comments of those in and out of the initiative. "Relative to non-team members, team participants consider themselves to be more empowered, sensed that more information was being shared by management, communicated more often with managers and supervisors within their work groups or teams, and communicated more often with workers outside of their work groups or teams," wrote the researchers. "In addition the survey findings indicate that participants in teams put more effort into their work. The evidence is equally suggestive that attitudes and thus potentially the behavior of team members was being affected in other ways. Thus we find some evidence for participants displaying stronger organizational commitment and more trust towards management. . . . Team members are more satisfied with their jobs (and) are more positive about the use and contributions of their knowledge and skills."[19]

The New York manufacturer was also a good site for research because the company keeps individual statistics on each operator's production, defect rate, and downtime. Employees in the "team" program averaged 3 percent higher production and 27 percent fewer defects. While the company had to invest additional time to gather input, the results bolster the case that "employee involvement will produce improved enterprise performance through diverse channels, including enhanced discretionary effort by employees."[20]

Somewhere beyond the grave, Henry Noll is smiling.

Susan Jewell spent her first months in Diagnostic Imaging listening to people, trying to understand their opinions and gathering facts about the wait-time problem. Among her conclusions: Some of the people currently managing employees had lost credibility with the staff and needed to be let go or reassigned; she needed to be a strong advocate for the department to the rest of the hospital; several areas needed to be remodeled to improve patient flow; and the working hours of the imaging machines needed to be lengthened. But ultimately, nothing was going to improve much with the dissension between techs and nurses.

"I knew that we could say, 'Okay, we have to extend the hours until 11 at night,' and I might as well just shoot myself and leave because that was not going to go over well," she said. "I had to get really engaged, enthusiastic people to really appreciate what we needed to do." Dr. Babyn agreed that employee engagement was a prerequisite to improved efficiency. "You have to have motivation of the employees to encourage them to recognize that we may need to go through a little bit of pain to get to the next level," he said.

Among the meetings Jewell convened was one between Pratt, who leads the nurses in the CAT scan area, and Guila BenDavid, who manages the techs. The director said she wanted them to exemplify the cooperation she intended between the two professions. "We have to leave that baggage aside. I want to see you two hand-in-hand, skipping down the CT hallway." To coincide with renovations in the CT area, the three of them decided they needed to hire a facilitator and organize a retreat in hopes of getting the techs and nurses working together better.

Those who attended the meeting that day say it started like the typical all-day session. There were ice-breaking exercises to help the group begin to feel comfortable interacting. There were ground rules — one speaker at a time, no blaming, speak in headlines, give constructive feedback. And, the facilitator emphasized, say what needs to be said: "Put the moose on the table."

One technique that seems to have worked was a role-playing exercise in which the techs played the part of the nurses and vice versa. Through exaggerated misperceptions and a certain amount of ribbing, the two groups got to some of the real issues between them. "Oh, could you try this kid without sedation? He's really cute," said one tech pretending to be a nurse. Another tech-turned-nurse sat down and began reading a magazine. Not to be outdone, one of the nurses playing the role of a tech deadpanned, "I don't care. Sedate them!"

Jewell and her managers pounced on the dramatic play. "I see that you guys are making jokes about this, but there must be some truth to it," said BenDavid. "There's no joke that doesn't come from somewhere, right?" Using the humor as a springboard, the techs and nurses started discussing the real issues: why they recommended for or against sedation in certain situations, how both professions felt a lack of respect, where a failure of communication or courtesy interfered with the work, and how they could make improvements.

BenDavid recalls getting hopeful when one of the toughest nurses, who could be expected to put up brick walls in defiance of change — "It's just her personality; it's who she is" — started voicing support. "She was all for getting the group to work better. She wasn't about taking the soapbox or saying, 'Nurses are this' and 'Nurses are that.' I was really, really shocked and happy to see it." Jewell noticed a sense of relief that people had a chance to acknowledge the problems and address them.

Much of the discussion focused on who should be responsible for various aspects of the process. In the end, they agreed that only one function, sedation, was the sole domain of nurses, and only one other, scanning, had to be done by a tech. "Other than those two distinct roles, everything else should be fluid," said Pratt. "It isn't a tech's job to make up the bed following a scan any more than it's a nursing job to solely do some other task." They made a pact to stop hanging back and work as one team rather than as two autonomous groups. They agreed to communicate better.

They pledged less negativity and more praise in the department. When they took an assignment to write a short note of praise to the people on either side of them, "everybody was really shocked and I think a few people were kind of really floored by what the people beside them wrote," said BenDavid. The department secretary, who thought no one noticed her work, was stunned to get a note that said the department could not get through the day without her.

"I think they really learned about each other," said Jewell. "Then we really put some tangible plans together around how they were going to work together better and what specifically they were going to do in terms of combined roles, communication, and expectations. I've got to say that retreat was probably the turning point."

Her staff credits a willingness of nearly all the employees to stick by the agreements of that day to their subsequent success. "Everyone assumes you want to be on the same page, but it's different to actually try to do it," said tech Christine Billanti. Many small gestures, such as nurses hanging around the control room with the techs and both professions meeting the other more than halfway, ensured the good feelings of the retreat were translated into action. "It's like any other relationship; it was the little things," said Billanti. "But it was a huge difference," added tech Nancy Padfield.

The employees say glowing things about Jewell's leadership. "It's Sue's X-ray vision," said Pratt, no pun intended. "It's as though she can see inside and knows where you thrive and where you don't and doesn't want you to be in something that you don't love doing every single day." Dr. Babyn praises her ability to help a team focus on the right goals. Gibney, her boss, said simply, "I think she has an innate management style."

"She has the ability, whether she knows it or not, to have people feel like they're important, that they count," said Charkot. "And she did that in a very subtle way. It's not like she came in and everybody suddenly began to feel like it's a great place to work and 'I want to stay here and I know that my input will be valued.' It happened gradually, but it happened very significantly. I don't think there's anyone who could say that they feel like she doesn't see them as a person who is contributing to the entire system."

Only when she had an engaged group did Jewell approach them with the need to extend Diagnostic Imaging's hours to handle more patients. Once the friction inside the group was reduced, most of the employees could better focus on their passion for helping their young patients, a fervor evident in many of the small touches throughout the department.

The overhead curve of the CT scanner is peppered with stickers for the kids to stare at. Stickers are the common currency to entice non-sedated patients to hold still. If that's not enough, a disco ball hangs in the corner. One of the techs uses bird whistles. Others sing. Every nurse and tech has their favored technique for relaxing a nervous child. "I usually say, 'You're going into the doughnut, the Tim Horton's doughnut,'" said tech Maria De Stefano Reusse. (Tim Horton's coffee and doughnut shops are as common in Canada as Starbucks are in the United States.)

At one point the team decided to hold a special Saturday clinic for eight children who, because of breathing problems or other issues, could not be sedated. They would have to either hold still long enough for a good image or go under a general anesthetic, a slower, riskier process.

Pratt brought in her grandchildren to allay the patients' fears. "Somehow, with a kid talking to a kid, you can get them to do things," she said. "So my granddaughter would say, 'Come on! Come for a ride with me!' And she'd lie there and the bed would move in and out." The staff painted the kids faces and gave toys as rewards. One patient dressed as his favorite comic book hero, prompting the tech and patient to sing the familiar "Spiderman! Spiderman!" theme as the boy was being readied. "It was a fun day and we had eight-for-eight success, so that was really good," said Pratt.

Life has improved for the employees as well. "Before the meeting, it was organized chaos," said Padfield. "Now, there's not an 'us' and a 'them.' We have to work together. Everyone is just more courteous toward each other." Instead of leaving the building separately, they take Friday lunches together in the control room. The chief radiologist said he's noticed the difference in the work atmosphere: "It's a louder environment."

Increasing engagement and dissipating the nurse-versus-tech animosity was key to reducing wait times. Although they bounced up a bit,

MRI wait times declined from 41 to four weeks at one point. CT wait times dropped to from 27 weeks to three days. Without making the employees feel their opinions count, "we never would have reduced the wait list in MR and CT. Never!" said Jewell. "There would have been no reason for the staff to put out the extra effort, because they didn't look to their immediate leader or to me, frankly, as somebody who cared enough to make their environment better, so why would they bother?"

Because of the stakes for their patients and how deeply most of the employees feel about their work, the improvement is a major accomplishment. The staff talks about how the patients' young ages can mean many sad stories, but their youth also mean there's a chance to help change an entire life. "I couldn't see myself doing anything else," said Jewell. "These kids mean everything to us."

THE EIGHTH ELEMENT:

A Connection With the Mission
of the Company

WHERE WOULD THEY GET THE WALLEYE?
The guy who was supposed to supply that species for the aquarium of the soon-to-open Cabela's store hadn't come through. So the store manager dispatched a couple of employees in a special truck to retrieve some fish. That would have worked fine, "but somehow they turned up the oxygen too high in the tank and over-bubbled the fish," said Store Manager Mike Boldrick. "By the time they got here, we only had one little lethargic walleye."

As if that weren't enough, the bass also had to be popped. They had been fished from too great a depth, and their air bladders had expanded, so the extra air had to be vented to save them. Still, all that was simple enough, if fish were the only problem. But how could they get the small airplane to be hung from the ceiling up the stairs? Where could they put all the merchandise from the grand opening tent that couldn't be set up because of the cement that wasn't poured because of the record rainfall?

How could the managers stay awake in their 5 p.m. meetings when they were exhausted from 100-hour work weeks? Where were the three dozen radios to give to the spotters the fire marshal said were now required because the water tower was drained due to a broken water main?

And would it be okay if the President of the United States stopped by in, say, 20 minutes?

On August 12, 2004, Cabela's opened a 175,000-square-foot show-case store in Wheeling, West Virginia. Dignitaries, customers, and employees — so many that the state patrol had to shut down the new highway exit — gathered to see the unveiling of a large statue in front of the store depicting a mother bear with cubs fighting off two eagles. Little did they know the challenges that Boldrick and his team of hundreds fought off behind the scenes to make that day happen. By marshaling a force of men and women who were committed to the mission of their new employer, Boldrick and his team of managers surmounted a staggering number of challenges to set a company record for the speedy launch of a new store. In doing so, they also created incredibly high levels of employee engagement under circumstances when morale might have collapsed.

Wheeling was the 10th "destination store" for Cabela's, a nationally known catalog merchant of outdoor equipment, rapidly expanding its physical retail presence in the United States. In 1961, Dick and Mary Cabela launched Cabela's as a kitchen-table business selling a package of fishing flies advertised in *Sports Afield* magazine. Cabela's is now a $1.5 billion firm that in the last few years went public in hopes of out-distancing competitors such as Bass Pro Shops, Gander Mountain, and Dick's Sporting Goods. A lot of hopes ride on each new store. Prior to its opening, the Wheeling store and its projected performance frequently came up in company discussions with Wall Street analysts. Boldrick and his management team were under no small amount of pressure as they prepared for opening day.

A 15-year retail veteran, Boldrick had been with Cabela's only about two years when he was offered the chance to establish the Wheeling store. He impressed the managers he recruited as energetic, but calm under pressure. "This guy is genuine; he's down to earth. He believes in this, and that's what helps him sell it to everybody," said Loss Prevention Manager Michael Rock. Boldrick warned prospective managers about the trials ahead and turned away a few who seemed intimidated. "You're going to be working 12- and 15-hour days. You're going to work harder than you've ever worked," he told them. "But you're going to have more fun and see more accomplishment in a shorter period of time than you ever have."

"We kind of vetted people through that interview process," said Boldrick. "If people looked at me funny, then I knew that this person might not be up for the challenge."

While the building was going up, Boldrick and his managers worked from trailers on the construction site and a nearby hotel, interviewing people for 400 front-line positions. For those who would be on the sales floor itself, outdoor experience was more important than retail experience. "You give me somebody who's dedicated and has a love and a passion for the outdoors, and I can teach him what he needs to know about retail," said Troy Gatti, receiving manager during the grand opening period. For many of the applicants, their hobbies had never been so useful to their careers. "What do you like to do on your weekends?" they were asked. "Where do you like to fish?" "What kind of shotgun do you like?" Applicants were sorted by their area of outdoor interest, and the best were hired in each until the departments were full.

Then came the hard part.

The Eighth Element of Great Managing is captured by the statement, "The mission or purpose of my company makes me feel my job is important." As with the rest of the 12 Elements, the degree to which a team agrees with this statement is predictive of its performance on a wide array of measures, many of which would prove to be crucial to the opening of the West Virginia Cabela's store. For instance, business units in the top quartile of Gallup's engagement database on this element average from 5 to 15 percent higher profitability than bottom-quartile units. Mission-driven workgroups suffer 30 to 50 percent fewer accidents, and have 15 to 30 percent lower turnover.[1] Employees who feel connected to the mission of their company are also more likely to report that humor or laughter plays a positive role in their productivity.[2]

The strange thing about the Eighth Element is how extraneous it is to the job itself and the employee's material well-being. The absence of many of the other elements — job clarity, the proper equipment, a match with one's talents, consistent feedback — become real obstacles to actual production. It's easy to see why they are required to get the job done. The same cannot be said for the Eighth Element, which is strictly an emotional need, and a higher-level one at that, as if the employee can't energize himself to do all he could without knowing how his job fits into the grand scheme of things.

The data say that's just what happens. If a job were just a job, it really wouldn't matter where someone worked. A good paycheck, decent benefits, reasonable hours and comfortable working conditions would be enough. The job would serve its function of putting food on the table and money in the kids' college accounts. But a uniquely human twist occurs after the basic needs are fulfilled. The employee searches for meaning in her vocation. For reasons that transcend the physical needs fulfilled by earning a living, she looks for her contribution to a higher purpose. Something within her looks for something in which to believe.

Sometimes, this wrinkle in human nature causes people to elevate the most pedestrian of products, as they did in the odd document issued in 1922 by the Pacific Ice Cream Manufacturers Association that begins: "We believe in ice cream."

They called it their "Declaration of Principles." It ascribes lofty ideals to an unusually common product. "We believe," it continues "in the great future that lies before the industry, because ice cream is the one product which contains all of the life-giving, body-building properties peculiar to milk, combined with a variety and palatability found in no other milk product."[3] Beyond the 1920s-style boosterism, the Pacific Ice Cream Declaration of Principles reveals a much deeper and older feeling, not about what it means to make and sell ice cream, but to be humans looking for meaning in the mundane.

From one perspective, ice cream is just ice cream, just one of many desserts, hardly worth glorifying. But to someone who buys the cream, runs the factory, agonizes over the right flavors and gets a thrill out of seeing a little boy or girl savor a double-scoop cone, being in the ice cream business is a way to make a small contribution to the quality of life — the happiness — of their customers. So when Blue Bunny Ice Cream calls its flavor mixers "colossally creative artisans" who work not just in the small city of Le Mars, Iowa, but in "The Ice Cream Capital of the World," making "America's favorite treat," most of them really mean it.[4] People cling to greater purposes. Ice cream makers "believe" in ice cream.

Companies routinely adopt high ideals as part of their mission. Lowe's Home Improvement stores aim not just to sell lumber and hardware, but to offer "practically everything customers need to build, beautify and enjoy their homes."[5] Kodak doesn't just sell film; it "continues to expand the ways images touch people's daily lives."[6] Kellogg's aspires to do more than make cereal; instead, "we make the world a little happier by bringing our best to you."[7] Siam Commercial Bank in Thailand seeks to "dedicate ourselves to the quality and righteousness of our work, to work as a team so that we shall provide the best of services, to respect human values, and to participate to the best of our ability in our society and nation."[8]

As in the Ice Cream Declaration of Principles, there are large dollops of marketing syrup in these statements. There is also a reason why such statements appeal to customers and, when backed up by the company's culture, why they strongly motivate employees. Workers thirst for something noble in which to believe and invest themselves.

Claremont Graduate University Professor Mihaly Csikszentmihalyi tells a story of teaching seminars on midlife crises to high-level executives, employing "the best theories and research results in developmental psychology." The seminars were well received, but something was missing. "I was never quite satisfied that the material made enough sense," he wrote. Dr. Csikszentmihalyi decided to try starting the sessions by reviewing Dante's *Divine Comedy*, the more-than-600-year-old poem that begins, "In the middle of the journey of our life, I found myself in a dark forest, for the right way I had completely lost." The professor hoped instilling his discussions with greater meaning would help with the teaching. "I was rather concerned about how the harried business executives would take to this centuries-old parable. Chances were, I feared, that they would regard it as a waste of their precious time," he wrote. "I need not have worried. We never had as open and as serious a discussion of the pitfalls of midlife, and of the options for enriching the years that would follow, as we had after talking about the *Commedia*."[9]

Stories like Dr. Csikszentmihalyi's hint at why quantitative studies are finding that the motivating power of salary, commissions, and even awards is limited. "The most recent evidence suggests that money is losing its power as a central motivator, in part because the general population is realizing, in greater numbers, that above a minimum level necessary for survival, money adds little to their subjective well-being," wrote researcher Amy Wrzesniewski.[10] It's not uncommon for employees of highly engaged workgroups, from entry level to senior executives, to mention having turned down higher pay to join or remain with a company they believed would provide more meaningful work with a more enjoyable team.

Why people gravitate toward a larger purpose is a mystery. One is unlikely to get an acceptable reason for it outside of places of worship (which may be why religions last longer than businesses). The need appears to be nearly universal. When respondents to a 1990 Gallup Poll were asked, "How important to you is the belief that your life is meaningful or has a purpose?" 83 percent said "very important" and 15 percent said "fairly important."[11] Belief that one is doing something meaningful is important to a person's psychological and even physical health.[12] It's not necessary that managers understand why people need to dedicate themselves to an endeavor greater than themselves, only that they appreciate and work to fulfill this need.

Just how deep these connections go has surprised even professional researchers of "meaningfulness" in the workplace. In 1993, University of Utah doctoral student Melissa M. Koerner conducted interviews with health care workers who helped the underprivileged in an unnamed western United States city. As she talked to the physician's assistants, nurse practitioners, and a doctor, she found their connection with their job bordered on feelings of "sacredness." "The study's original focus was to explore the nature of the relationship between health care providers and their patients; the presence of sacredness in the relationship was not initially an area of inquiry," wrote Koerner. "However, during the investigation, anecdotes and comments with religious undertones were so prevalent among informants, that sacredness eventually became the centerpiece of the study."

A 41-year-old nurse practitioner named Linda described how helping a family get through several crises created a deep affection for them and made her feel her job was important. "I met her family when her husband came in very sick. He ended up having pancreatic cancer and dying within about three or four months of the time I met him. She was pregnant with their first child. I took care of her little girl after she was born, and then I took care of her. I just really liked her. I enjoyed the whole family," said Linda. "To be involved in the whole dying process, and the whole birth and life process of other folks — it makes you feel like what you're doing is really useful and good."[13]

Koerner found that patients and health care providers routinely mentioned many of the aspects of good service traditionally observed: responsiveness, empathy, and assurance, for example. "In contrast, when describing their most positive medical experiences, both provider and patient-informants' descriptions often emphasized sacred, rather than secular, qualities," she wrote. "They discussed 'special relationships' based on 'real, deep, basic human connections.' One told 'a magical kind of story;' others talked about 'really making a difference.' . . . One patient-informant repeatedly used the word 'weird' to describe her unusually positive relationship with her health care provider. Both providers and patients viewed their best health care experiences and relationships as extraordinary, significant and meaningful."[14]

It is not difficult to understand how health care workers could see their work as important. They are, after all, in the business of preserving lives, delivering babies, and directly improving the quality of life for their patients. Because of this, health care organizations typically have higher scores on the Eighth Element. So do schools, those working in the justice system, and environmental quality organizations. What's puzzling is how someone working at a clinic or hospital would feel their job is not important. And yet some do: One-third of hospital workers give a low score to this element. Less than half of workers in any industry feel strongly connected to their organization's quest.[15]

Equally surprising are the high percentages of workers in less than life-and-death careers who feel a strong connection to the goals of their organizations. In the Gallup database, one quarter or more of the workers in the retail trades, in finance, and in chemical manufacturing strongly agree the purpose of their company makes them feel their job is important. While it is somewhat easier to find a mission-inspired employee in stereotypically altruistic vocations such as teaching and healing, a sense of meaning in a job is less a function of the industry than of the work environment itself.

It can happen in any job, no matter how seemingly common. Recently a businesswoman reported that when she had a flat tire on the road, a Good Samaritan stopped to help her put on the spare. "I used to be a tow truck driver," he said while loosening the bolts on the flat. "I miss it. It was great to be in a job where you knew every day you would get the chance to help people."

Conversely, high-profile professionals sometimes find that perks and high pay are not enough. "I have been an experienced hire in consulting firms that have no culture," the leader of an international strategy firm complained. "They have no culture because they are composed of experienced hires who have built no connection, commonalities, or common processes. They are, in fact, cultures of cohabiting independent contributors. . . . You do not feel that you fit because there is nothing to fit into."[16]

A small group of sociologists specialize in the study of occupations they call "dirty work," the messy, distasteful, or stigmatized jobs on the other end of the spectrum from the astronaut, doctor, athlete, and scientist answers kids commonly give to the question, "What do you want to be when you grow up?" Dirty work typically includes jobs such as sanitation workers, prison guards, hotel maids, shoe shiners, and psychiatric ward attendants.[17] One might think that type of job would diminish a person's self-image and be largely lacking in meaning.

Arizona State University Professor Blake Ashforth thought that among those doing dirty work he would find a subculture of depressed and angry employees. Instead, he was surprised at the strength of their drive to make their jobs meaningful. These workers often throw off the social stigma and see the everyday value of what they do. "When somebody's stopped up," said one septic service owner, "they're pretty happy to see you."[18] One woman told a New Jersey newspaper she quit a personnel job she'd held for seven years so she could work at an animal shelter worker, despite the fact she must euthanize many dogs and cats. "The paycheck (at the old job) no longer was enough. I wanted more," she said. Because of the heartbreak, "there are days I go home and hug my dog for dear life. Every single day you come back fighting again."[19] A corrections officer told *The Wall Street Journal* he knows "it's not smart" to work in a prison, but likes the mission "to protect the public and protect your coworkers and protect the inmates from themselves."[20]

There is no such thing as an inherently meaningless job. There are conditions that make the seemingly most important roles trivial and conditions that make ostensibly awful work rewarding. "One implication of the motivated and socially embedded desire and search for meaning is that *any* task, job, or organization can be imbued with meaningfulness. The desire spawns the reality," wrote Ashforth and fellow researcher Michael G. Pratt.[21]

One view of this phenomenon separates people's views of their employment into three categories. The least engaged group sees their work as simply a job: a necessary inconvenience and a way of earning money with which they can accomplish personal goals and enjoy themselves outside of work. The second group sees their work as a career. They enjoy the increased pay, prestige, and status that come as they work their way up the corporate ladder. The third group considers its work "callings." "In callings, the work is an end in itself, and is usually associated with the belief that the work contributes to the greater good and makes the world a better place," wrote researcher Amy Wrzesniewski.[22] As with Koerner's research on "sacredness," the term "calling" doesn't necessarily have a religious definition. Each person filters the world through his own lens. "It is the individual doing the work who defines for him- or herself whether the work does contribute to making the world a better place," she stressed.[23]

No matter how the employee makes sense of the world and her role in it, if she sees a connection substantial enough to consider her work a calling, she gets more out of work and the organization gets more out of her. "Only for those with callings is work a wholly enriching and meaningful activity," wrote Wrzesniewski.[24] Because of this connection, they more strongly identify with the team, have less conflict, trust management more, are more committed to the team, work through things better, and put in more time at work, whether compensated or not.[25] Here, too, the job itself doesn't determine its meaning. "A school-teacher who views the work as a job and is simply interested in making a good income does not have a calling, while a garbage collector who sees the work as making the world a cleaner, healthier place could have a calling," wrote the professor.

The data do not indicate that every employee wants his or her job to be filled with cosmic interactions. For many, it will be enough knowing their work helped the company make a better batch of cattle feed, deliver millions of packages on time, or sell a new line of clothing. However, having large proportions of employees who are there just to draw a paycheck and who don't care about the larger purpose of the business can be a tremendous drag on retention, customer attitudes, safety, productivity, and — ultimately — profitability.

In general, and contrary to many senior executives' overestimation of their influence, companies do not have a homogenous culture. Company leaders don't have as much influence on workers as do front-line managers. The Eighth Element is the most dramatic exception to this trend. How executives feel about the company's mission is strongly correlated with the assessments of mid-level managers. How those managers feel about the Eighth Element is strongly correlated with the assessments of front-line employees. Unlike most of the other Elements of Great Managing, this one cascades from the top down, losing strength along the way, but is still closely tied to how much commitment to the corporate mission exists at the top.[26]

The second half of the Eighth Element statement — "The mission or purpose of my company *makes me feel my job is important*" — requires more than just persuading employees that their employer is in a worthy line of business. The most highly motivated and productive employees push hard because they feel their work makes a difference to attaining those worthy goals. Despite the high correlation between senior leadership and front-line commitment to the mission, more than any other element, this one loses the most power along the way. While two-thirds of executives in a typical company strongly agree with the mission question, less than one-third of street-level associates do. The employees are plugged in, but they frequently find little juice reaches the outlet by their cubicle. Given that a customer is far more likely to see a front-line worker than a member of the senior team, this loss of power makes it difficult for an enterprise to convey its passion to customers.

So at the same time that Mike Boldrick was trying to schedule electricians to wire the new Cabela's store, he needed to ensure the desire to be "the world's foremost outfitter" was fully transmitted to every member of the Wheeling team.

On July 8, it was time for the Cabela's team to begin turning the new building into a store. But the building wasn't finished. "All that was done was Fishing, and then Camping and Gifts," said Boldrick. "The rest of the store was still uncarpeted. We had giant lifts in here. They were putting tile in. They didn't have the register pods in up front. There were still about 500 or 600 pallets of construction material in the building."

That was Monday. The merchandise was going to start arriving on Wednesday. "The builders weren't done, so we had to work around them," said Clothing Manager Susan Sacks. As the merchandise was loaded on trucks bound for Wheeling, the fixtures to hold those products lay unassembled. The first test of the new team was whether they could assemble them in 48 hours. "The vendor that provides the fixtures came in and said, 'Can you give me eight people?' We brought everybody in," recounted Boldrick. "Instead of taking two days, we got everything built, not just the fixtures for the sections that were being turned over to us. We generated a ton of excitement because it was our first time in the building, and our employees looked like a NASCAR pit crew."

Only those who have been in a Cabela's store can fully appreciate what happened next. As trucks arrived with fishing lures, fly rods, and bait buckets, so did the first of a veritable Noah's ark of taxidermy animals — deer, mountain goats, bears, lions, zebra, water buffalo, and dozens of other species. "We would have thousands of fishing rods coming in one door and full mounts of lions and rhinos in the other door, so it was quite a sight," said Troy Gatti. "Everything in the building came through the back doors in receiving. Even the elephant came in three parts through the back end." Space was at a premium. Thirty truck trailers were parked on the site as the team struggled to move into the not-quite-finished building.

Early in the process, Boldrick established a schedule of all-employee meetings every day at 7 a.m., noon, and 5 p.m. Part news broadcast, part pep rally, and a chance to introduce associates to one another, the meetings brought order to the chaos. "There was a lot of confusion," said Vern Kidwell, a product specialist in the hunting department. "The meetings kept us whole and kept us going." As work to set up the store spread from one department to another, the meetings also grew. In the early meetings, Boldrick simply shouted to the group. Then he progressed to using a bullhorn. Finally, managers moved up the stairs so they could address several hundred people at once. "Sometimes there'd be 500 or 600 people in the building, and it was working! The meetings were absolutely fantastic," said Gatti. After the electrical work was finished, Boldrick used the store's intercom system.

Boldrick and his managers used "show and tell" to familiarize the staff with each other and the merchandise. Employees were encouraged to stand on a ladder during the meetings, introduce themselves, display a product, and talk about what other items would be sold with it. In one of those meetings, Boldrick sparked a little competition among the departments by asking which department would be ready for the grand opening first. "Who's going to be first?" he yelled from the mezzanine.

"We will!" proclaimed Travis Glover, the assistant sales manager in the firearms department.

"Did you hear that?" said Boldrick. "Travis said he will wear a dress and do shopping carts the first day if you beat him." Although Travis's department lost, he wasn't held to the statement, "because he didn't say that; I said it," said Boldrick.

Although the store was progressing quickly, not everything was going according to plan. "We must have had 90 percent of the electricians in Ohio County working on the building," said Boldrick, but the wiring and lights were not finished. Large lifts for installing track lighting had to be moved through the departments, so the merchandise had to be moved. "We were handling some of the merchandise two or three times," he said, doubling and tripling what was planned. Meanwhile, the merchandise kept arriving. Before the fishing department was fully in place, hunting products were being unloaded. Employees were doing all they could to keep up. "When you had your two days off and came back, you wouldn't believe how much the store had changed. Mountains were moved," said Kidwell.

As other departments fell into place, the clothing areas still had a long way to go. "We didn't have carpet," said Sacks. "Our kiosks weren't set up. We were the last ones to get our product — thank God — but we were also the last ones to get done. We had no electricity in our department. It was frustrating for us because we wanted to get our employees used to the computer system, and we couldn't get anything up and running."

Shane Etzwiler was senior merchandising manager over apparel. He recalls they were about halfway through the four-and-a-half weeks of store preparation when the clothing began arriving. Had there been more time, the camouflage clothing, pants, ski jackets, and other articles would have arrived at a measured pace, with time to take inventory of what had arrived and what additional items were needed. "Instead, they just bombarded us with it all at once," said Etzwiler. "How do you get through two hundred black collapsible containers of [unsorted] merchandise, and then the next day get through another hundred, and the next day another hundred, and the next day another hundred?" It was too much. "Eventually we had 250 black collapsibles of clothing merchandise in the back room. It was like 'Holy smokes!'"

Etzwiler needed to travel to Owatonna, Minnesota, to close the sale of his home there. He left instructions about how to plow through it all but returned to find little progress and now even less time. "I'm thinking, we are in deep doo-doo here," said Etzwiler. "So basically, I just pulled the team together and said, 'This is the game plan; this is what we're doing going forward.'" Only by concerted teamwork and a two-stage process of sorting the merchandise did they get back on schedule.

As they moved into the home stretch, the pace was wearing down the managers. Boldrick was getting six hours or less of sleep each night. Many of the managers were working 100 hours a week. Etzwiler and Boldrick decided to ease off a bit. "I told Mike, 'We're killing the managers. Let's change it; let's do some things," said Etzwiler. "In the five o'clock meeting, you'd see some of them starting to drift off," Boldrick recalled. "I went to my senior managers and said, 'Schedule everybody a half day off, and I want to try to give everybody a full day off before we open.'"

Boldrick himself decided to head home at 1 p.m. on a Saturday for some badly needed sleep. An hour later, he was dozing off when he got a call from the store's marketing manager. "I'm sorry to wake you up, but I just got a call from the head of the advance team for the White House. He's stopping by, and he said maybe the President wants to visit sometime later."

"I better come in," said Boldrick.

"We can handle it."

"No, I'll come in."

Boldrick got onto the interstate to find it filled with traffic. Police were closing the exits, forcing cars to drive past the Cabela's exit. On arriving at the store, Boldrick was greeted by four Secret Service agents and the "advance" man. "Mr. Boldrick, the President of the United States wants to come visit your store," said the White House official. "Would that be all right with you?"

"Well, absolutely," said Boldrick. "When?"

"In about 20 minutes."

Because of all the work to prepare the store for its opening, there were about 100 pallets of construction material near the front door, right where the President would enter. "You never saw people move a hundred pallets faster in your life," said Boldrick. Passing through between campaign stops, President Bush arrived even sooner than expected. "Sure enough, his buses pull up, and he came walking out and met me at the door," Boldrick said. "We shook hands, and he went through the crowd, shook hands, and signed autographs. He was here about twenty minutes."

"We're at war, and they're asking him questions about things," said Rock. "Just to witness and take in the whole entire thing — it was an awesome spectacle to behold," said Rock.

Presidential visit or not, the store still had to meet its opening date. "The press releases were out. Everything was out. That was the date we had to live by," said Boldrick. But events beyond their control were conspiring to make it tough. Record rains meant they didn't have a parking lot or cement walks in front of the store until very near the end. The electricians were behind. Inventory scanners weren't working. The town drained the water out of the water tower, so the building did not have the water it needed if there should be a fire. The 680 pieces of taxidermy had to be secured in place. Through sheer hard work and teamwork the Wheeling employees pulled if off. One of the key drivers turned out to be the engagement of the employees. "It wouldn't have mattered if the building had fallen down on us. We would have propped up a corner and started selling because of how well they treated us," said Kidwell.

Cabela's mission statement reads: "As the world's foremost outfitter, we passionately serve people who enjoy the outdoor lifestyle by delivering innovation, quality, and value in our products and services." When the employees of the Wheeling store were surveyed by Gallup on the 12 Elements, their connection to that mission stood out. More than 60 percent strongly agreed that the "mission or purpose of Cabela's makes me feel my job is important." Fewer than 10 percent of workgroups in Gallup's database give such strong scores on the Eighth Element. Those who work at the Wheeling store say that their mission and drive come from hiring people who love the outdoors, then managing them to bring out their best.

The Wheeling team members say that they pushed so hard to make the opening date because they were eager to work in a store that matches their own enthusiasm for outdoor recreation. "It's not just a job to them," said Rock. "It's something that they like to do outside of work, so work is like a playground to them." Photos of outdoor adventures adorn nearly every office and cubicle in the staff offices at the store. Ask almost anyone why they like working there, and they wax poetic about family memories of outdoor activities. "It's a bond," said Sacks. "My grandfather was always the most important person to me. That's what we did. We fished together. Every Sunday, we'd go up to the lake together. If you enjoy what your family enjoys doing, you're going to spend a lot more time together. That's what I get out of the outdoors."

You don't have to prod Tabatha Klug much to get her to talk to about her hunting experiences. "I shot my first doe when I was seven," she said proudly. One day, she showed off a beautiful mounted turkey to a coworker, the 681st piece of taxidermy in the store. She not only shot

it; she also did the preserving and mounting. Klug seems to take particular pleasure in surprising male customers who don't anticipate that
she has, for example, shot a moose in Alaska or landed the longest gar
in West Virginia. Men sometimes challenge her. "What do you know
about camo? You're a girl," they say. "What actually are you looking
for?" she replies. "I'm sure I can help you." After she gives them some
expert advice, their impression begins to change. "They ask me how I
know so much about the camo," said Klug. "Well, I hunt, I fish, and I'm
a licensed taxidermist." In a few cases, they ask her out. "They actually
want to take me home. They ask me if I'm married." She is, she hastens
to mention.

A shared passion about their outdoors lifestyle and their new employer kept the Wheeling team moving through hundreds of difficulties.
"When you've got engaged employees, they're trying to drive [the busi-
ness] for you, and there's a lot less coaching and time out on the floor
training," said Etzwiler. "They've got the buy-in that Cabela's is a great
place to work."

The Wheeling team met its deadlines. The store opened as planned.
"We had a certain sales number we wanted to hit that very first day of
our grand opening, and we just crushed it," said Etzwiler, who has since
been promoted to store manager. "It was like, 'Yeah, we're flying here
now!'"

Dead fish. Sleep deprivation. A lack of working scanners, computers, and water. An unassembled elephant. All these bring fond memories
to Boldrick, who, since the store's opening, was promoted to become
the company's second regional manager. "It was fun," he said. "I never
doubted we'd do it. It was the most fun I've had in a job. I'd do it all
over again."

THE NINTH ELEMENT:

Coworkers Committed
to Doing Quality Work

R UNNING A BEST BUY STORE IS NO EASY JOB. A typical 45,000-
square-foot location is filled with thousands of different products, from key-chain-sized computer microdrives to refrigerators,
washers, and dryers. It's open 77 hours a week and is staffed by 120
employees, many of them young adults in their first or second jobs. The
complexity of the products demands a high level of training, and the
many distractions that tempt college-age employees keep the turnover
potential high.

An average store sells tens of millions of dollars in consumer electronics, computers, CDs, DVDs, and other merchandise in a year. But
because it's a low-margin business, Best Buy keeps only a fraction of
each sale.

At the center of every Best Buy store is a general manager — a
young, friendly, air-traffic controller who is ultimately responsible for
every aspect of its performance. In the summer of 2003, the manager at
the center of Store 484 in Manchester, Connecticut, was Eric Taverna,
a 13-year retail veteran and Sam's Club expatriate in his third year

with Best Buy. Less than a year after he assumed responsibility for the Manchester store, one of Taverna's most important challenges was to harness the energy of the people in his store. Many associates thought their opinions didn't matter much to management and believed their colleagues weren't committed to doing quality work.

As with any retail enterprise, there's a fine line between profit and loss at a Best Buy store. Staying on the right side of that line requires a manager who can balance many competing aspects of the business at once. Is staffing sufficient to meet customer needs, yet lean enough to keep prices competitive? Is security high enough to stop theft without irritating honest customers? Is everything clean and bright? Is everything properly stocked and labeled? Beyond these basic and tangible aspects are more subtle, equally crucial issues of employee engagement. Are the employees deeply committed? Are associates, often young people with one eye on the job and the other on this week's mid-term exam or this weekend's concert, getting what they need from the company? Are they motivated to do a good job? These were not trivial questions. Extensive research conducted by Gallup analysts found that employee engagement was a crucial component of the performance of a Best Buy store, affecting everything from customer attitudes to the percent of merchandise lost to theft to profitability itself. For this reason, Taverna and his hundreds of counterparts across the country are judged in part by how well they maintain morale.

The 12 Elements results for July 2003 showed that the Manchester store was at a good, but not great, engagement level. When compared to Gallup's database of workgroup engagement scores, Store 484 barely made the top third. Employees gave particularly low ratings to the Seventh Element ("At work, my opinions seem to count") and the Ninth, which is measured by the statement, "My associates or fellow employees are committed to doing quality work." Worse yet, although the overall engagement level had increased since the previous administration, scores on these two elements went down.

"It was honest, and it hurt," Taverna said. "Getting feedback like that is gut-wrenching. That "opinions count" thing really worried me. That just tells me we're not good listeners." Moreover, he added, "Many of the managers at my store have just been promoted to management for the first time, while others have been in the business for 20 years but have never focused on people or culture." Getting his entire management team effectively focused on the people issues "was a huge challenge."

To Taverna, the ability to motivate a team is a key part of managing. "Developing people skills, for myself and my managers, is the most important thing, because they in turn steer the whole ship," he said. "The store is virtually run by 21-year-old kids," said Bob Gaudette, merchandising manager, "and the amount of knowledge that they have for being such young people is staggering."

Taverna and his team of five assistant managers brought these issues up during their next quarterly all-employee meeting. The general manager took the employees through a simple straw-poll exercise that asked them to put a sticky note next to one of the 12 Elements they believed the whole store should emphasize. Not surprisingly, the notes accumulated around the item: "My associates or fellow employees are committed to doing quality work." On the notes themselves, many associates suggested a solution. "We want 'team close,'" said some of the notes, meaning that employees wanted to close the store together. "We want everyone to be treated the same, and we want to walk out together as a team."

One of the complexities of running any retail business is closing the business for the day. When the last customer leaves, there's a flurry of activity to close down the registers, secure the day's receipts, and prepare for the next day. "You close to open," Taverna said. At closing, everything needs to be cleaned. Shelves must be restocked. Hundreds of display items must be checked and turned off. And everything has to be ready to greet tomorrow's first customer, often less than 12 hours after today's last customer leaves. During the holidays, there's even more to be done and less time to do it because of the store's extended hours.

The situation in Manchester was complicated by differences in how one assistant manager or another would close the store. If an associate worked in a smaller department, he might be able to finish his area and be on his way faster than his colleagues in the larger departments — or maybe not, depending on the manager. Although the Manchester store closed at 9:30 p.m., it was not unusual for some associates to be in the store until almost midnight, while other employees were long gone.

By practice, if not by design, Store 484 stumbled into one of the most discouraging situations for any team: allowing some people to shoulder less of the burden while requiring the others to carry the bulk of the load.

Phoning it in. Free-riders. Cheaters. Hitchhikers. Deadwood. Slugs. Drones. Asleep at the switch. Cowards. Barnacles. Slackers. Con artists. Deserters.

They go by dozens of scornful labels. During a career, everyone encounters at least a few of the people who strive to do the least they can do without getting reprimanded. Few factors are more corrosive to teamwork than the employee who skates through life taking advantage of the much harder work of others.

The frustration is evident in the comments of employees who give a low score to the associates-committed-to-quality-work statement. "I don't like the quality of people who are hired and just don't care, don't make an effort, and just show up for a check," one employee complained in a note attached to her 12 Elements responses. "We need to do a better job of filtering out those individuals who bring down what others work hard to achieve."

"I do not like coming into work and having to baby-sit coworkers who have little or no regard for their job," said another. "I dislike having to constantly tell people how to do their job. It becomes my job to fix what they neglected to do correctly in the first place." Other comments from the low end complain about "people not showing up on time for their shifts," "not doing their jobs and making me do the lion's share of the work," and "no one wanting to take responsibility for anything."

The problem is not new. One hundred years ago, French agricultural engineer Max Ringelmann conducted one of the first studies of how teamwork affects performance. He asked men recruited for the experiment to pull a rope as hard as they could. He did this with various numbers of men on the rope at one time. Not surprising, two men pulled harder than one, three men pulled harder than two, and so on. However, when the force exerted on the rope was divided by the number of those pulling, Ringelmann discovered the force-per-man decreased as the number of men increased. The larger the group, the less the average man pulled.

Assume that the force one man can pull is equal to 100 percent. If two men are pulling, the average guy exerts himself at 93 percent. When four men are pulling, they average only three-quarters of their real capacity. By the time the eighth man is added, each man is pulling on average only half what he could. In fact, eight men on the rope pull no harder than seven, because the other seven relax enough to subtract whatever the eighth man adds.[1] "One of the truly remarkable things about workgroups is that they can make 2 + 2 = 5," states one organizational behavior textbook. "Of course, they also have the capability of making 2 + 2 = 3."[2]

Given how desertions can snowball into devastating defeats, military commanders have always forcefully guarded against them. As George Washington prepared his troops to surreptitiously place cannons, fortifications, and themselves on Dorchester Heights to drive the British from Boston in 1776, he issued orders that "if any man in action shall presume to skulk, hide himself, or retreat from the enemy, without orders from his commander, he will be instantly shot down, as an example of cowardice."[3] Because 5,000 men of the Continental Army instead worked hard and harmoniously through the night, first light on March 5 found the British completely surprised, one American general remarking "perhaps there was never so much work done in so short a space of time," and a British officer surmising the feat must have required 15,000 to 20,000 men.[4]

In 1986, when the United States federal government changed the way taxes were calculated, the rate of compliance was discovered to have no correlation with whether a citizen's taxes were going to go up. But they were influenced by whether their neighbors, relatives, and friends said they supported and planned to comply with the changes to the tax code.[5] In a similar vein, the state of Minnesota discovered higher reported income and fewer deductions among residents who were sent a letter telling them that tax compliance was actually higher than public opinion polls were showing.[6] The lesson from these disparate sources is what makes it so important that a team can positively and strongly respond to the Ninth Element. If a team lacks a strong work ethic and a sense of responsibility to each other, the group becomes a convenient place to hide a little slothfulness, to push a little work to the other guy, or to point fingers when a project doesn't hit its deadlines.

In an average team, about one in three employees strongly agrees that her associates are committed to doing quality work. But the Ninth Element is highly sensitive to the presence or absence of one or more slackers. When a team perceives one of its members is dragging his feet, the proportion that rates the Ninth Element high drops to only one in five. If a team is free of deadwood, the proportion that strongly agrees with the statement jumps to half of the team, with most of the rest giving positive, although slightly less emphatic, responses.[7]

Responses to this element are remarkably similar across industries and type of job. But like the other 11 elements, it varies dramatically from one team to another. There are plenty of workgroups in which no one feels their fellow employees are committed to quality and those in which everyone on the team perceives a kind of universal allegiance. The consequences apply to more than just pulling rope. At an Australian bank, variation in the Ninth Element accounts for a 14-percent difference in profitability across its many branch offices.[8] For a food manufacturer in Europe, assessments as to whether everyone is doing his part account for a 51-percent range in on-the-job accidents.[9] The many companies' performance data matched to Ninth Element scores show that people who feel part of a solidly committed team are routinely safer, better with customers, less likely to quit, and more productive.

Law professor Dan M. Kahan illustrates the challenge facing managers with a large bell curve representing the typical team. On the far right are the most helpful of the group, those "dedicated cooperators" who by personal conviction will contribute their best to the common cause without worrying much about what the rest are doing. On the far left are a few "dedicated free-riders," people who in almost any situation will let the others do the heavy lifting and keep their own resources for themselves. In between the extremes are those who reciprocate to various degrees. This majority of people will meet cooperation with cooperation and selfishness with selfishness. Therefore, in the beginning, every team is poised to go into one of two vicious circles, one spirals downward into "every man for himself," the other spirals upward into "all for one and one for all."

In the lab, scientists have created the conditions and observed the consequences of rapid breakdown so often that the phenomenon is now axiomatic: Bring together a group of people and give them a chance to earn more by making contributions to the general welfare. If you do not incorporate any way of stopping the hitchhikers, more and more people will give up until almost no one contributes to the common good.

Swiss researchers Ernst Fehr and Simon Gächter organized people in groups of four, then gave each some money and the option to keep it or contribute all or some to a pool of funds that would be increased by 40 percent and divided equally among the participants, regardless of whether they contributed some, all, or none of their initial stake. At the beginning of the game, most players invested some of their money; the average was a little over 9 out of 20 points. But as the game continued, players who were contributing realized others were free-loading. "Subjects strongly dislike being the 'sucker,' that is, being those who cooperate while other group members free ride," wrote the researchers.[10] The more helpful players gave up. Slowly and steadily, they reduced what they would put in the common pool until, 10 rounds later, the average contribution was only 3 points. The average participant, convinced he was being taken advantage of, kept nearly all his money to himself.

The researchers then added one condition. In the next set of rounds, players could spend some of their money on "punishment" points that would reduce the funds of the slackers. Even though spending money to punish another player reduced the punishers' own funds, they were quite willing to pay the price. At least now they could do something to counteract the free-riders.

The desire for revenge is a potent psychological force, arguably more powerful than many incentives companies put out there to get employees to just get along or to overlook an associate's lack of work ethic. "Just pay attention to your own job," simply doesn't cut it in the mind of an employee who sees a bum in the office next door. With the help of positron emission tomography to watch the workings of the brain, scientists in recent years have begun tracking the neurological mechanisms of revenge. One study found that the dorsal striatum, a portion of the brain that processes anticipated rewards, lights up when a test subject thinks of getting even. Although punishing someone else may be costly, many times it is psychologically worth it. Striking back "provides relief and satisfaction to the punisher and activates, therefore, reward-related brain regions," wrote seven researchers in the respected journal *Science*.[11]

Adding the chance to even the score changed the whole game for Fehr and Gächter's subjects. Although the average contribution during the second set of interactions started near the same point where the first began, it grew from there until it sometimes reached 20. With accountability, "full cooperation emerges as the dominant behavioral standard for individual contributions." Average contributions reached 18.2, with 82.5 percent of players investing everything in the common pool.

It does not surprise scientists that people are often selfish and don't work together well during an experiment in which there are strong incentives to keep the money. In fact, traditional math-based predictions of behavior anticipate much more selfishness than shows up in real life. But there are four intriguing aspects to these kinds of experiments that have theorists rethinking their ideas of human interaction. These little surprises are crucial for a manager to understand if she wants to increase teamwork in her own business unit.

First, even though there are incentives to free-load from the very beginning, a large proportion of people start by venturing some of their money, maybe to test the waters, maybe out of a sense of morality. They arrive at a job fully prepared to cooperate with the group — if they find cooperation to be the norm.

Second, without any way of holding team members accountable for their work on the group's behalf, some will coast. Taking advantage of the group in this way creates resentment that causes many of those originally willing members to withhold what they control, and this snowballs into an almost perfectly selfish workgroup that loses the chance of making solid profits. For these experiments in teamwork without accountability, "it is well known that cooperation strongly deteriorates over time and reaches rather low levels in the final period," wrote Fehr and Gächter.[12] "In view of these facts there can be little doubt that in the no-punishment condition subjects are not able to achieve stable cooperation."

Third, even when it is personally expensive to punish another team member, many participants will "invest" in keeping the game fair. Researchers call this "altruistic punishment" because it requires a player to spend his own money to enforce the group's interest. "A subject is more heavily punished the more his or her contribution falls below the average contribution of other group members," wrote the researchers.[13] This suggests that even with performance-based bonuses that create a risk of neglecting their own rewards for a while, employees' attention can be seriously diverted when a bad apple is in the barrel.

Fourth, if team members can be punished for slacking, the slackers behave better and the naturally cooperative people, seeing a fairer system, become more willing to invest. The group's profits rise.

For a manager, the contrast cannot be clearer. Would he rather go easy on the foot-draggers and allow his team to become disheartened, possibly sidetracked by the powerful emotions of "altruistic punishment," or maintain work standards so the group enjoys the benefits of ever-higher levels of individual investment in the team's accomplishments? Faced with one or more drones, a team has two avenues for relief. They may use various forms of social coercion to correct the behavior, or they must rely on the manager to punish lazy associates.

The first option, self-policing, is not uncommon, but it has limits in the normal course of office, retail, or factory work. Off the coast of Maine, lobstermen illegally cut the buoys from traps set in a fellow lobsterman's unofficial waters. One Oakland (Michigan) University professor issued advice on how to keep "hitchhikers" from hiding inside an otherwise diligent study group. "Set your limits early and high, because hitchhikers have an uncanny ability to detect just how much they can get away with," she cautioned.[14] Personal ostracism, refusing to work with someone else (where that's an option), a serious talk over coffee, and ceasing to send electronic copies of a carefully crafted PowerPoint all help set limits on those who always seem to make it home in time for dinner. Sports teams often have a player who helps lead and even reprimand. However, self-policing is limited by the authority of those who want to employ it.

Ultimately it may require the coach to pull someone off the field. The second, more powerful, and most obvious answer inside a business is for the manager to police the problem. The best managers know in their gut what social researchers have locked in through hundreds of experiments in cooperation. "The prevalence of this sort of strong reciprocity is supported by a vast body of evidence," wrote Kahan. "So-called "public goods" experiments — laboratory constructs designed to simulate collective action problems — have consistently shown that the willingness of individuals to make costly contributions to collective goods is highly conditional on their perception that others are willing to do so."[15] One of the worst one-two punches to a team's *esprit de corps* and productivity is having a slacker in their midst and a manager who lacks the spine to do anything about it.

A less flammable, but still frustrating, situation is created when team members seem to be trying, but just don't have what it takes to perform "quality work." Gallup asked a random sample of United States workers which made them more frustrated: a colleague who tries hard but doesn't have much ability (a bungler), or a colleague who has the ability and doesn't try (a slacker). By a margin of six to one, workers are more upset with a slacker than a bungler.[16] Still, the level of frustration with an incompetent is high, and can drop the level of those strongly agreeing with the Ninth Element question to one in four. Although the heart of many miscast employees may be in the right place, and they therefore may be candidates for different jobs in the same company, they cannot be left in a position where they can't maintain the same levels as the rest of the group.

A good manager must continually ask herself whether her team tips that maybe-I-will/maybe-I-won't newcomer toward jumping in with both feet. This assessment was among the first questions asked by Nancy Sorrells, the Marriott hotel manager profiled in the first chapter of this book. "Who is the worst employee at this hotel, and how long have they been here?" she asked. Why did she want to know? "Whoever is the lowest sets your standard, no matter what you say to the contrary."

Faced with weakness in the Ninth Element in Best Buy Store 484, Eric Taverna and his five assistants developed a threefold plan for responding to their employees' concerns. First, all the managers had to be on the same page. "When I'm not in the store, and an associate comes to management with a problem, we all need to speak from the same shared values," Taverna said. "In reality, managers have days when they have to say 'no' to associates. If associates think they can go to another manager and get a 'yes,' that's a problem. We had normal struggles with that, and it's still a work in progress."

Second, associates who were not pulling their weight were asked to leave Best Buy.

Third, and most directly in response to what the employees of Store 484 requested, Taverna and his lieutenants designed a "team close" procedure. "We had to make sure, one, that all the managers understood it, were bought into it, and agreed it was the right thing to do," he said. "Two, we didn't just flip a switch and do it. We had to make sure we scheduled it properly. The last thing I wanted was to schedule someone until 10:30, then tell him, 'You have to stay until 11:30.' Then we went out to the store and started explaining, 'This is what we've come up with, and this is why.'"

Reaction to the three-part plan was generally positive, but Taverna and his managers encountered some resistance, particularly among those who were satisfied with the time they were leaving the store. "Out of 120 people, maybe 10 percent might say, 'I don't like that.' Maybe another 20 percent might say, 'We'll see.' Maybe 70 percent would buy into it. That's normal, and we understood that," Taverna said. "The turning point was that all the managers and all the supervisors supported it."

The new plan was put into action as the 2003 holiday season approached. There was some friction. "Occasionally you'd hear some rumblings, or one of the supervisors would come up to us and say, 'So-and-so's walking around the store saying this 'team close' really stinks,'" said Gaudette. But, adds Taverna, "The message needed to be, 'We're one store, one team, and we've got to help each other out.'"

Other employees appreciated that their idea had created an important change in the store, and few could argue with the logic. "The majority jumped on because it was an idea they'd had themselves," said Mike McCormick, inventory supervisor. "It was something they wanted to see happen."

The "team close" concept needed to be refined after its introduction. "In the beginning, everyone was made to stay," McCormick said.

"We realized that you needed to schedule for 'team close,' but the people who were scheduled to go home two hours before close needed to go home. We can't have the whole store staying because then you're running into too many labor hours."

The real measure of whether "team close" — and whether the risk Taverna and his managers took in listening to their employees — was a success came with the next 12 Elements assessment in January 2004. "It was nerve-wracking because we tried to do something we hadn't done before in the store," Taverna said. "We were concerned that we were going to get some backlash."

The results confirmed the value of listening to employees and making changes in response to their suggestions. Store 484's employee engagement score jumped from good to great, reaching the top 10 percent of the workgroups in the Gallup database. And there were solid increases for both the Seventh and Ninth Elements. Not coincidentally, the Manchester store was performing well against budget and, in a high-churn business, substantially lowered its turnover.

"When I heard our new scores, shivers went through my body," Taverna said. "Maybe when people took the survey, they were able to look back and say, 'You know what? It was the right thing to do.'"

THE TENTH ELEMENT:
A Best Friend at Work

D R. SURESH NAGESH WONDERED HOW he found himself in such a mess.

He arrived in January of 2004 to lead DaimlerChrysler's Vehicle Engineering and Quality Unit in Bangalore, India. Instead of a team, he found six individual engineers working essentially alone.

They didn't have good rapport with Nagesh's predecessor. The stress of a tough customer seemed to be taking its toll. Their desks were separated across several floors of the building, so while they might have called or e-mailed each other with a question, they seemed to interact as little as possible. At lunch time, each went his separate way. Nagesh didn't even see them saying "hello" to each other or having normal professional discussions in the hallway. Employee engagement scores for the group put them lower than 60 percent of the teams in the global database.

"They were quiet," said the manager. "I very soon realized that there was no homogeneity in the team. The chemistry itself was not there. This guy complains about that guy; that guy complains about this guy; and nothing was happening — no motivation whatsoever."

The members of the team certainly weren't happy with the situation. "My previous company had a different culture. We were all fishermen and good friends," said Keshavanand Prabhu. "But when I came here, I didn't find that. The idea of confiding in someone was pretty far away. I wasn't really comfortable that way."

Largely because of this disunity, and despite the long hours put in by the engineers, the work was not getting done on time. Poor performance put the entire center under scrutiny from DaimlerChrysler executives. Nagesh's team, such as it was, was a leading example of what was wrong in Bangalore. For the 43-year-old manager, who holds a doctorate in computational mechanics and has had an accomplished career at General Electric and DaimlerChrysler, it was an unprecedented challenge. "Every group has some issues, but this was absolutely strange to me," he says. "I never thought I'd end up in this sort of situation."

The supervisor summoned everything he knew about human nature and managing in an attempt to make his collection of engineers into a real team. Some of the remedies were quite basic. The team needed better organization of its processes. More engineers needed to be hired. The employees needed more direct and involved managing. Everyone needed a greater feeling of connection with the mission of the company.

Nagesh started by changing the regular department meetings. Where in the past some employees simply came, sat through the meeting without talking, and left, Nagesh required that everyone talk about what they were working on and what they had ahead of them. "The first thing that changed was the communication," says Prabhu. "He was very transparent. He told us everything. He gave us some motivation that this is our team, and we have to work toward attaining the goal. The customer deadlines and targets which had seemed very difficult were looking far more achievable to us."

There was quite a bit of dissension over the recognition system, with some of the group feeling it was unfair or subject to favoritism. Responding to their concerns, Nagesh began a new system based on objective criteria circulated to the entire team.

But the gaping need was to strengthen the ties among the workgroup. Nagesh's team needed to become better friends.

★

The most controversial of the 12 Elements is the Tenth: "I have a best friend at work." When a company's executives receive their first briefing on employee engagement results from Gallup, the presenter typically asks if any of them has a question about the statements asked of their workers. Invariably, one of the business leaders says, "Why do you ask that 'best friend' question?" Sometimes their tone of voice communicates real curiosity. Sometimes it carries a tone of derision. Physicians bristle at it; it offends their clinical perspective. Attorneys scoff; "irrelevant," they object. Accountants consider it too far removed from the financial statements.

A good share of the press coverage of *First, Break All the Rules* betrayed surprise that Gallup asked such an apparently strange question and said it was predictive of performance. "A best friend at work?" wrote a *Washington Post* columnist. "What is this? High school?"[1] *Time* magazine called it a "more subtle variable" than many of the other 12.[2] The *Chicago Tribune* warned managers to be careful: "Friendships at work can lead to jealousy, envy and sloth."[3]

Clearly, the conversational form of the statement seems to invite skepticism. How does one define "a best friend?" Wouldn't it be easier to rate a statement about trust, or about the harmony of intra-office relationships? The problem is that complicated, and formal questions often fail to get at the heart of the issue. "Standard survey questions about trust do not appear to measure trust," but rather trustworthiness, concluded a National Bureau of Economic Research paper. "This means that most work using these survey questions needs to be somewhat reinterpreted."[4]

On executive row, reactions were more caustic and skeptical than those in the press. One company cancelled a 12 Elements survey because it had just sent out a memo discouraging friendships.[5] Others asked if the survey could be administered with just 11 of the 12 statements, omitting the "best friend" item. That such a simple and, indeed, business-related question would prove to be so provocative shows how deeply a "Theory X," leave-your-personal-life-at-the-door philosophy still pervades the business world.

One company requested a Gallup expert face its legal team's interrogations about the Tenth Element. The group's scores showed they had modest levels of friendship, with one attorney scoring friendships at work as low as possible (anonymously, of course). "Disregard for a moment whether you feel someone ought to be able to answer 'strongly agree' to this element," said the researcher. "If you strongly disagree with this statement, you are lonely at work. Someone here is trying to tell you he or she is isolated and miserable." After the legal team's grilling, the expert was contacted by one of the lawyers. "I am the one person you were talking about," he said. "You were right. I feel no connection here. I have no one to confide in. I'm working on getting a job somewhere else."

Gallup itself would have dropped the statement if not for one stubborn fact: It predicts performance. Something about a deep sense of affiliation with the people in an employee's team drives him to do positive things for the business he otherwise would not do. Early research that identified the 12 Elements revealed a very different social bond among employees in top performing teams. Subsequent large-scale, multi-company analyses confirmed the Tenth Element is a scientifically salient ingredient in obtaining a number of business-relevant outcomes, including profitability, safety, inventory control, and — most notably — the emotional connection and loyalty of customers to the organization serving them.

When tested against a number of alterative ways of asking the question, "I have a best friend at work" proved best able to discriminate between groups in which friendships are sufficiently supportive and those that have only surface relationships unable to withstand adversity. Measuring friendships is susceptible to what scientists call "social desirability," the tendency of a respondent to give an answer that casts him in the best light. The same bias makes people sometimes tell pollsters they read the newspaper when they didn't, say they voted when they didn't, or report they didn't watch a lot of TV when, in fact, they and a bag of potato chips were on the couch for two hours the night before. Simply asking people if they have friends is not enough, as most people prefer to think others like them, or are loath to confess their isolation. It took a quirky twist to the survey question to elicit the type of meaning that makes a measurable difference in organizations.

While the Tenth Element is the most controversial, it is not the toughest on which to achieve strongly positive answers. A little less than one-third strongly agree they have a best friend at work, a higher frequency than the Seventh Element (feeling one's opinions count) and about the same as the Fourth (recognition and praise). Maybe executives don't see the need because they tend to have more friendships at work than do front-line employees. It is especially ironic when senior teams gather for off-site retreats during which they golf, fly-fish, play tennis, and socialize together, but during the meetings at those retreats question the need to address friendships on their employee survey.

Prior to seeing the group's Tenth Element results, a personnel representative from a consumer product company said, "Our policy is to not have close relationships at work. Our executives frown on it." The results showed policy was being flouted with abandon, with close friendships being more prevalent in the business than in the average organization. In the battle between company policy and human nature, human nature always wins. The evidence suggests people will fulfill their social needs, regardless of what is legislated. Companies do far better to harness the power of this kind of social capital than to fight against it. Business units in the top quartile on this element achieve profitability a full percentage point or two higher than that of bottom-quartile, unfriendly environments.[6]

Numerous qualitative studies of employee engagement suggest customers not only sense the level of camaraderie where they shop, but also that it makes a large difference in their experience, if for no reason other than its natural contagiousness. In the service industries, the customer ratings of workgroups with strong Tenth Element levels are 5 to 10 percent higher than those of impersonal or acrimonious groups, explaining the difference between success and failure in many organizations.[7]

Other connections between the "best friend" statement and business outcomes are less intuitive, at least at first blush. At one electric utility, friendships among team members proved to be responsible for lower accident rates. When the workers were asked for the reason, they said the answer is simple: People look out for their friends. A friend reminds his buddy to put on his hard hat. In the few seconds before a fall might occur, a friend is more likely to spot the hazard and rush to steady the ladder. A friend guards his comrade's safety as much as he does his own, and shudders at the thought of having to ride to his coworker's house to inform his family, whom he probably knows well, that there has been an accident at work. It isn't as though team members want to see accidents occur to those who are not their friends. Rather, where there is not a close bond, it is less likely there will be the level of vigilance that can make the difference between a close call and a mishap. A team that has two-thirds of its members strongly agreeing they have a best friend at work averages 20 percent fewer accidents than a team with only one in three strong on the Tenth Element.[8]

One of the statistics over which retailers obsess is called "shrink." Assume a store takes delivery on 100 laptop computers. One month later, records show the store sold 25 of the computers and has 73 more in stock. The two missing laptops are defined as shrink. What happened to them? Sometimes one is shoplifted by a customer. Occasionally an employee steals one. Shrink dramatically reduces or destroys the profitability of a store. It requires the profit margin from many items legitimately sold to make up for one item purchased at wholesale and then simply gone. In several analyses of stores that keep good inventory records, the level of friendships among the salespeople was shown to affect shrink. The connection was puzzling at first. The people at the stores were less perplexed. "You don't steal from your friends," said one. There also appears to be a higher level of coordination among team members and vigilance against customer theft in the more cohesive groups.

The workplace holds a unique position for most employees in a society widely regarded as having lost much of the social contact of prior generations. Sociologists note a decades-long decline of people joining clubs, participating in the PTA, attending a town meeting, working for a political party, going to church, or informally socializing, such as going to a neighbor's house for dinner. Each successive generation has a lower level of trust in those around them than did their elders.[9] One of the most disturbing findings is that between 1985 and 2004, the number of people in an average person's network dropped from roughly three to two and "the number of people saying there is no one with whom they discuss important matters nearly tripled."[10]

What people today are doing more than did earlier generations, and what seems to go hand-in-hand with the decline in neighborliness, is watching television. "The American house has been TV-centered for three generations," wrote architecture scholar James Kunstler. "It is the focus of family life, and the life of the house correspondingly turns inward, away from whatever occurs beyond its four walls. . . . At the same time, the television is the family's chief connection with the outside world. The physical envelope of the house itself no longer connects their lives to the outside in any active way; rather, it seals them off from it. The outside world has become an abstraction filtered through television, just as the weather is an abstraction filtered through air conditioning."[11]

TV does bad things to a person's social ties. Those who say TV is their primary form of entertainment are less likely to attend church, to write letters to relatives and friends, to attend a club meeting, or to volunteer for a worthy cause. There are, however, a few things heavy TV-watchers are more likely to do. One of them is giving "the finger" to someone else on the road.[12]

One sociologist contends television actually tricks viewers into thinking they have more friends than they do. In evolutionary terms, wrote Satoshi Kanazawa, the tube is such a recent phenomenon that the brain's emotional centers don't really know how to distinguish between watching an episode of "Friends" and having a real group of friends in one's living room. Analyzing survey data on people's satisfaction with their friendships against their TV watching, and controlling for their level of real interactions, Kanazawa found evidence that "watching certain types of TV shows increases the respondents' satisfaction with friendships in exactly the same way" as real socializing. "Watching TV *is* our form of participating in civic groups," he concluded, "because we do not really know that we are not participating in them."[13]

From one perspective, none of this matters to business. No matter how pathetic it may be, if people want to substitute imaginary friends for going out to dinner with flesh-and-blood pals, who cares? As long as they show up for work on time the next morning, does it really matter? But because a half-century of changes to the culture outside of work make it less connected and friendly, the workplace, once just one of many venues for social interaction, is now becoming relatively exceptional. Where else does one interact with a group of people from various walks of life organized around a common mission? Where else does one spend so much time with real people and away from TV? Where else is one so dependent on the efforts of others?

"Professionals and blue-collar workers alike are putting in long hours together, eating lunch and dinner together, traveling together, arriving early, and staying late. What is more, people are divorcing more often, marrying later (if at all), and living alone in unprecedented numbers. Work is where the hearth is, then, for many solitary souls," wrote Robert D. Putnam in *Bowling Alone*, a 2000 book replete with data documenting the decline of social cohesiveness in the United States.[14] "As more Americans spend more of their time 'at work,'" wrote another commentator, "work gradually becomes less of a one-dimensional activity and assumes more of the concerns and activities of both private (family) and public (social and political) life."[15]

People generally still have their closest comrades outside of work. Few men and women have the luxury of working side-by-side with their former college roommates, their hunting buddies, their childhood friends or others to whom they might, say, consider donating a kidney. "In the most careful study," wrote Putnam, "when people were asked to list their closest friends, less than half of all full-time workers put even one coworker on the list. On average, neighbors were more likely to appear on the list than coworkers. When people were asked to whom they would turn to discuss 'important matters,' less than half of all full-time workers listed even a single coworker."[16]

The issue is not whether office friendships overwhelm bonds in private life, but to what degree a certain level of affiliation — "a best friend" rather than "my one best friend" or "most of my friends" — creates beneficial effects for the business. It's less surprising that other friendships take precedence over work relationships than almost half of workers listed a coworker as someone to whom they would turn for crucial advice. It's not a huge leap to assume from these studies that particularly where work issues are concerned, a close colleague is an invaluable resource. "Many studies have shown that social connections with coworkers are a strong predictor — some would say the strongest single predictor — of job satisfaction," wrote Putnam. "People with friends at work are happier at work."[17]

Another indication of how friends can make a work obligation more enjoyable comes from "day reconstruction" studies conducted by Daniel Kahneman, a psychologist who won the 2002 Nobel-Prize for economics. The research technique asks respondents to recall the various events of their day and evaluate the enjoyment of each activity. Commuting to work is consistently one of the least enjoyable common activities — unless one commutes with a friend. Then it becomes one of the most enjoyable.[18]

Friendship is not without hazards for productivity, nor is it effective without the other elements, such as coworkers being committed to doing quality work or clear expectations for each member of a team. Without clear direction, tight-knit teams can lose themselves in socializing and ignore customer or business needs. Friendships tend to be very strong among union workgroups preparing to strike, an us-versus-them mentality that serves neither group well. A group needs more than cohesion; it needs "norms" of high performance. Research dating back 50 years shows that cohesive groups that have standards of low performance do in fact perform at a low level.[19] But these are the exceptions, situations in which a team rates high on the Tenth Element, but low on most of the others. Most of the evidence suggests that the more interconnected a group, the better they will perform routinely and under pressure.

Research on workers in various settings has shown that friends are more likely to invite and share candid information, suggestions, and opinions, and to accept them without feeling threatened.[20] Friends tolerate disagreements better than do those who are not friends.[21] The good feelings friends share make them more likely to cheer each other on.[22] Friends are more committed to the goals of the group and work harder, regardless of the type of task.[23] Group members who identify most closely with the team are more likely to monitor its performance against the goal.[24]

One of the most intriguing studies of how friendships help a team excel was conducted in 1995 by professors Karen A. Jehn of the University of Pennsylvania and Priti Pradhan Shah of the University of

Minnesota. They wanted to know not just whether friendships boosted performance, but also why. To investigate the process, they separated 159 students into 53 groups, each with three team members. Twenty-six of the groups were friends. In these triads, each participant had volunteered the names of the other two as his or her friends. The other 27 groups were composed of mere acquaintances.

The groups were given two tasks. One was cognitive, requiring the students to review the applications of six people who applied to the university's M.B.A. program. Their goal was to estimate whether the person was admitted or rejected by the school's admissions committee. The second task involved working as a team to build from Styrofoam balls, glue, Popsicle sticks, aluminum foil, macaroni, string, and Tinker Toys as many models as possible that matched a diagram supplied by the professors. To capture as much information as they could about how the teams worked together, the researchers analyzed audio recordings of the student's conversations during the experiment, video recordings of their actions, and their actual output. They also conducted a survey of the students' attitudes after the work was completed.

The groups composed of friends "produced significantly more models" and "also matched more admissions committee decisions." The friends were more encouraging of each other. In the post-experiment survey the friends expressed more commitment to their groups.[25] "Friendship groups appear to engage in behavior and interaction patterns beneficial to the task they are performing. This suggests a feedback mechanism that may be more common in friendship groups than in acquaintance groups," wrote the researchers. The friends "helped each other complete their task components more in the motor task (model-building) and engaged in more critical evaluation in the cognitive task (reviewing the applications) than did acquaintance groups, who attended to work independently on both tasks. Thus, one implication of this study is the adaptability apparent in friendship groups."[26]

Even when convinced of its importance, managers often challenge the Tenth Element by asking, "What am I supposed to do about this 'best friend' question? It's not like I can be everyone's buddy. I am the manager, after all."

The best managers encourage friendships in the workplace by creating the conditions under which such relationships thrive. For example, new employees at one home improvement store are required to spend some time working in each department as part of an orientation tour. As far as the training is concerned, it usually doesn't matter where they start. So one astute manager inquires into the interests of his new employees and tries to start them in a department where another employee shares the new recruit's hobbies. "We want to put together personalities that will gel," he said. "It's important to put people together who probably could communicate, first of all, but secondly be friends."

One of most effective ways Suresh Nagesh fostered friendships among the Vehicle Engineering and Quality (VEQ) team in Bangalore was quite simple: He moved their work areas together. The engineers' works areas had been spread across various points on the first and second floors of DaimlerChrysler's building in Bangalore. In one of his first decisions, the manager brought all the team members together in one part of the second floor.

"We could interact more with each other," said Prabhu. Instead of e-mailing across the building or between floors, "whenever I need to talk to anybody, I just had to stand up and talk to him — just like that. There was a lot of personal interaction. Face-to-face contact was something very important." Although this also increased the amount of non-work topics people discussed, the higher degree of professional collaboration increased the speed of the work.

The VEQ group "builds" complex virtual components or complete vehicles, prototypes of those to be built for real in the next few years. Sometimes they are looking for weak spots in a vehicle's design, ferreting out sources of noise, vibration, or structural chinks. On other projects they "crash" or tip over the computer model of a bus to see whether and where it needs reinforcing to protect passengers or to meet European, Japanese or American government standards. As long as the computer models reflect damage in the same way a real one would — something verified by wrecking both and comparing the results — the virtual tests have the benefit of allowing numerous cycles of simulation and design modification at a fraction of the cost and time. A computer the size of an ice cream freezer, posted with warnings that it not be touched, sits in Nagesh's office, performing the millions of calculations from his team's workstations.

The work is specialized and complicated, and therefore not easy to learn. "If I had done it all myself, I would have made a lot of mistakes," said engineer B.V.R. Sanjiv, pointing out the need for the engineers to help each other.

Members of the team say there were many communication barriers that needed to be broken down if the team was going to function better. The veteran employees weren't interacting very well among themselves. The size of the team doubled in roughly six months, so there was a gap between the established employees and the new recruits. A bit of a generation gap separated the older and younger workers. Nagesh decided he needed something to shake up the group and force them to depend on each other.

Soon after arriving, Nagesh summoned all the VEQ unit employees for what was ostensibly a routine team-building session. The only hint of what was to come was that he told them to "come ready for anything." For a half-day, the meeting progressed predictably enough, with a facilitated session on the benefits of team cohesion and group discussion about ways to work better together.

Then Nagesh told everyone to get up and get ready to go white-water rafting. The announcement caught the engineers off guard.

"I'm not a good swimmer," says Dr. K.S. Ravichandran, one of the team members. In fact, many of them didn't know how to swim. "I've gone swimming in a pool, but I never imagined myself getting into water that is flowing with such rapids."

"We didn't know how this could have been a team exercise and how this could make us a cohesive team," says Prabhu. For many of the team, it sounded like a good way to drown an engineer or two. In fact, such traditional "team-building" activities are no panacea for a lack of cohesion. Stories abound of such adventures going awry, ending in fist fights, injuries, or permanent acrimony. Nor are they essential to forming enduring bonds in a workgroup; many highly engaged teams learn to rely on each other through the normal course of business seasoned with social events the manager decides will best strengthen friendships in that team. But for the VEQ group, Nagesh determined they needed something dramatic.

A healthy dose of nervousness was precisely what he intended. "I wanted them to get into trouble and see how they can help each other," he said. Nagesh took the team to the Kali River, about 500 kilometers northwest of Bangalore. The team was fitted with life jackets and helmets for the ride downstream.

"When I got there, I was not too sure that the life vest was going to keep me afloat and I was not too sure that the raft in which we were going to be put in was all that safe, considering the rapids that were before my eyes," says Chandran.

With their advanced degrees, even the non-swimmers in the group certainly understood the physics of floatation and the safety of the exercise. But the visceral reaction was a combination of excitement and fear. Photos of the event show two rafts full of nervous smiles as the VEQ team went afloat.

To test his life vest, Nagesh insisted he be thrown in first, and emphasized he was relying on the team to pull him out if he had problems. To force the issue, when he hit the water, he pretended not to know how to swim. His employees pulled him from the water. One by one, each employee took a mandatory plunge in the water to get the feel for how his life vest would bring him back to the surface. As each jumped in, the rest of the team cheered him on.

"It became very clear to us that now we have to work as a team," says Prabhu. "When we used the paddles, we had to handle them as a team. Those who were swimmers said, 'Okay, come on, jump in and I will help you if anything happens.' It was amazing to see people believing in each other and jumping into the water. I think the ice broke there and we started realizing that we can be very good friends, believe in each other and get along very well."

One of the first sets of rapids was the worst. A raft hit the waves at the wrong angle and dumped the men into the water. "These guys had to pull each other up," says the manager. "I saw each of them struggling to try to come to the raft, each of them trying to pull each other inside. It was something. Once they got in, they were so happy. It's something that I don't think I'll forget in my lifetime."

As they became more comfortable traveling down the Kali, the two rafts became competitive, racing each other, poking each other with their paddles, and pulling each other from the rafts. They had the time of their lives. "Toward the end of the rafting expedition," says Ravichandran, "one of the guys from the other raft, which was pretty close to me, pulled me on the neck with the stick that he had and I fell into the water, with no idea of what was the cause. But I was so used to it, I was actually laughing."

When they returned to the office the next day, something had changed. They were eager to take on more work. They had learned they could rely on each other, and they had a memorable and positive shared experience that brought them closer together. The group now draws parallels between their rafting adventure and their reliance on each other in the office.

"If you don't know swimming and you're in the water, even if you have a life boat, the people around you are the ones that inspire confidence in you," says Ravichandran. "I could see that even Suresh Nagesh was pulled into the water and he was in the same situation that I was in. The way that the person in the water reacts shows clearly that the people around you are the ones that you can rely on in times of difficulty."

"I know that I'm not going to be left alone and I'm not going to be blamed if anything goes wrong, because I will always have somebody to help me out, to take me out of the water if anything is wrong," says Prabhu. Since the river-rafting, the VEQ group has created green T-shirts bearing a logo of DaimlerChrysler trucks and cars forming the symbol for infinity. "Infinite possibilities," it reads. Turnover within the group is essentially zero. They now routinely go to lunch together.

As engineers, the Bangalore group is more conscious than most of the effect of friendships on their ability to get the job done. "Let's say I'm bugged by a personal issue. I can be bogged down," said Kaushik Sinha. "It could cut my efficiency by 50 percent. If you can transfer the weight by discussing the personal issue with someone, you feel better; your efficiency can immediately go up to 70 percent."

Friendships take time, time that could be spent working. But the DaimlerChrysler group says the bonds among them improve both the work experience and the quality of their work. "Ideally it should not matter," but it does, said Sanjiv. If one needs advice "it's always better for your friend to tell you, because he knows how to put it. With a third party, it could be an argument; with a friend, it can be a compromise." Sanjiv said people took him out to dinner from his first day there, and he came to know his colleagues "first as people," then as engineers. As a consequence, they were instrumental in giving him advice on what to read and how to approach various customers.

"Last week we worked two days and a night continuously," said Prabhu. "Anyone could have said, 'My job is eight hours a day," but we are such good friends that no one complains. I don't see any other way why someone would work those long hours."

"I have certain deficiencies," said Sinha. "A good friend will help me refine myself."

Ravichandran believes the "initial sense of *bon ami*" is seriously tested by situations when one employee needs to sacrifice for the team. "That's why I think the role of the leader is so important," he said. "It's very important for the daily manager to have his eyes and ears open. There is never a day when there are not interaction problems."

As the group became better friends, the complaining that marked Nagesh's first days there subsided. But he hoped for more than just a cease-fire. He hoped they would learn to sing each other's praises, and instituted a citation program in which one engineer can present a certificate to another for particularly hard or effective work.

The VEQ group is now taking on work creating mathematical models for the Mercedes brand. It requires that the attributes of the entire car be converted into a computer model that can be used to simulate durability tests and crashes during the development of a new model. Recently Mercedes requested the creation of six such models, one of them a crash version that had to be completed in the unusually short period of less than five weeks. Nagesh and the six original engineers worked until midnight and, to make sure they met the deadline, skipped the Bangalore center's annual outing for employees and the families. "We delivered with 100% quality," says Nagesh. "We are with you," the engineers told their manager. "We don't care if we don't go (to the outing) because this is more important to us. We'll come together."

"I just got feedback from our customer," says Nagesh. "He said this is extremely good work that has been done. This is something that I really feel happy about. It's a 180-degree turnaround."

In the relatively no-nonsense culture of Germany-headquartered DaimlerChrysler, Nagesh is considered something of a maverick. His dogged optimism for the Bangalore group stood in marked contrast to the bleak picture others were painting before the turnaround. Even members of the VEQ team admit they didn't know quite what to make of him when he first arrived.

Various observers in the company say several factors made him successful. He is modest, always asking questions, not assuming he has all the answers. His credentials are strong enough that he doesn't need to worry about job security, so he can take risks. His optimism is infectious, and — with the exception of keeping the river trip a secret — he is eager to share his thinking and motives with his team. Maybe most important, he does not believe in the traditional arms-length approach to management or the idea that friendships are restricted to time off the company clock.

Nagesh considers strong affiliations just one of the important factors in building an effective team. However strong, friendships cannot, for example, overcome concerns about job security or compensate for a lack of planning. Still, he said, "friendships are definitely very important to people. I don't believe that you just shake hands and just forget the other person. But friendship does not happen overnight. It takes a period of time for people to understand each other, to come together. It's like a flower: It does not blossom overnight; it takes some time. It's like nature. But once it blossoms, it really blossoms, and it's very, very important."

THE ELEVENTH ELEMENT:
Talking About Progress

N
O ONE ON PHILIPPE LESCORNEZ' TEAM of grocery sales specialists goes into a performance evaluation meeting expecting any
big news. If the manager has something that important to say,
he will just say it, rather than wait for the formal session.

While for other workgroups the yearly or semi-annual appraisal can
be an anxiety-laden confrontation between an employee and a company's official representative, in Lescornez' approach they are simply a
chance to summarize and commit to paper hundreds of discussions that
occurred along the way.

The veteran manager's team scores him among the top 20 percent
of supervisors worldwide on the Eleventh Element of Great Managing,
which is measured by the statement, "In the last six months, someone at
work has talked to me about my progress." Lescornez is considered one
of the best mentors in his company, and was recently recognized with its
"Line Manager Excellence" award for Europe.

How could it be that a manager who doesn't make a big deal of such
a traditionally important responsibility is considered the epitome of a
statement that many think has "good performance appraisals" written
all over it? Because the annual review isn't all it's cracked up to be, but

receiving regular, insightful, personal feedback is intensely powerful to workers. Lescornez understands the difference.

While Lescornez' evaluations are more *pro forma* than formal, his everyday discussions with his team are challenging and invigorating. No one is left guessing how he or she is doing. "The most important part (of discussing progress) was the informal part during the year, because he always kept us motivated," said former team member Hulya Hoke. "He was always giving us objectives and challenging us. He did it during the whole year and not only in the formal part of the evaluation, not only on paper, but continuously." His investment in the careers of his people is the centerpiece of their high engagement and performance.

Lescornez and his team work for Masterfoods in Brussels, a division of Mars, Incorporated, that sells snacks, dog and cat food, and human staples such as grains and sauces under such familiar brands as Uncle Ben's rice, Snickers candy bars, Dove ice cream, and Pedigree dog food. The team of "sales promoters" is assigned to fan out across Belgium and Luxembourg, calling on grocery stores to ensure Masterfoods products arrive on schedule and get enough prominence at the point of purchase. Results hinge on two factors: availability and visibility. Those hired are frequently young and ambitious. Sales promoters generally work alone and many kilometers from company headquarters, so the job requires strong personal motivation and can be isolating.

Unless, that is, one has a manager like Philippe. "He always calls his people in the car. He speaks with everybody at least once a week, often more," said Karin De Backer, a Masterfoods trade services manager and Lescornez' supervisor. "When people move to his team, at the beginning they need to adapt because he phones them all the time: 'How are things going? How are you? Everything okay?'" New hires sometimes complain, "He's always behind me," until they realize he calls because he cares. "It's feedback, feedback, feedback all the time," said De Backer.

The way some performance evaluations are conducted, the employee and the company would be better off without them.

Consider the case of "Don," an anonymous employee of an unnamed company, who posted his experience as part of an online contest looking for the worst appraisal. By the time February rolled around, past the deadline for conducting performance reviews for the previous year, Don was wondering when or whether his boss would make time for the discussion. It took him by surprise to get such ostensibly important feedback in the men's room.

"I happened to be entering the men's bathroom at the same time as my boss," he wrote. "Standing side-by-side at adjacent urinals, he remarked that he hadn't had a chance to go over my review with me, but now was as good a time as any." Don's manager told him he and others in the company were pleased with his work. The setting didn't quite convey genuine appreciation for Don's work. "All of this was bad enough, and a bit humiliating since we were not alone in there, but the summation was really priceless," he wrote. "Walking away from the urinal, he told me to 'keep it up' in the new year." Don doesn't work for that company anymore.[1]

His situation is extreme, but much of the humor in it stems from the problems with performance appraisals. Even when conducted in more typical settings, little in human nature prepares an employee or manager for the artificial aspects of the typical review. Whether out of a fear of confrontation or sheer workload, many managers detest appraisals and delay them, implying to the employee she is not important. The usual forms are just that: forms — impersonal, one-size-fits-all, procedural and lawyerly. Personnel executives like the consistency and assumed fairness of a uniform scoring system, without recognizing the results are so contaminated by human factors — tough versus soft managers, easy versus hard jobs, favoritism — that evaluations can backfire and reduce an employee's motivation to propel the company forward.

Although performance reviews have been in place for generations, until recently very little effort was given to understanding whether the process motivated employees or irritated them. "One may develop the most technically sophisticated, accurate appraisal system, but if that system is not accepted and supported by employees, its effectiveness ultimately will be limited," states one summary of the research.[2] Another finds that "a statistical review of the evidence supporting the use of feed-back (such as performance appraisal) suggests that providing personnel with feedback is like gambling in the stock exchange: On average, you gain, yet the variance is such that you have a 40 percent chance of a (performance) loss following feedback."[3]

Many organizations implement some version of a "balanced score-card" following the logic outlined in Robert Kaplan and David Norton's 1996 book of the same name. The book can be found in nearly every personnel department of the world's largest corporations. Its logic is watertight: Long-term profitability is the product of a multivariate equation; a company's managers must pay attention to, and the scorecard must incorporate, many different aspects of the business if they are to perform as well as possible. However, this ideal proves elusive when placed in the hands of human managers and employees. "Despite survey evidence that a growing number of firms are using balanced scorecards for compensation purposes, relatively little is known about the implementation issues associated with scorecard-based reward systems," wrote three University of Pennsylvania professors who scrutinized a bank that tried and then abandoned a balanced scorecard.[4]

In the case of the bank, the judgment given to managers apparently backfired when they monkeyed with the math, disregarding factors that were predictive of financial success and incorporating factors that were not, and changing the criteria from quarter to quarter. "This evidence suggests that psychology-based explanations may be equally or more relevant than economics-based explanations in explaining the firm's measurement practices," wrote the researchers.[5] Once again, human nature trumped the best-laid plans of corporate strategists. Such bumps along the way are not an indictment of balanced scorecards, any more than human idiosyncrasies nullify the rationale behind job descriptions, marketing plans, safety guidelines, or any area where company-wide standards are important for consistency or coordination. But they do demonstrate that any corporate strategy is only as good as the managers who bring it to life in the day-to-day routines of the teams they supervise.

Several recent twists make performance appraisals more interesting, if not more effective. For example, 360-degree feedback injects a juicy aspect of gamesmanship into the process, allowing underlings to fire back at bosses or sideways at colleagues. Such systems are more likely to grade style rather than substance, and usually focus on weaknesses

rather than strengths.[6] The practice of asking employees to assess themselves presents its own dilemma. "The idea of this workplace ritual that
is gaining popularity is to help managers and employees level with each
other, applaud achievements, set new goals and identify job-training
needs," wrote columnist Jared Sandberg in *The Wall Street Journal*. "But
these self-evaluations have instead been put on the list of annualized
torments, ranking up there with taxes and dental probes. There are, after all, an infinite number of ways to self-incriminate.

"Ostensibly," he continued, "you rate yourself on a scale from one to
five, usually in preparation for a follow-up interview. But let's be frank.
You really end up portraying yourself in one of two ways: A) Self-flagel-
lating lummox dumb enough to enumerate weaknesses that can be used
against you at a later date. B) Self-aggrandizing egomaniac who thinks
'no' means 'yes,' insults are a form of flattery — and you're pretty good-
looking to boot."[7] The caveat given by "Dilbert" creator Scott Adams
has plenty of truth in humor. "The key to your manager's strategy is
tricking you into confessing your shortcomings. Your boss will latch on
to those shortcomings like a pit bull on a trespasser's buttocks. Once
documented, your 'flaws' will be passed on to each new boss you ever
have, serving as justification for low raises for the rest of your life."[8]

More troubling, self-evaluations are likely to be terribly flawed.
"People are not adept at spotting the limits of their knowledge and
expertise," wrote four researchers from the Cornell University and
the University of Illinois at Champaign-Urbana in a report with the
confidence-building title, "Why People Fail to Recognize Their Own
Incompetence." "Indeed," they wrote, "in many social and intellectual
domains, people are unaware of their incompetence, innocent of their
ignorance. Where they lack skill or knowledge, they greatly overesti-
mate their expertise and talent, thinking they are doing just fine when,
in fact, they are doing quite poorly."[9] After administering a sophomore-
level psychology exam to 141 of their students, the four professors asked
them to estimate their absolute scores and their performance on the test
relative to the rest of the students.

The students in the bottom quarter of the class on the test thought
they were well above average. Those who did worst on the test overes-
timated their performance by about 30 percent.[10] The dilemma — the

"double curse," the researchers called it — is that some of the very abilities that make a person good at performing a job are the same abilities needed to realize whether he is failing or succeeding. If an employee isn't talented, knowledgeable, or skilled enough to do a good job, there's a good chance he's not talented, knowledgeable, or skilled enough to know he's blowing it, and floats around naively thinking everything is fine.

This form of unconscious incompetence is not restricted to taking psych tests in college. Other research has found the same problem with people's assessment of their ability to think logically, to write grammatically, or to spot a funny joke.[11] Hunters who don't know much about firearms think they know plenty.[12] Medical residents who have poor patient-interviewing skills think they are doing fine,[13] as do medical lab technicians assessing their knowledge of medical terminology and problem-solving skills.[14] Even if the researchers offer a $100 incentive for a subject to give them the cold, hard truth, people give inflated self-assessments, apparently because they sincerely believe they are that good.[15]

The Cornell and Illinois researchers also made an intriguing discovery on the other end of the scale. While those at the top of the class accurately estimated they did well on the test, they did not realize their accomplishment was unique. They suffered an "undue modesty." "Top performers tend to have a relatively good sense of how well they performed in absolute terms, such as their raw scores on a test," they wrote. "Where they err is in their estimates of other people — consistently overestimating how well other people are doing on the same test."[16]

These results show how imperative it is that a manager, a coach, or a mentor be able to hold up the mirror to an employee. The ray of hope in the "double curse" is that once a research subject is educated on the difference between good and poor performance, he becomes more conscious of where he is failing. "We gave roughly half of the participants a mini-lecture about how to solve this type of logic problem, giving them skills needed to distinguish accurate from inaccurate answers," wrote the social scientists. "When given their original test to look over, the participants who received the lecture, and particularly those who were poor performers, provided much more accurate self-ratings than they had originally."[17]

A recent study commissioned by the United States Army demonstrates the importance of considering the job, the kind of information being conveyed, and the nature of the person receiving the review when giving performance reviews. Responsibilities can be roughly divided into two categories: "promotion" jobs that require someone to think expansively, looking for new opportunities, and "prevention" jobs that require the workers to ensure that something negative does not happen. The job of the creative director of an advertising agency is largely promotion-focused; he needs to think up many ideas, some of which are bound to be stupid, in the hope that one of them will be brilliant and sell a lot of his client's products. The job of an airline mechanic is prevention-focused; he needs to look for every potential problem, some of which are bound to be no threat at all, in the hope of detecting every real flaw and avoiding a crash.

Experimenting with business and health-systems management students, the professors who conducted the Army study assigned different groups to two tasks. Half were given responsibility to generate new ideas, a promotion task. The other half were asked to spot errors, a prevention task. After working for a while, the students randomly were given positive and negative feedback and were asked to indicate how much effort they intended to exert when they returned to the task. Incredibly, the effect of the feedback depended on whether it matched the nature of the task. Those asked to generate ideas were more likely to redouble their efforts if they heard they were succeeding. Those who were asked to detect errors were more likely to try harder if they heard their work thus far wasn't good enough.

Supervisors need to consider the type of information that motivates a given employee, and realize it may be different from the types that motivate others on the team or the way the manager herself prefers to learn about how she is doing. "At the practical level, these findings suggest that no feedback system can fit all," concluded the study. "For [a] performance appraisal system to be effective it must be tailored for specific tasks, occupations and even personalities."[18]

Gallup inquired into the proper balance between a manager focusing on strengths and positive news or weaknesses and negative news in a manager's discussions with subordinates. The research found that a manager who focuses on his employees' strengths essentially inoculates them from being actively disengaged. Those who focus on weaknesses get more polarized results; the strategy rarely works as well as a more positive view, but the manager gets credit for at least "focusing" on the individual. The worst-performing managers were those who, by essentially ignoring their team, fail the Eleventh Element. One-fourth of all employees, and nearly two-thirds of those who are actively disengaged, say their boss is asleep at the switch.[19]

For all the complexity of performance appraisals — the balanced scorecards, the 360-degree feedback, the self-evaluations and forced grading systems — the statement that shows the best connection between perceptions of evaluations and actual employee performance is remarkably simple: "In the last six months, someone at work has talked to me about my progress." The statement does not specify that the discussion be an official review, but an appraisal can be one ingredient in creating the requisite feedback. The two are related, but not synonymous. More important to the employee and to the business is that he understands how he is doing, how it is being perceived, and where his work is leading. In some ways, this statement is a long-term complement to the Fourth Element of managing, which focuses on more immediate "recognition and praise."

There is nothing wrong with a formal evaluation process *per se*, and much to recommend it. Roughly seven in 10 working Americans say their company has a formal performance review process. The odds of creating high engagement are better, but far from perfect, in businesses with a formal process.[20] The deadlines, the forms and the threat of Personnel or a boss coming after them appear to force the issue with front-line managers, making many have a progress meeting with employees where none would have taken place otherwise (serendipitous encounters in the men's room notwithstanding). Companies that implement or tighten appraisal procedures typically see an increase in the Eleventh Element from poor to modest levels, but they never achieve high levels on the strength of appraisals alone.

With any formal appraisal cycle that links ratings to pay, which is the case for 54 percent of U.S. workers,[21] there is an ever-present risk that the system will have enough real or perceived flaws that it actually erodes employee engagement. One study of government workers in a Midwestern U.S. county found that "burnout" was more likely among those employees who believed their new appraisal and merit pay system were unfair. "Employees need to think that how they will be compensated by a system is based on merit, rather than other, extraneous factors," said the study.[22]

Four out of five employees whose companies have a formal review system feel it is fair. However, these perceptions are strongly affected by what happens between the appraisals. The proportion feeling the system is fair drops to two-thirds if they feel no one has talked to them about their progress. Conversely, if a manager can maintain a strong, regular discussion of progress, nine in 10 workers will consider the review system fair.

The consequences on either end of the scale are important. Where a manager is regularly checking in with an employee, she is more likely to consider herself properly compensated for her work, more likely to plan on staying with the company, and more than twice as likely to recommend the company to others as a great place to work.[23] When compared with business results, the Eleventh Element turns out to be particularly powerful in driving productivity and safety. Business units in the top quartile on this element realize 10 to 15 percent higher productivity and 20 to 40 percent fewer accidents than bottom-quartile business units.[24] Yet less than half of employees in the global database strongly agree that someone talked with them about their progress in the last six months. Even among executives and senior managers, the proportion is only one-half.

On a purely functional level, an employee appraisal is quite simple. Observe her progress over the course of the year, record it carefully on the company-supplied form, inform her at the required interval of the results, and expect her to make the necessary corrections to improve next time around. If only she were a machine, the program would work perfectly. In practice, a good performance evaluation is a form of interpersonal art that requires managerial talent and careful preparation.

Whether the employee feels she has a voice in the process — the Seventh Element of "my opinion counts" applies here as much as it does anywhere else — is even more crucial than the functional aspects of her participation.[25] A manager must maintain a delicate balance between giving candid, objective feedback and not crushing the employee's spirit and confidence. The research indicates that positive feedback charges up a worker, but negative comments sap the job of some of its intrinsic motivation.[26] Comments from peers or subordinates must be interpreted carefully, filtered of grudges, jealousy, and erroneous observations. A good reviewer needs to avoid the natural inclination to give too much weight to the outcome regardless of whether the employee did the right thing to get there or just got lucky.[27]

And, most of all, the discussion must be tailored to the personality, the circumstances and the potential of the employee. A drive-by performance evaluation just doesn't cut it.

For Philippe Lescornez, one of the challenges of motivating his team is seeing the potential of each employee and deciding what progress would be most meaningful. Consider the case of Didier Brynaert.

Brynaert works in Luxembourg, 230 kilometers from Masterfoods' Belgium headquarters and, of course, a country away from his manager and the rest of the team. Brynaert was considered a good sales promoter who was doing what was generally expected from sales promoters. Lescornez decided that Brynaert's job could be made more important if he were seen less as just another sales promoter and more as an expert on the unique features of the Luxembourg market.

"It's a small country that's very profitable. It has 5 percent of the population of Belgium, and it makes up 15 percent of Masterfoods Belgium's business," said Brynaert, who rattles off other observations about unemployment rates and consumer preferences. "The economic situation in Luxembourg two years ago was not so good. And now, after my experience here, the business is growing."

To help Brynaert progress, Lescornez asked him for information he could share with the home office. He hoped that by raising Brynaert's profile in Brussels, he could create in him a greater sense of ownership for his remote sales territory. "I started to communicate much more what he did internally to other people because there's quite some distance between the Brussels office and the section he's working in. So I started to communicate, communicate, communicate. The more I communicated, the more he started to provide material," said Lescornez. As Brynaert received more recognition, he began to excel, fighting for more business and building large, high-quality displays of Masterfoods products in the grocery stores he serves. Account and marketing managers rely on him for expertise on the market. "Now he's recognized as the specialist for Luxemburg, the guy who is able to build a strong relationship with the Luxemburg clients, where volumes and inventory turnover for the company are guaranteed and even still growing."

Brynaert said the regular connection to his manager is crucial to his success, and that he enjoys being able to easily phone Lescornez with a question or to relate an experience. "It's very important to me to have a good manager, because I like to work without supervision and with a lot of freedom," he said. "Philippe gives me a lot of freedom."

In sales promoter Ilse Van der Weeën, Lescornez saw great potential, but he also found her too stern and unapproachable, enough so that he thought those traits would handicap her progress. "It was probably the most important thing for her to improve," he said, "but it's not the easiest thing to do. How do you tell someone she has to smile more?"

After Lescornez got to know her well enough that he thought she might take the advice, he gave her his opinion. She accepted the criticism solely because she knew her manager was trying to help. "I wouldn't have accepted it from just anyone," she said, "but he was my line manager. He was the one who knew me best. And he had in mind good things for me."

Wendy Dekens has been a sales promoter for four years. She knows the job well. But for a number of reasons, a promotion does not seem imminent. She was at risk of stagnating and candidly acknowledged that her career track is uncertain.

"There was a certain comfort zone, some routine, coming," said her manager. Lescornez decided to capitalize on her expertise and her interest in training to make the job of a sales promoter more fulfilling and to give her a sense of progress. "I know my job and I know it 100 percent," she said. "I would really like to share all this information with my colleagues. I love to explain things. I love to give training."

Lescornez asked Dekens to prepare a manual that could be given to new hires, who are likely to be assigned to ride along with her in their first weeks on the job. She "took with both hands" the chance to create the manual. "It made my job more attractive, innovative, and interesting than the job that I know through-and-through." Where it will lead, she doesn't know, but her manager's creativity sparked greater engagement than if she were left to do just the job of a sales promoter.

Hulya Hoke is known for her exuberance and extroversion. "The energy I may have taken from my culture," she said. "I come from Turkey and maybe people there are more open." Her clients loved her because of the excitement she brought along. "She was very, very respected by her clients," said Lescornez. "It was always a very amusing day to go with her into the field to see her clients."

Her greatest talent was also a liability, however. Hoke brought such energy to the job that she was also susceptible to going in too many directions at once, spreading herself too thin. "I saw the potential and the drive she had," said her manager. "It was in a rather unstructured way. She was doing plenty of things with big doses of energy, but her balance wasn't that strong."

Lescornez needed to help her focus without diminishing her natural enthusiasm. He did so first by spending plenty of time riding along with her to visit her clients, and then by praising her abilities enough that she felt comfortable taking direction from him. "We spent a lot of time together in the field, a lot of discussions, a lot of talks," said Lescornez. "I always made it possible that she could take risks and speak freely." The manager says he discovered that if he spends enough time with his team members helping them, talking and joking, they will invite feedback, asking him what they can do to improve. This is when an employee is most receptive to coaching.

After calling on one grocery store with Hoke to discuss the visibility of Masterfoods' products, Lescornez shared his thoughts about how the visit had gone. He made sure he began by praising what she had done well. "Praise is very important," he said. "Once you get people on a positive track, you can tell more and more things to them. You have to praise people. You have to talk in a positive way and then you can redirect things that need to be redirected."

Lescornez felt that for all her positive emotional connection with the customer, Hoke meandered, "jumping from the left to the right," during the negotiation. He told her she might want to spend more time preparing for the meeting, introducing more facts and figures and relying less on personal rapport. "He is a funny man, and so the way to explain things was also wonderful. He has an easiness in the way he explains things," said Hoke.

She took his counsel to heart, improved quickly, and was selected soon thereafter to expand her abilities by working in the vending part of the business. Turnover is an issue for Lescornez' team — not because team members quit, but because they get tapped for new responsibilities. In his 18 years as a manager, Lescornez estimates, he managed 125 sales promoters ("I've seen some characters," he adds), 60 percent of whom eventually were promoted.

It's not unusual for each person on his team to feel he or she receives special attention, said De Backer. In fact, he does that for everyone. "If I do my job well, it's thanks to Philippe, because he taught us to set priorities," said Hoke. "We have lots of things to do. You can't manage everything at the same time," she said, preaching the message her manager taught her. "We have to say, okay, this is a job; we have to do A, B, C, D, E, and so on. But you have to begin with the A."

Mieke Demeyer hasn't reported to Lescornez for more than a year-and-a-half, but was among those who recommended him for his award because of his patience and knack for helping people participate in solving the problems they presented to him. "He makes you think harder, just trying to get to the next step yourself, being a coach, standing on the sideline, but doing the thinking with you," she said.

A typical coaching session is prompted by a sales promoter calling Lescornez when he or she is "stuck," not knowing what to propose in negotiating for display space. The manager begins by reviewing the situation. He is, by all accounts, a patient and careful listener. "He would try to make you think what could be the options and not give the answer right away," said Demeyer. If the employee needs a little help, he'll drop a hint or two. That's usually enough, she said, "then you could build upon that and it was fantastic, because he took the time to really build up a new solution and you had the feeling that, 'Yeah, I came to a solution myself!'"

The hallmark of Lescornez' leadership is the responsibility he gives his team and how he makes them struggle a bit in finding answers. "He could do it quickly, so it's easy and it's done," said De Backer, his manager. "He never does that. He always challenges back and says, 'What would you do?' He gives them a lot of trust. They learn by committing mistakes, and then he coaches them. He's always there to look after them, but he will not do it for them."

She recalls soon after she assumed responsibility for Lescornez and his team that she commented the sales promoters' fact books were insufficient. Lescornez told everyone to bring their fact books with them to the next meeting. De Backer assumed he would have them leaf through the manuals and examine them for the required pages in a fairly authoritarian fashion. Instead, he asked the employees to pair up, review their colleague's book, and present to the group the good points of that book. "At the end, they had tremendous ideas to improve their fact books," she said. "It was in a very positive, constructive way. Everybody learned something good from another person. It was a simple thing, but for me it was a great example of how you should do it."

Lescornez' approach certainly took longer, but it yielded more. De Backer anticipates the sales promoters will do more with the material in their fact books than if their boss dictated the contents to them. But she doubts Lescornez ever considered the alternative. "I'm sure Philippe never did it any other way."

"He's an inspiring person," said former sales promoter Dieter Van den Brande. "He's funny. He's informal. He makes you challenge yourself." In his 18 years of managing at Masterfoods (he is so much a company man that his dog is trained to reject a competitor's bone in favor of the Pedigree-brand bone his team markets) Lescornez has built a reputation as someone who will work to accelerate the careers of his people. "He is the one you want to work for," said Van den Brande.

With so much direct coaching, there isn't much drama left for the formal evaluations, which are as much required at Masterfoods as they are at many companies. "The formal paper part of it was more like,

'Okay, now we have to do the paper part. We're going to do it together and fill it out and then you can tell me if you are all right with what I've written down,'" said Demeyer.

"There was no surprise," said Hoke. "It was very, very easy to do because it was exactly what we had done during the year."

"Performance evaluations should not be a surprise," said Lescornez. "If they don't know where they stand before that meeting, there is a big problem. One of the two hasn't been doing his job — probably the manager."

Van der Weeën said she appreciates Lescornez' ability to understand each person's individual strengths and weaknesses, and to ultimately determine the needs of the person he is coaching. "I don't think any of us want to feel I am just a machine being told to 'Sell, sell, sell!' I am a person — not always perfect," she said.

One of the first things that came to mind when De Backer was asked about Lescornez was a conversation she had with him about a manager's responsibility for an employee's progress. "People often judge other people quickly," she said. "We tend to do that at Masterfoods. But he always says if somebody is not good, you should question yourself as a boss and ask, 'What did I do to improve, to coach, the person, to help him, to teach him?' Always be sure that you did everything that you could."

THE TWELFTH ELEMENT:

Opportunities to Learn and Grow

THROUGH NO FAULT OF HER OWN, and without anyone intending it, Colleen Saul's career at B&Q got off to a rocky start.

With her new management degree, and having worked for the company briefly once before, she approached the British home improvement retailer in hopes of landing a management job and ultimately working in the buying department. There were no openings that fit her aspirations, the company said, but there was an urgent need for help in the "revamp" of the store in Bangor, Wales.

"It will be good experience for you," the regional manager told her. And it was. Managing the stock clearance process, Saul got valuable insights into what it takes to remodel and run a store. But in going directly to Bangor, she had to skip the requisite training that management-track employees typically receive in their first four months. She was not offered a management job in Bangor because newly refurbished stores are not set up to provide the training she lacked.

Instead, she was asked to supervise the gardening department in B&Q's Ellesmere Port store. While that store was closer to Saul's home, she still needed her training. By oversight, in the rush of regular business, or through the reluctance of managers to give her the needed time,

Saul could not get those orientation sessions scheduled. "Nobody made provision for me to do my training; they just thought I was basically good to go," she said.

She found herself facing a "sink or swim" onslaught of customers during a holiday weekend in a part of the store that had gone without a manager for three weeks. She was struggling without the basic information taught during training: how to account for cash received, how to close the store, how to order more inventory. "I managed to run the gardening department when I'd never run a department before, but there were things that obviously weren't right, certain things that went wrong because I didn't understand the ordering processes," Saul said. "I managed to keep my head above water, and in my spare time went to other stores to learn the processes I should have been taught."

Saul was languishing. She was frustrated, wondering if she made a mistake in joining B&Q. Her self-confidence was diminished. She wasn't making a very good impression within the company. "I felt like if I did something wrong it would be picked up on, but maybe not necessarily mentioned to me, but mentioned to other people, so then I never felt like I was learning properly." She even considered looking for another job.

That's when Saul met Simon Gaier, manager of the store in Wrexham, Wales, just six miles west of the border with England. Regional Manager Paul Randles suggested Saul move to the Wrexham store because of Gaier's well-regarded people skills. If anyone could help her get back on track, he was the one.

"He came to see me before I left the other store," she said. "He really sought out what was the best way to work with me, was interested in what I wanted to do and what my aspirations were." He also said he'd make sure she got her training.

At 28 years old, Gaier is often not believed when he introduces himself to customers as the manager of the Wrexham store. But employees at B&Q say Gaier has a real knack for managing. They describe him in terms common to the managers profiled in this book: laid-back and approachable despite an unquestioned commitment to achieving results, completely candid, investing time in getting to know each individual employee's opinions about the job, continuously promoting a sense of team-wide responsibility for the store, rarely missing an opportunity to recognize good work — a consummate "people person." One of the areas in which Gaier particularly excels is the Twelfth Element, which is measured by the statement, "This last year, I have had opportunities at work to learn and grow." The 58 people who work at the Wrexham store rank in the top one percent of business units in the Gallup worldwide engagement database.

"If I were to move Simon," said Randles, "they'd probably lynch me, because they love the guy." Much of their attachment to Gaier is because he took a store with many long-term employees who felt stagnant and gave them a chance to grow.

For 54 years, the Pulitzer-Prize-winning author Theodor Geisel delighted children with his imaginative illustrations and their accompanying rhymes. Under the pen name Dr. Seuss, he wrote and illustrated a small library of best-sellers such as *The Cat in the Hat*, *How the Grinch Stole Christmas* and — on a bet to prove he could write a book with a vocabulary of only 50 words — *Green Eggs and Ham*.

His last book threw people a little because it didn't fit the pattern of the rest. It didn't have any strange characters with silly names. It didn't have a plot. While it had the surreal imagery one would expect from Dr. Seuss, the book's only characters were the narrator and "you," the reader. Instead, the book waxed poetic on overcoming obstacles and the possibilities of future accomplishments. He titled the book *Oh, the places you'll go!*

Where were the imaginary animals? asked the reviewers. After a half-century parade of Thidwick the Moose, Yertle the Turtle, Zinn-a-zu Birds and Fuddnudler Brothers, this book seemed, by comparison anyway, so serious. The publisher's jacket copy suggesting it was for "upstarts of all ages," "raises quizzical questions about the story's intended audience," pondered *The New York Times*.

"But seriously now, who's got the punch line?" continued the newspaper. "Where's the sly beastie waiting to toss a big dollop of gooky green oobleck on this path to success? Horton, old pal, can you hear us?"[1]

This really isn't a storybook at all, said the *Orlando Sentinel*, but a lesson about life. "For this book, Seuss has abandoned his traditional fable format in which the lesson can be found in the silliness," wrote that paper's reviewer. "Instead, our hero here never gets a name. He is us; we are him."[2]

Seuss himself said he wanted the book to communicate a theme of "limitless horizons and hope" because he was concerned modern children did not think beyond their problems.[3] The book hit a nerve with more than children. It remains a staple for many send-offs, particularly high school and college graduations. Special Seussian sunglasses and photo frames are bought to amplify the optimistic message of the book. In his inimitable way, Seuss captured the uniquely human quality of striving to accomplish something new, something better.

Experts in many disciplines struggle to define just what it is about us that creates this need to progress. Abraham Maslow theorized that humans have a hierarchy of needs much like an ancient pyramid, the pinnacle of which is "self-actualization," fulfilling one's potential. "What a man *can* be, he *must* be," he wrote.[4] In the 1960s, MIT professor Douglas McGregor argued a "Theory Y" approach to managing allows businesses to tap into the natural desire of employees to do well and reach their potential. More recently, researchers have proposed employees have innate needs for "self-determination,"[5] for chances to "thrive,"[6] to "flourish"[7] or to create the best possible self-image through achievement.[8]

This drive is so basic that evidence of its existence confronts us every day. What mother has not been shocked by how vociferously her toddler insists on doing something himself? A person naturally looks forward to learning to ski, getting a driver's license, college, his first real job, buying a house, and thousands of new challenges that create a feeling of advancement. Funny how quickly interest in a sports team diminishes once it is eliminated from post-season play, and how quickly the fan's mind moves on — "Maybe next year." Backers of the Chicago Cubs, the Minnesota Vikings, or Spain's national soccer team can explain the frustration of never accomplishing the goal.

The dictionary definition of a career revolves around the idea of successively greater accomplishments:

> Career: Professional *progress*: somebody's
> *progress* in a chosen profession or during that
> person's working life.[9]

For many people, it is progress that distinguishes a career from employment that is "just a job." Employees who have an opportunity to learn and grow at work are twice as likely as those on the other end of the scale to say they will spend their career with their company.[10]

"The fullest representations of humanity show people to be curious, vital, and self-motivated," wrote University of Rochester professors Richard Ryan and Edward Deci. "At their best, they are (self-directed) and inspired, striving to learn; extend themselves; master new skills; and apply their talents responsibly. That most people show considerable effort, agency and commitment in their lives appears, in fact, to be more normative than exceptional, suggesting some very positive and persistent features of human nature."[11]

Neuroscientists are only beginning to understand the mechanisms within the brain that create the drive to succeed. In a 2004 study, 10 researchers, most from the University of Wisconsin at Madison, compared brain scans of volunteers with the subjects' self-assessments of how strongly they felt "interested," "alert," "attentive," "excited," "enthusiastic," "inspired," "proud," "determined," "strong" and "active." High scores indicate "a state of high energy, full concentration, and pleasurable engagement," precisely the kinds of emotions a manager needs from his employees. The researchers "documented a modest but robust relationship between lateralized (left) activation over a posterior region of the superior frontal cortex" and the 84 subjects' feelings of engagement with life. The early evidence suggests this portion of the brain is crucial for employees continuing to pursue a long-term goal despite the inevitable setbacks. Such a mastery over one's self and circumstances appears to be an important component of living a full life.[12]

This research points out important distinctions between the kinds of pleasurable but transient experiences that may not help a business reach its goals (eating all the doughnuts at a meeting or being allowed to goof off) and the deeper sources of stimulation and meaning that create a sense of accomplishment for the employee and also advance work of the company. As they might with any of the 12 Elements, the most cynical managers could question why they should worry about the employees' well-being. "Let them figure out their life on their own time," they might say, or, "Why should I care whether my team feels a sense of progress so long as they get the job done?" This view is both short-sighted and not that uncommon.

A wealth of research — at least 200 studies — proves that challenging employees to meet goals motivates higher performance. "Performance increases have been documented using tasks ranging from cognitive, such as solving anagrams or thinking of creative uses for a common household object, to physical, such as cutting logs and pedaling a bicycle," concludes one summary.[13] "Loggers cut more trees, and unionized truck drivers increased the logs loaded on their trucks from 60 percent to 90 percent of the legal allowable weight as a result of assigned goals," states another. "The drivers saved the company $250,000 in nine months. A subsequent study saved $2.7 million in 18 weeks by assigning unionized drivers the goal of increasing their number of daily trips to the mill."[14] One of the most interesting wrinkles in the research is that employees perform better when they are working toward a specific difficult-to-attain target than when they are told simply "do your best."[15] What are commonly called "stretch goals" are psychologically invigorating and good for business.

Whether a particular accomplishment is meaningful depends on an employee's unique perspective. As with the rest of the 12 Elements, the way the human mind makes sense of events may not seem perfectly logical. "I think if I was an Olympic athlete I would rather come in last than win the silver," said comedian Jerry Seinfeld. "You win the gold, you feel good. You win the bronze, you think, 'Well, at least I got something.' But you win that silver, that's like, 'Congratulations, you almost won.' Of all the losers, you came in first of that group. You're the number one . . . loser. No one lost ahead of you."[16]

Seinfeld was closer to the truth than he may have realized. Interviews with 1992 Olympic medalists found that those who got a bronze medal were, in fact, happier than those who won silver, for precisely the reasons the comedian speculated. This tendency not to look at an accomplishment just in absolute terms, but also relative to what might have been, is a fundamental principle of psychology, said the study's authors. "A person's objective achievements often matter less than how those accomplishments are subjectively construed," they emphasized.[17] Other sociologists found that because people need to see themselves in a positive light, if they fail, they are likely to rationalize that they never had a chance anyway.[18]

These are just a few of the all-too-mortal aspects people bring to this element and yet another reason why maintaining employee engagement requires the judgment of front-line supervisors constantly "getting inside the heads" of their team members. Because each person is unique in her talents, strengths, situation, hopes, and personality, it is incumbent upon the employee and her manager to chart her future progress. Whatever those decisions — whether they include formal training, a mentor, chances to assume new responsibilities or simply informal opportunities to learn the nuances of a job — it is imperative they create that feeling of personal improvement.

When employees feel they are learning and growing, they work harder and more efficiently. This element, while linked to nearly every important outcome Gallup has studied, has a particularly strong connection to customer engagement and profitability. On average, business units in the top quartile on the Twelfth Element surpass their bottom-quartile counterparts by 9 percent on customer engagement and loyalty measures, and by 10 percent on profitability. These superior customer relationships and profits may occur because employees who are learning and genuinely interested in their work have better ideas — which is another demonstrated correlation to the Twelfth Element.[19]

The importance of the learning and growing may be best appreciated when they are not there, when — as Seuss called them — "Bang-ups" and "Hang-ups" leave a person stalled short of his goal. Something about human nature hates to be stuck in one place. During the commute to work, a driver's level of frustration has less to do with the amount of time it takes than with how frequently she ends up just sitting in traffic.[20] The same is true once she arrives at the office. Getting stuck in one place — George Orwell called it being "smothered under drudgery"[21] — is as unnatural for adults as it is for children. Researcher Barbara L. Frederickson even theorizes that positive emotions "are evolved psychological adaptations that increased human ancestors' odds of survival and reproduction."[22]

"Developmentalists acknowledge that from the time of birth, children, in their healthiest states, are active, inquisitive, curious, and playful, even in the absence of specific rewards," wrote Deci and Ryan. "The (idea) of intrinsic motivation describes this natural inclination toward assimilation, mastery, spontaneous interest, and exploration that is so essential to cognitive and social development and that represents a principal source of enjoyment and vitality throughout life."[23]

Yet almost everyone hits a bump in the road sometime during his or her career. "Despite the fact that humans are liberally endowed with intrinsic motivational tendencies," wrote the University of Rochester professors, "the evidence is now clear that the maintenance and enhancement of this inherent propensity requires supportive conditions, as it can be fairly readily disrupted by various nonsupportive conditions."[24]

That's exactly what happens to many employees. Raised through a childhood in which each new year brought novel opportunities, playing at ever more difficult levels of sports, growing physically, educated in a system of cleanly delineated grades — freshman, sophomore, junior, senior — many employees find themselves several years into their career wondering what happened to the momentum they used to enjoy. Being both conditioned and naturally wired to look forward to differences between seventh and eighth grade or high school and college, many workers are disappointed to discover there will be no dramatic difference between their experience as a 25-year-old employee and their experience as a 26-year-old.

Helping adults learn and grow is admittedly more difficult than moving children through the grades. "Traditionally, we have known more about how animals learn than about how children learn; and we know much more about how children learn than about how adults learn," wrote adult learning expert Malcolm Knowles. "Perhaps this is because the study of learning was taken over early by experimental psychologists whose canons require the control of variables. And it is obvious that the conditions under which animals learn are more controllable than those under which children learn; and the conditions under which children learn are much more controllable than those under which adults learn.[25]

Sitting in the same cubicle, doing the same job in much the same way without any meaningful new challenges, causes employees to languish personally and professionally. "I'm just like a sponge and they're drying me out," one employee responded when asked about whether he was getting chances to learn and grow. A study of over 3,000 adults between the ages of 25 and 74 found that 12 percent of the population is "languishing," and only 17 percent were "flourishing." "Languishing is associated with poor emotional health, with high limitations of daily living, and with a high likelihood of a severe number of lost days of work" and, when at work, lower productivity, wrote the study author Corey Keyes.[26]

Similar results show up in the Gallup employee engagement database. Nearly one-third of the 10 million employees in the files are lukewarm to ice cold on the question of learning and growing. This issue is worse yet in government offices, utilities, communications, information services, insurance offices, banks, transportation, and manufacturing. A sense of learning and growing is more common in accommodation and service jobs, and in restaurants.

It may be that the leadership of many companies is blind to the problem. Executives are roughly 20 percent more likely than managers and 70 percent more likely than employees in general to feel they are progressing. Some executives almost certainly assume they are different than the troops, that while they struggle to make senior vice president or chief marketing officer, the people on the front line do not share their sense of aspiration. While people differ dramatically in their drive to advance in a career, the need for progress seems to be nearly universal. Other executives may take a dim view of employee growth after formal education. The idea that "you can't teach an old dog new tricks" still circulates despite the fact it is false both for canines and when used as a metaphor for adults.[27] There is plenty of evidence progression accelerates when properly nourished by regular opportunities and supportive managers.[28]

★

Simon Gaier needed his employees to succeed and progress, both for their own sakes and to meet the needs of the store. He had a number of management positions open, yet few of the employees had been prepared to assume those responsibilities. He filled the management jobs with people from outside B&Q or from other stores. It was a cumbersome process complicated by the fact that those who were hired from outside the company had to learn the B&Q culture. The move had predictable effects on those already at the store. "They felt very, very disengaged," said Gaier.

"I wanted to do more. I didn't want to just work on checkout," said Ceri Jones, a six-year veteran of the store.

"When we brought the external people in," said Gaier, "Ceri was really frustrated and really annoyed because she wanted to progress. But no one had actually done the feedback with her, done the development plan with her, actually spent the time with her." The manager resolved to make sure those already working there, many of whom had been at the store for a long time, had opportunities to get promotions in the future.

There is no way to match a worker with the right opportunities, Gaier said, unless the manager has a deep understanding of a person's strengths and hopes for the future. Region Manager Randles called Wrexham one afternoon looking for Gaier and was told he was not there. Gaier didn't call back until 3 p.m. His boss questioned him about it.

"I want to work with the night crew tonight," said the store manager.

"Why are you doing that?"

"I just haven't done it for a while," he responded.

"That might not seem like a lot," Randles said of the incident, "but, believe me, if I could get all my managers to see the importance of working with the night crew as well as the day crew, our stores would work a lot smoother." Turnover is highest among the night crews because they can often be forgotten.

Through a series of individual conversations with each employee, the manager learned what each of his 58 employees wanted to accomplish in the future. As with any large group, not everyone wanted to become a manager.

Among those learning and growing in his current position was Mike Jones. The cracked skin on his fingers bears testament to the long career he had as a carpenter before a stroke disabled him. "I couldn't climb stairs," he said. "I can't walk backwards; I lose my balance." As if that weren't bad enough, when he was trying to recover, his former employer called to ask when he was leaving, and to inform him he had been over-paid £1.60 (about $3).

Hiring Jones and Gareth Ingman, a former building tradesman who lost one of his legs in a motorcycle accident, gave B&Q's Wrexham store two in-house experts on home improvement. It gave the men the fulfill-ing second careers they had a hard time imagining when circumstances forced them to leave the construction business. Through the transitions, the two middle-aged workers found that chances to learn and grow are not restricted to the young, and that the inside of a retail business is a much different place than a construction site.

"It's so interesting dealing with people," said Jones. "This woman came in one day and said, 'My husband sent me for a whatsit.'" The men learned patience and listening skills as they interacted with people who know much less about completing a project than they do.

Sitting between the two men, their friend and coworker Shereen "Queeny" Evans interjected, "One customer asked me, 'How much wall-paper do I need in my bedroom?' 'How big is your bedroom?' I asked her. She said, 'Average.'"

While computers were not used on job sites, they are integral to running B&Q, so the men learned how to use them. "I learned a lot more about the retail trade than I ever thought I would," said Jones. "It exercises your mind." And the former building tradesmen restrained their job-site vocabulary a bit. "Not swearing" is very important, said Jones.

In his conversations, Gaier discovered one employee was stretched thin trying to split her time between her job at B&Q and her work at a day-care center. The stress of working with the children was affect-ing her sales and her happiness. He drew up a plan that showed if she improved her sales at the store, he would give her more hours and she would no longer need to work both jobs. "She's now gone over to being the top sales consultant in the store and one of the top in the region," said the manager. "It was just a matter of sitting down and breaking down some of those barriers."

Ceri Jones had been turned away several times for B&Q's "Fast Track" program that prepares employees to be managers. For that reason, she said, "I was a bit dubious in going to Simon." But he encouraged her to undertake the six- to nine-month program. She still recalls her first shift as "duty manager," taking charge of the store for several hours. "It was scary. It was good," she said, a smile on her face. "Simon told me he was proud of what I'd done."

The discussions helped him solve the succession problem. Once he knew all the staff's aspirations, he was able to sketch out a plan that had one or more potential successors for every managerial position in the Wrexham location. "He has a proper, robust people plan," said Randles.

In the interviews, one of the people who caught Gaier's attention was Adam Williams. A somewhat reserved person, Williams had been working at B&Q for several years, beginning in college, when he worked a four-hour shift ending at midnight to earn pocket money. After college, he began working full-time. Like Saul, some of his first experiences were being called in to other stores that needed extra help during revamps. Revamps are a large part of B&Q's strategy to attract more customers and boost profits during a difficult time in the United Kingdom's home-improvement economic cycle.[29]

By the time Gaier first sat down with him, Williams had done a tour of revamps throughout the region, eight to 10 weeks at a store, then on to the next. Riding the circuit gave him many chances to earn overtime pay, but he didn't feel he was moving in the right direction.

"The two years traveling took its toll on me," he said. "I wanted to be based close to home and actually think toward a career." Gaier asked him the same questions he asked everyone else: What did he want to do? Where did he hope to be in the future? Williams wanted to be done with revamps. As chance would have it, just as Gaier was working on repatriating him to the Wrexham store, it went through a revamp. The manager suggested Williams spend this remodeling period in the warehouse, as he would need that experience in the future if he were to become a manager.

As he got to know Williams better, Gaier expressed some concern that without some bolstering, his shy side might handicap him. Williams' assignments in the night shift, in revamps, and in the warehouse didn't put him in contact with nearly as many customers and other employees as a regular day shift on the main merchandise floor. "He was always someone who, if he knew you, if he'd known you for a long period of time, he could talk to you intelligently and he could communicate very well," said Gaier. "But if we had an external visitor to the store or a new manager came into the store, he'd struggle with that because basically he was a little bit shy."

Gaier was direct with Williams. "He won't hide anything from you," said Williams. "If it's stuff that you need to know, then he will obviously tell you. He told me, 'There's no way out of it. You need to communicate with as many people as you can to run a department.'"

Meanwhile, having received her training, Colleen Saul flourished over the prior year while managing the gardening center of the Wrexham store. Gardening center sales increased by 20 percent. Saul knew all the procedures, such as how to track what sold and what didn't. "I felt comfortable with what I'd done, what I'd achieved, and how stuff worked," she said. With the gardening center working well, Saul had the operational experience she needed to keep take the next step. She was finally in a position to ask about the possibility of moving into the department that buys products for the entire company.

"Simon offered me roles in the store where I could be promoted, but I knew that wasn't the career path that I wanted to go down," said Saul. "I requested to have any chances where I could shadow somebody (in the buying department) and just see if it was something that I wanted to pursue, because I only had a theory of what the job was about." With some work by the company's human resources department and Gaier arranging for a week of relief from her responsibilities in Wrexham, Saul spent the time learning about the wholesale purchase of home furnishings for the company's 329 stores in the United Kingdom, Europe, and Asia. "It was a really good experience," she said.

"Simon saw things in her that people — including me, I have to say — hadn't seen in her," said Randles. There were no open positions in the buying department at that time. Moreover, Saul was needed back in Wrexham, because the store was still going through its revamp. But once the store was fully refurbished and the regional managers came for one of their visits, Saul got her chance.

"They knew who I was because of what I had done," she said. "I don't think anybody before had actually gone and chatted with somebody or shadowed someone at the head office. So they were asking about my future career path. I said that I wanted to go into buying and I wanted a position at the head office. A couple of days later they gave me a call to say that there was a position in Store Closures, that it ran until the end of January and if I did this, I could make the contacts I wanted with Buying."

Gaier had seen to the progress of Saul, but because her career path took her outside the store, he made tougher his own job of keeping the management ranks staffed. Now he needed a new manager of the gardening center. He had just the person in mind — Adam Williams.

Gaier said he knew Williams had "loads of potential." Once he was pulled off the road and given some coaching, he became a tremendous supervisor. As for the shyness, "he can now speak to anyone — the first time they meet him, he comes across as really confident," said Gaier. "He'll tell them exactly what he's doing, exactly what he's about, what he wants to do, and where he wants to go."

The store manager said he was particularly pleased to hear how Williams handled himself during Gaier's Christmas vacation when the regional managers and directors came to visit. Not only did Williams confidently lead the tour; he even rebuffed a challenge from one of the executives. About a particular procedure, "one of the regional managers said, 'Well, that's good, but maybe you should do it a little bit differently.' He was able to say, 'Well, actually, no; the reason we're doing it is this," and was able to challenge back, which was fantastic!" say Gaier. "That is just such an improvement over the last 12 months."

Williams gives much of the credit to his manager. "I would honestly say that Simon has offered a lot more opportunities to members of staff than what I've seen and what I've heard of other managers that we've had here," he said. "I've been here three years. I don't know any other manager that will stand by you, give you all the time in the world and say, 'Well, this is the plan that I've got for you and we'll do it over this amount of weeks,' talk to you step-by-step through what he intends to do. That's why I say the interaction is spot-on with him."

Having moved from a position in which she felt stagnant to another in which she is growing at the same company within just a few years, Saul is able to compare the two quite well. "I'd spent all these years and all these thousands of pounds on an education. I had a brilliant theory but had no practice, and so it was very, very easy to get stuck," she said. "To hit a brick wall — it's mind-boggling. You don't set yourself up for things like that. It knocked my confidence a hell of a lot. I went through quite a lot of different emotions. I thought maybe I'm just not good at getting on with certain people."

Gaier's combination of pep talk, forthrightness, confidence in her, and his plan for her future made all the difference. "Working for him, I loved going into work. I loved being in work. I loved all the stuff that we were doing, and it was just really interesting. Results were getting produced and he was very supportive," said Saul. "He just gave me loads of confidence and I felt like I could do stuff. I suppose he gave me back the thing that it wasn't me; it was just maybe the situation I was in before."

"I've seen managers come and go," said Evans, an 18-year employee of B&Q. "Simon will listen to you. He's honest. He's trustworthy. You can talk to him in confidence. He's fair to his staff." The mostly Welsh employees in the border town of Wrexham speak in especially fond terms of Gaier given that — as Ceri Jones said — "The Welsh and English don't get on" and their manager is English. "It's not a problem with Simon," she said. "He's just being himself. He's quite approachable. It doesn't bother us."

"Unless we lose at rugby," adds a coworker following the conversation a few feet away.

The store ultimately became self-sufficient in replacing managers. Williams, for example, was training his own possible successor should he move to a new position. The staff understood that if they prepared themselves for it, the new opportunities would present themselves.

Although the initiative required a large investment of his time, Gaier found that helping his employees learn and grow allowed him to delegate more and spend more time on other aspects of improving the store. But Williams suspects it's far more personal than that for Gaier. The manager is so interested in the progress of his people that "I think he doesn't want us to fail because he'll take it as himself failing."

An Element Unto Itself:
The Problem of Pay

IN **April 2006, British newspaper writer Polly Toynbee** published a column on the peculiarities of compensation. She noted that doctors in the United Kingdom had seen their average pay double since 2000, but were no happier than before. Raises were no guarantee against workers "rubbishing their employers," she wrote in the Manchester *Guardian*. "If higher pay does not lead to happiness or gratitude, how people feel about their pay is complicated and exceedingly important," she correctly concluded.

Then Toynbee dropped a rhetorical bomb. Part of the problem, she argued, was in keeping pay private. Referring to a controversy over pay for British Broadcasting Corporation radio personalities, Toynbee argued: "The BBC should reveal all (salaries) to ensure there really is a genuine market in talent out there. And that should be a general rule, not just in public bodies but everywhere. People do know more or less what everyone else earns in the public sector, so why not make it compulsory for all?"[1]

Norway and Finland make tax returns public, she observed. Toynbee cited research finding that fairness and "transparency" are more important than the actual amount of one's salary, so why not — as the column's headline said — "Throw open the books so that we can see what everyone earns." "After the initial shock," she assured her readers, "people would soon get used to the idea."

The day the piece appeared, a blogger wrote to the columnist, asking, "How much do you earn per annum?"

She refused to answer the question. "An organisation has to go public all together."[2]

As much by her own silence as by her column, the *Guardian* writer made her point: Pay is complicated.

In fact, pay is so thorny that it behaves like none of the 12 Elements. Companies frequently ask why Gallup does not include a compensation statement when assessing employee engagement. The answer is that while an employee's response to each of the 12 Elements predicts how he will perform in the future, his answer to a pay question is so bundled up in psychological complexities that asking it usually causes more problems than it solves. Pay is a status-laden, envy-inspiring, politically charged monster. Getting it right is crucial, and that begins by not underestimating its hazards or lumping it in with other aspects of an engaging workplace.

On one level, this seems counterintuitive. If any aspect of work should be logical, amenable to straightforward formulas and public agreement, shouldn't it be the most quantitative of the company's rewards? Ideally, compensation is simply the market value of a person's work. At least on a superficial level, pay is a matter of applied mathematics. If it were only that easy.

In its irrationality, pay is like many of the 12 Elements — ideas that seem logical on the surface, yet are both surprising and exceptionally complex when processed through the human mind. But compensation is much messier than any of the 12 Elements. A number of basic truths about the psychology of pay demonstrate why managers must view their compensation strategies through an emotional lens if they want to maximize how well they motivate workers.

Higher pay does not guarantee greater engagement.

A supervisor might assume going in that the more she pays her team, the happier they will be. But there's a lot of truth to the old saying that "Money doesn't buy happiness." It doesn't necessarily buy engagement either.

One of the sociological puzzles that presented itself in the last few decades is why, if people spend so much of their energy in pursuit of higher incomes, the attainment doesn't bring the hoped-for result. "Increases in our stocks of material goods produce virtually no measurable gains in our psychological or physical well-being. Bigger houses and faster cars, it seems, don't make us any happier," wrote Robert H. Frank in his book *Luxury Fever: Why Money Fails to Satisfy in an Era of Excess.*[3] Five leading researchers writing in the journal *Science* concluded, "The belief that high income is associated with good mood is widespread but mostly illusory. People with above-average income are relatively satisfied with their lives but are barely happier than others in moment-to-moment experience, tend to be more tense, and do not spend more time in particularly enjoyable activities."[4]

Good and bad employees are equally likely to think they deserve a raise.

Most employees are less than completely satisfied with the pay they are receiving.[5] This should not come as a shock, given people's desire to progress, ability to find things to buy, and awareness of their every sacrifice for their employers. But the real fly in the ointment is that when asked a pay question, the worst performers are not very objective. They are just as likely to say they should be paid more as the best employees. At one company, when employees were allowed to set their own salaries "it was a disaster: the good workers set them far too low, and the bad ones set them far too high," wrote the company's chief executive.[6]

In posing any question to its associates, a company sets up an expectation that it will do something about the results, an expectation that can backfire if the issue is not addressed. If you ask a friend whether he'd like to go to the baseball game with you, he's likely to not just say "Yes" but also "When do we leave?" If you ask whether someone is happy with her pay, she will likely not just say "No" but also "Where's my raise?" Although some employees in almost any company "deserve" an increase in pay, asking every employee his opinion neither identifies who should get a raise nor gives any useful information to company leaders.

Three professors ran into this problem in their 2001 study of one company's plan to "scientifically" revise its pay structure and to incorporate employee feedback in the process. Retained to help implement the new system, the researchers anticipated satisfaction with pay, its administration and its structure would increase. It didn't. "Neither the pay plan implementation nor the degree of participation in the process had an effect on the satisfaction measures," they wrote. The lack of effect was, they said, "somewhat puzzling given the presumed value of (the open, structured process) for enhancing pay satisfaction."[7] The presumption turned out to be wrong.

Some incentives can backfire, decreasing employee motivation.

When companies slice incentives into too many small pieces, they have the opposite of their intended effect. Paying for a small act communicates to the worker, "You wouldn't normally want to do this, so we're going to pay you to do it." While logically the reward should be a further inducement, it instead decreases motivation. What is meant as a bonus the mind unconsciously takes as a bribe. "When people are rewarded for doing an interesting activity, they are likely to attribute their behavior to the reward and thus discount their interest in the activity," wrote professors Edward L. Deci, Richard Koestner and Richard M. Ryan after analyzing 128 studies of how rewards influence behavior.[8]

When children are asked to collect money for a charity, those who receive a higher reward do, if fact, collect more than those offered a smaller incentive. But children whose only inducement is the knowledge they are doing something good for someone else collect more than either the high- or low-reward groups.[9] If a small payment is given to induce more blood donations, the number of people who show up at the blood bank is less than if there is no payment at all.[10] "The stipend turned a noble act of charity into a painful way to make a few dollars, and it wasn't worth it," wrote Steven Levitt and Stephen Dubner in their book, *Freakonomics*.[11] In the scientists' terminology, the piecemeal rewards "crowd out" the "intrinsic motivation" of the task itself. That joy of doing the work, separate from pay, is part of what makes the Third, Fourth, Eighth, and Twelfth elements so powerful.

Sales commissions and piecework pay are sometimes the best ways to hold people accountable. Pay-for-performance tactics can help keep workers' eyes on the goal and can even build engagement.[12] But when used as a catch-all strategy, paying for doing can just as often backfire. Managers who tack a dollar figure on all the overtly productive acts should not be surprised if employees lose the enjoyment of the job among all the chits and avoid doing anything for the company that does not have cash attached to it.[13]

Money without meaning is not enough compensation.

The most dramatic demonstration that work is not just about the money was an unintended consequence of a contract negotiated between General Motors and the United Auto Workers in 1984. With their contract up for renewal and auto workers nervous about automation, GM proposed an "employee-development bank" to train or find jobs for senior UAW workers displaced by technology or higher productivity.

In the back-and-forth of negotiations, the "Jobs Bank" grew to be a massive job guarantee program. It was not, however, a guarantee of being able to build cars. "The UAW told its workers their jobs were 'more secure than ever in history,'" wrote *The Wall Street Journal* in a 2006 front-page story on the program. "The UAW view, which continues to this day, was that the Jobs Bank would force GM and other auto makers to find work for union members because no company would keep paying people not to work."[14] But, as Detroit's sales declined, that's just what happened. Auto workers whose services are no longer needed, but whose salary is guaranteed under the Jobs Bank clause, could do volunteer work, could train for another job or they could just sit for a full workday in a space the workers call the "rubber room," a windowless storage shed with tables and chairs for 400 employees. To get full pay, employees didn't have to do anything except show up at 6 a.m. and stay until 2:45 p.m., with 45 minutes for lunch.

Even at his full pay of $64,500 a year, being in the room "makes you want to bang your head against the wall," Jerry Mellon, one of the UAW workers, told *The Journal*. "I couldn't take it. I need to be doing something." In search of greater meaning and to escape the rubber room, Mellon and many of his fellow union members ultimately opted to do volunteer work in return for their pay. If work had been just a means to the end of earning money, the rubber room would not have been such torture. Because it failed on every one of the 12 Elements even while paying full salaries, the Jobs Bank sapped the life from its participants.

Pay is more about status than about paying the bills.

Numerous studies show that a person's satisfaction with his pay is affected more by how much he out-earns those around him than by the absolute level of his pay. Assuming the purchasing power of a dollar is the same in the following two situations, which would you prefer? (A) Your yearly income is $50,000, while others earn $25,000 or (B) Your annual income is $100,000, while others earn $200,000? Given that choice, half the people will choose a lower absolute salary that puts them at the top of the heap.[15]

Columnist Toynbee argued that shining light on everyone's salary would lead to greater equality, "trust and social glue." Several pieces of evidence suggest just the opposite. Publicly traded companies in the United States are already required to report the compensation of their CEOs and the four other highest-paid executives in the business.[16] It may be that executive compensation has grown incredibly fast not in spite of the disclosures, but because of them, as corporate leaders fought for position on published lists of the highly compensated. If the goal of disclosures is restraint of executive pay, "history is not promising," wrote columnist Floyd Norris in *The New York Times*. "The rise in executive pay began after more disclosure was required and bosses could see what others were getting. Their standard of comparison went from what others in the company were getting to what other bosses got. And every boss deemed himself above average."[17]

Whole Foods Market touts the fact that it limits its CEO's compensation to 14 times its average worker's pay. In 2005, Chief Executive John Mackey received a salary and cash bonus of $436,000, just shy of 14 times the average worker's $32,000 salary. However, *Forbes* magazine reported, favorable coverage in the business press of the restricted range "omitted one thing: stock options." Mackey "made $1.8 million exercising stock options, and received another $460,000 because of a company error that allowed stock options to expire unexercised. The grand total: $2.7 million. Another $4.4 million of options have vested, so he can exercise them if he wants."[18]

As much as people like to think they are above it, status remains one of the most important organizing principles in any culture. "In a Stanford University study, groups of male college freshmen put in a room and given a problem to solve needed less than fifteen minutes to sort themselves into hierarchies," wrote Richard Conniff in *The Ape in the Corner Office.* "The appetite for rank and status is so intense that we seem to re-create the highly codified hierarchies of the playground wherever we go for the rest of our lives. We fret endlessly about who's got the best office, the biggest budget, the hottest BlackBerry, and other minutely calibrated workplace distinctions."[19] And, of course, who gets paid more.

This truth may have been best expressed in a 2005 "Dilbert" comic strip in which Wally negotiates his compensation with the boss. Wally states, "Research has shown that happiness is not related to one's absolute level of wealth. What matters is one's relative wealth compared to other people. So," he says to the boss, while pointing at Dilbert, "if I do a good job, could you cut this guy's pay?"[20]

Pay comparisons among employees spark intense emotions.

People are fascinated by what other people make. Like few other attributes, pay allows the rank ordering of individuals, an unvarnished display of where each stands in the hierarchy. Lists of moneymakers, whether *Forbes'* compilation of the richest people in the world or a local newspaper's list of CEO pay in the market, are always splashed on the cover.

Once a year, *Parade* magazine, the Sunday insert in many U.S. newspapers, publishes a special issue headlined, "What People Earn." It shows a sampling of salaries from stars and political leaders to everyday workers, a little financial voyeurism into data usually considered impolite or taboo at a lesser distance. One of the attractions of *Parade's* version is that, in finding the salaries of ordinary Joes and Janes, the reader can see who makes more or less than he does. It's one of the publication's best-read issues.[21]

When the comparisons are closer to home, such lists change from fascinating reading to potentially explosive information. *The Wall Street Journal* told the story of one woman who found on the office copier a document containing the performance ratings, base compensation, raises, and bonuses for 80 of her colleagues. She was "outraged that a noted screw-up was making $65,000 a year more than more competent colleagues, while some new hires were earning almost $200,000 more than their counterparts with more experience," said the story. "The discovery led her to question why she was working weekends for less pay than others were getting. 'I just couldn't stand the inequity of it,' she says. Three months later she quit."[22]

Vigilance against inequity is part of the Ninth Element: coworkers committed to doing quality work. Something about the way humans are wired makes them intensely angry to see someone getting disproportionately large rewards for sub-par effort. Most people are organically incapable of following advice to "mind your own business" and not weigh their reward-to-work ratio against those in the adjoining offices. A sense of justice or "inequality aversion" is one of the most basic and common emotions in humans and primate animals.[23] Shortly after they learn to speak, children have the ability to complain about inequities; "That's not fair!" is one of their first sentences. Even monkeys dole out rewards proportionate to the amount of work required of a compatriot.[24]

Many compensation managers have learned the hard way that the logical elegance of a new pay plan is no guarantee that the populace will not storm the castle with torches and pitchforks.

In most countries and companies, people consider their pay a private matter.

As much as people are fascinated by the rank order of compensation levels, and maybe because of the emotions behind that fascination, most are intensely private about it. Relative pay levels are often a touchy subject even between husbands and wives in dual-income families. "Money is the great taboo. People are more likely to reveal intimate secrets of their sex lives than ask someone what they earn," Toynbee wrote in her column before refusing to reveal her own pay. It's not unusual for companies to outlaw, on threat of termination, discussing one's own compensation with colleagues.

The reasons for these hang-ups are numerous. For those who make relatively little, having their salary broadcast is humiliating. For those who make top dollar, disclosing their pay invites challenges — "You're paying him how much?!" — that require justifications, all of which is disruptive to getting the work done. Publicizing individuals' pay is apt to start unproductive chattering, jockeying for position and disenchantment, no matter how well-reasoned the formula for reaching those figures. As much as human nature predisposes people for cooperation, instinct also spurs jealousy, conceit, and a discounting of others' accomplishments, making pay comparisons volatile. Like the lead characters in the movie *A Few Good Men*, one part of an employee says, "I want the truth" about the pay of his colleagues while another side of his nature "can't handle the truth."

While individual pay usually should not be public, compensation criteria should be.

While individual pay is usually best kept confidential, common knowledge of established salary criteria is important to feelings of fairness. Workers need to know, as one study found, "how pay plan goals are established, the pay plan goals themselves, how the plan goals are evaluated, and how the payouts are determined."[25] Only from such widely understood information can the workgroup have a belief in what social scientists call the "procedural and distributive justice" of the system. Without it, the organization is exposed to perceptions of favoritism, opportunism, or discrimination.

A hypothetical *Harvard Business Review* case study lists several of the disparities that can creep in over time: the new hires lured in with more money than veterans make, substantial salary differences between departments, and the higher salaries better negotiators gain over those who agitate less, to name a few. In the entertaining case study, a computer-savvy employee decides to punctuate her departure by e-mailing the salary file to the entire company, creating predictable angst.[26]

The question for decision-makers is how large of a riot would be sparked if all pay were public. If a company can honestly say that based on a common knowledge of how it calculates pay, most employees would not find huge surprises in such a leak, the business has this base covered.

Compensation works in concert with each of the 12 Elements.

Although Gallup typically does not ask about pay on employee censuses, the organization often fields a wage question in surveys of the general population, where chances of getting a more candid answer are improved by the fact that the survey is not commissioned by the respondent's employer. Even prompting respondents not to think self-ishly by prefacing the question with the phrase, "from my most objective viewpoint," few can strongly agree with the statement, "I am paid appropriately for the work I do." Yet within the less than exuberant responses, perceptions of pay are strongly colored by the 12 Elements. Paid the same amount, an engaged employee is happier with her pay than a disengaged worker.

The power of money is limited by itself. It works only in combination with all the non-financial drivers of employee engagement. "Any organization believing it can solve its attraction, retention, and motivation problems solely by its compensation system is probably not spending as much time and effort as it should on the work environment — on defining its jobs, on creating its culture, and on making work fun and meaningful," wrote Stanford business professor Jeffrey Pfeffer in the *Harvard Business Review.*[27]

Further evidence that work is not just about the money comes from the work of professors Leaf Van Boven and Thomas Gilovich, who designed two surveys and a laboratory experiment to determine whether life's experiences or one's possessions bring greater happiness. Experiences won out. In all three inquiries, respondents were more positive about what they did than what they had.

"Happiness is advanced more by allocating discretionary income toward the acquisition of life experiences than toward the acquisition of material possessions," they wrote. "'The good life,' in other words, may be better lived by doing things than by having things."[28] If spending money on experiences outside of work makes one happier than using the same money to accumulate more belongings, wouldn't it also make sense that foregoing some income for the experience of an engaging job makes one happier than working harder at a more frustrating job just to earn more money?

All the evidence agrees that a worker's actual compensation is composed of wages, benefits, and — just as important — the numerous psychological rewards of an engaging job.

Most employees who feel generously compensated repay the gesture.

One truth reemerges in various permutations throughout this book. It is that human behavior usually doesn't conform to the logical or mathematical assumptions behind many personnel strategies. This certainly holds true of the tug-of-war over an employee's salary.

The traditional view assumes that a company should pay as little as possible to secure someone's services, whether that amount is just a little more than a competitor would pay or the lowest amount for which the worker will settle in his salary negotiations. The often-overlooked flip-side of that strategy holds that the employee will do the minimum required to make his salary and his bonus. The company wants maximum work for minimum pay, while the employee wants just the reverse. Between these competing forces, the wage is settled, giving both sides a tolerable, antagonistic compromise.

But a funny thing happens in experiments where one person offers a wage and another person decides what level of effort to give in return. If the "employer" offers an above-market wage, the "employee" usually matches it with more effort, even when the worker can get away with doing less. "This suggests that on average people are willing to put forward extra effort above what is implied by purely pecuniary considerations," wrote researchers Ernst Fehr and Simon Gächter.[29] With conscientious, engaged employees, generosity of pay begets generosity of effort.

While money itself does not buy engagement, it appears an employee's perception that the company is aggressively looking out for his financial interest leads to productive reciprocation. More than just the money, the thought counts. The research points to a choice that executives must make. Do they want a workforce that thinks, "I have to fight for every extra dollar they begrudgingly pay me," or one that feels, "If I look out for my company, they will look out for me"?[30] Simple questions reveal where a company stands. If a talented employee does something extraordinary or repeatedly distinguishes herself, will it be her manager or the employee herself who initiates discussion of a raise? Does the company spend more to attract outside stars than to cultivate internal ones? Does the company realize its talent is underpaid only after a competitor woos them away?

In matters of pay, as with the 12 Elements, what employees enthusiastically do for the company depends heavily on what the company eagerly does for them.

What Great Managers Need

W E ARE OFTEN ASKED WHAT MAKES GREAT MANAGERS perform so well.

Some of it is pure talent — a natural ability to discern an employee's mindset, a persistent optimism, or a strategic acumen difficult to duplicate. Some of it is a deeply held personal mission to change the world for the better.

Much of it also requires that a front-line supervisor have the same experience with the 12 Elements as those he directs. One of the most fundamental needs of a great manager is . . . a great manager.

As obvious as that statement may be, there is an undercurrent running through many organizations that assumes recognition and praise, a mentor, clear expectations, and the rest of the 12 are required only for the front lines. The best managers, so this line of thinking goes, are more self-aware and self-contained, impervious to such forces, and able to maintain a steady course without much regard for the circumstances.

The evidence is just the opposite. The engagement of managers ebbs and flows just as much as it does for anyone else. Moreover, the engagement level of a manager correlates strongly with the attitudes of her team. No one is an island.

We were reminded of this fact most poignantly in the transcript of an interview with a high-performing manager identified through the database. His own supervisor, of whom he thought highly, left the company. He didn't know what to expect from the new supervisor. He no longer felt he had the resources he needed.

Try as he might to shield his own team from the problems with which he was wrestling, the group was increasingly unsettled. Some were blaming him, even questioning his honesty. As larger forces fought for control of various divisions within the company, the effect on the bread-and-butter workgroups was forgotten. "In their power play, we are suffering," he said. The story may sound familiar; the situation is common.

The anecdotes and, more important, analyses of manager performance point out that one of the best things a senior executive can do to motivate the entire population in a company is to first look out for the enterprise's supervisors. Before a person can deliver what he should as a manager, he must first receive what he needs as an employee.

A Final Note:

The Heart of Great Managing

"**O**UR PEOPLE ARE OUR GREATEST ASSET."

It is the strangest line in business today. No one knows who started it, but it proved to be so contagious that nearly every CEO says it at some point. It's a nice sentiment to work into a speech. It's comforting. It makes the executive seem more in touch, more humane.

But the statement has become a joke. Few companies have the kind of chief executive or culture that backs up the declaration, even though all the evidence says the statement is true. Hearing the line from a company leader who had no such personal convictions, one mid-level manager turned to his friend and said it reminded him of the apocryphal story of a children's radio show host who finished the broadcast and, not realizing the microphone was still on, said, "That oughta hold the little bastards!"

The same detachment showed up several years ago at the executive presentation of 12 Elements results for a Fortune 500 financial company. "Watch out for the CEO," a colleague warned the presenter. "He's going to go after you."

The presentation proceeded without incident until it reached a slide highlighting the huge spread of engagement levels within the company. "You have at the same time some of the most engaged and least engaged workgroups in the entire Gallup database," he said.

At that, the chief executive pounced. "What you just said means nothing!" he asserted. "Having some of the best and some of the worst has to be true of just about every company in the world."

The CEO was right. It is, in fact, not unusual for a large company to have its least engaged team at the 2nd or 3rd percentile, worse than all but a few percent of the worldwide scores. Nor is it unusual that a big organization's most committed team is more engaged than 99 out of 100 in that repository.

The presenter conceded the point and countered, "You're absolutely right. It happens all the time. But if I were to come in here and say you have some of the most profitable groups we'd ever seen and some of the biggest money-losers, would you say that's meaningless just because that also happens at other firms?"

"I get your point," said the business leader.

Somehow that point gets lost on many executives. The title of manager is too often doled out as a reward for tenure and connections, for solid performance that demonstrates no particular ability to deal with people, or as the sole path of progress in a company that does not know how to create highly valued non-managerial positions. Enterprises that wouldn't think of letting an accounting school dropout run its finances, a Luddite run IT, or a klutz supervise safety routinely let dislikable, insincere, or aloof men and women assume stewardship for a crew of the company's ostensibly greatest assets.

In a seminar Gallup conducted for a regional bank, the middle managers in attendance were asked to write a speech to a hypothetical group of honor students extolling the virtues of the company in hopes of attracting them to join. The speeches were what one would expect: boilerplate language about the prominence of the company, chances for advancement, and the generous benefits package. After the managers had delivered these addresses to their classmates, they were challenged with a question one of these honor students might ask: "If I join your bank, can you assure me I'll have a really good manager?" The room fell silent. They looked around and shrugged. For all the grand oration they just completed, these leaders had to admit they could not guarantee this most basic benefit to a new recruit.

Casually ask "Who's ripping off the company?" at an evening reception and you will get puzzled stares. "No one that I know of," they respond. Ask "Who in this company is a lousy manager?" and the stories just keep coming. Just as people will admit to being bad with math more than they will admit illiteracy, business tolerates interpersonal incompetence where it would never allow financial malfeasance. And yet, barring a few headline-making examples of high-level fraud, companies lose far more to employee disengagement than they lose to theft.

This relative negligence is the reason that while those companies actively working on employee engagement see appreciable increases, the overall trend in quality of work experience is flat. The proportion of engaged workers in the United States has ranged from 26 percent in 2000 to 31 percent in 2002, to 28 percent in 2005.[1] Levels of engagement appear to change dramatically not with macroeconomic swings, but only through better managers — and the aggregate quality of managers isn't improving. The same can be said for other countries Gallup has randomly sampled over the years. The national and global results indicate employee engagement is being destroyed in some places as fast as it is being improved in others. It's a real blind spot in the corporate world, a rare situation in which, never mind the moral considerations, executives aren't even being selfish very well. The failure to make work more invigorating has industry leaving a lot of money on the table. The cost of lost productivity due to disengagement, conservatively expressed, is $300 billion in the United States, 90 billion Euro in Germany and 3 billion SGD in Singapore, to name a few. The estimates are high for every country Gallup has studied.

Despite the flat aggregate trend, changes at the company level are often substantial and lasting. For the publicly traded organizations cited in the introduction who achieved top-quartile status in the Gallup database, and who realized superior earnings per share growth, it was typical to see dramatic change in engagement over time. Many of these organizations started with less than one-fourth of their workgroups in the top quartile of the engagement database. By the fifth year of holding managers accountable for the 12 Elements, it was not unusual to find 60 percent or more in the top quartile. In the space of just a few years, the ratio of engaged to actively disengaged employees had doubled as a result of managers' sincere efforts.

Ask the best how they excel on these dimensions and you get stories like the dozen we've told in the earlier chapters. But ask them why they do this, what motivates them, and you get the most non-financial of root causes for the string of ultimately profitable events.

"Oh, I love them to death," said one supervisor. "Honestly and truthfully, from the bottom of my heart, there's not anyone who works on my staff that I have any hard feelings with. I feel like if I had to go to battle for them, I would, and I'll stand beside them any day for any thing."

"People are more important than facts and figures," said Philippe Lescornez, the manager profiled in Chapter 11. "People are very important to my happiness; I could not be happy on my own."

"Well, they're like my family," said another manager. "I want them to be as happy working here as I am. I love my job, and I've worked here for 17 years. I've always wanted to be a store manager. And I want them to always come to work and be happy."

In our studies of hundreds of thousands of managers and work teams across the globe, it is very clear that great managers have an instinctive awareness that what they are doing is contributing more than profit. Great managers achieve sustained profitability because they make a connection to something beyond profit. They see the result of their work in the life of each person they manage.

Their impact transcends mere business. For many it is an almost spiritual issue, no matter their particular faith. Their motivation stems from deeply held beliefs about their responsibility to those around them. Whether they believe it is Providence or pure chance that puts them in the same office or factory with their team, these managers understand viscerally the scientific truth that what they do will have a large effect — maybe a lifelong effect — on their colleagues. They realize, given the percentage of waking time their teams spend at work, how much influence they have, not just over their people's "work life," but their whole life.

Most will tell you management is a solemn responsibility, something from which they take tremendous satisfaction, but it also weighs heavily on their consciences because they take it so seriously. With it, they say, rests not only the fiduciary responsibilities of protecting other people's money and striving for a good return, but a special kind of stewardship over people's lives. Employees say that both sides of the coin, the personal and the professional, depend on a manager who can give them the guidance, support, advocacy, and resources that motivate them to reciprocate with their best efforts.

"These are people's lives. I have an obligation," said Pete Wamsteeker, the manager profiled in Chapter 6. "I can't make mistakes with that. I really have an obligation to do it right, and I'm going to invest the time to do it right."

Therein lays the irony. The managers who are best at getting the most from people are those who give the most to them. Those who create the greatest financial performance start with the least pecuniary motivations. They work hard to do the right thing for their people, and they end up doing well.

That is the heart of great managing.

Source Notes

INTRODUCTION:

The Value of Employee Engagement

1   Peters, T. (2001, March). Leadership is as confusing as hell [Electronic version]. *Fast Company, 44*, 124-41.

2   Kent, S. (2005, September 6). Manager's journal: Happy workers are the best workers. *The Wall Street Journal*, A20.

3   These figures are based on Gallup's meta-analysis of 12 Elements data and the corresponding absenteeism data from all client firms that supplied such records.

4   Gallup scientists compared top-quartile business units to bottom-quartile units. Harter, J. K., Schmidt, F. L., Killham, E. A., & Asplund, J. W. (2006). Q^{12} *meta-analysis*. Omaha, NE: The Gallup Organization.

5   Ibid.

6   In addition to our own research and observation of turnover costs for organizations we have worked with, we reviewed the literature on estimates of turnover costs, including studies published by American Management Association, the Department of Labor, Corporate Executive Board, Aetna, Nobscot Corporation, and The Jack Phillips Center for Research.

7   Harter, J. K., Schmidt, F. L., Killham, E. A., & Asplund, J. W. (2006). Q^{12} *meta-analysis*. Omaha, NE: The Gallup Organization.

8   Ibid.

9   Ibid.

10 Harter, J. K., Schmidt, F. L., Killham, E. A., & Asplund, J. W. (2006). Q^{12} *meta-analysis*. Omaha, NE: The Gallup Organization.

11   Gallup scientists conducted an extensive study of the earnings per share trends of organizations in its database. Scientists collected 12 Elements responses, earnings per share, and competitor data for 36 organizations. 565,185 employees were surveyed, and earnings per share data collected for 263 competitors (7.3 per organization). Researchers compared the engagement levels of publicly traded organizations for which census engagement surveys were conducted (average 83% response rate). Eighteen top-quartile organizations averaged four engaged employees for every actively disengaged employee (the ratio doubled from 2001 to 2004). Their median EPS was 2.4% above the competition in 2001-2003 and improved to 18.0% above the competition in 2004-2005. Below-average organizations averaged one engaged employee for every actively disengaged employee. Their median EPS was 2.9% below the competition in 2001-2003 and improved to 3.1% above competition in 2004-2005 (the companies in the below-average engagement group also worked on improving engagement). The growth trend, relative to the competition, for top-quartile engagement organizations was 2.6 times that of the below-average organizations.

THE FIRST ELEMENT:
Knowing What's Expected

1   Smith, A. (1994). *The wealth of nations*. (E. Cannan, Ed.). New York: Modern Library.

2   Employees are asked to rate themselves on a one-to-five scale where one is "strongly disagree" and five is "strongly agree."

3   Hatch, M. J. (1999, Winter). Exploring the empty spaces of organizing: How improvisational jazz helps redescribe organizational structure. *Organization Studies*, 20(1), 75-100.

4   *Carrier at war* [Television broadcast]. (2002, January 26). Atlanta, GA: Cable News Network.

5   Rossiter, M. (Producer). (1997, January 7). *Aircraft carrier* [Television broadcast]. Boston: WGBH.

6   Rochlin, G. I., LaPorte, T. R., & Roberts, K. H. (1987). The self-designing high-reliability organization: Aircraft carrier flight operations at sea. *Naval War College Review* 40(4), 76-90.

7   Frantom, T. (2005, June). Earning yellow. *All hands*. Retrieved May 15, 2006, from www.news.navy.mil/media/allhands/flash/ah200506/feature_2/

8   Roberts, K. H., Rousseau, D. M., & La Porte, T. R. (1994). The culture of high reliability: Quantitative and qualitative assessment aboard nuclear-powered aircraft carriers. *The Journal of High Technology Management Research*, 5(1), 141-161.

9   United States Navy. (n.d.). *Rainbow wardrobe: A guide to the color-coded jerseys on an aircraft carrier*. Retrieved May 20, 2006, from http://www.navy.mil/palib/ships/carriers/rainbow.html

10   Frantom, T. (2005, June). Earning yellow. *All hands*. Retrieved May 15, 2006, from www.news.navy.mil/media/allhands/flash/ah200506/feature_2/

11   Pool, R. (1997, July). When failure is not an option [Electronic version]. *Technology Review*, 100(5), 38-45.

12   The "chemistry sport" term is from Joe Soucheray, columnist for the St. Paul, MN, *Pioneer Press* and commentator on radio station KSTP-AM.

13   Berman, S. L., Down, J., & Hill, C. W. L. (2002). Tacit knowledge as a source of competitive advantage in the National Basketball Association. *Academy of Management Journal*, 45(1), 13-31.

14   Ibid.

15   Huckman, R. S., & Pisano, G. P. (2006, April). The firm specificity of individual performance: Evidence from cardiac surgery. *Management Science*, 52(4), 473-488.

16   Ibid.

17   Ibid.

18   Analyses conducted across 152 hospitals reporting mortality and complication statistics within Gallup's employee engagement database. 2002 engagement was compared to 2003 mortality and complication statistics. Mortality and complication indices were calculated as a ratio of actual to expected rates (based on type of disease and risk) for each hospital.

The Second Element:
Materials and Equipment

1   Muschamp, H. (1994, October 16). It's a mad mad mad ad world. *The New York Times*, Section 6, p. 64.

2   Ibid.

3   Malmo, J. (1995, March 5). Ad man reinvents the office: No desks. *The (Memphis) Commercial Appeal*, p. 2C.

4   Muschamp, H. (1994, October 16). It's a mad mad mad ad world. *The New York Times*, Section 6, p. 64.

5   Berger, W. (1999, February). Lost in space. *Wired*, 7(2), 76-81.

6   Ibid.

7   Ibid.

8   In addition to having personal space, being able to "personalize that space to make it your own" explained differences in engagement. Gallup Workplace Poll, based on telephone interviews with a nationally representative sample of 1,002 employed adults, aged 18 and older, conducted in October 2005. *For results based on the total sample of employed adults, one can say with 95% confidence that the maximum error attributable to sampling and other random effects is ±3 percentage points.*
    See also Krueger, J., & Killham, E. (2006, March). Why Dilbert is right: Uncomfortable work environments make for disgruntled employees – just like the cartoon says. *Gallup Management Journal*. Retrieved July 20, 2006, from http://gmj.gallup.com/content/default.aspx?ci=21802&pg=1

9   Pinker, S. (1997). *How the mind works*. New York: W.W. Norton.

10 Ibid.

11 Carr, C. (2003, August 3). Cue the stapler! [Electronic version]. *Time*, *162*(6), p. A12. Retrieved May 25, 2006, from http://www.time.com/time/insidebiz/article/0,9171,1101030811-472856,00.html

12 Spotlight reviews: Office Space – special edition with flair (widescreen edition) (1999). Retrieved May 26, 2006, from http://www.amazon.com/gp/product/B000AP04L0/102-3514557-8664915?v=glance&n=130&n=507846&s=dvd&v=glance

13 Schlotz, W., Hellhammer, J., Schulz, P, & Stone, A. A. (2004, March/April). Perceived work overload and chronic worrying predict weekend-weekday differences in the cortisol awakening response. *Psychosomatic Medicine*, *66*(2), 207-214.

14 Pratt, M. G., & Ashforth, B. E. (2003). Fostering meaningfulness in working and at work. In K. S. Cameron, J. E. Dutton, & R. E. Quinn (Eds.), *Positive organizational scholarship* (pp. 309-327). San Francisco: Berrett-Koehler.

15 From Gallup Workplace Polls in the United States (October 2005, n=1,002), Brazil (December 2004, n=1,000), Canada (December 2004, n=1,006), and Japan (February, 2005, n=1,000). Gallup obtained random samples of the working population in each country for workers aged 18 and older. Respondents were asked whether stress at work has caused them to behave poorly with friends or family three or more times in the last 30 days.

16 Based on analysis of Gallup's International Employee Engagement Database of 4.8 million workers from 2003 to 2005.

17 From The Gallup Organization's Employee Engagement Business Impact Database. Percentage difference varies by organization, depending on its base level of employee turnover. Based on analysis of Second Element scores and turnover across organizations in Gallup's database.

The Third Element:

The Opportunity to Do What I Do Best

1   Slate, J. H. (2004, December 27). Tree power. *The Llewellyn Journal*. Retrieved May 30, 2006, from http://www.llewellynjournal.com/article/748

2   Christopher, J. Y. (1994). Swept away. On *Yanni: Live at the Acropolis* [CD]. Los Angeles: Private Music.

3   Pinker, S. (2002). *The blank slate: The modern denial of human nature.* New York: Viking Penguin.

4   Vonnegut, K. (1998). Harrison Bergeron. In *Welcome to the monkey house.* New York: Delta.

5   National Basketball Association. (n.d.). *2004-2005 NBA player survey results.* Retrieved May 31, 2006, from http://www.nba.com/news/survey_height_2004.html

6   United States Department of Health and Human Services. (2004, October 27). *Mean body weight, height, and body mass index, United States 1960-2002* (Advance data from vital and health statistics No. 347).

7   Witelson, S. F., Kigar, D. L., & Harvey, T. (1999, June 19). The exceptional brain of Albert Einstein. *The Lancet, 353*(9170) 2149-2153.

8   Pinker, S. (2002). *The blank slate: The modern denial of human nature.* New York: Viking Penguin.

9   Segal, N. L. (1999, September/October). New twin studies show … the career of your dreams may be the career of your genes. *Psychology Today, 32*(5), 54-58, 69-70. See also: Bouchard, T. J. Jr., Lykken, D. T., McGue, M., Segal, N. L., & Tellegen, A. (1990, October 12). Sources of human psychological differences: the Minnesota Study of twins reared apart, *Science, 250*(4978), 223-228 and Bouchard, T. J. Jr. (1997). Genetic influence on mental abilities, personality, vocational interests, and work attitudes. *International Review of Industrial and Organizational Psychology, 12*, 373-395.

10   Pinker, S. (2002). *The blank slate: The modern denial of human nature.* New York: Viking Penguin.

11   Based on hundreds of studies of tens of thousands of employees. See: Schmidt, F. L., & Hunter, J. E. (1998). The validity and utility of selection methods in personnel psychology: Practical and theoretical implications of 85 years of research findings. *Psychological Bulletin, 124*(2), 262-274.
Schmidt, F. L. & Rader, M. (1999). Exploring the boundary conditions for interview validity: Meta-analytic validity findings for a new interview type. *Personnel Psychology, 52*, 445-464.
McDaniel, M. A., Whetzel, D. L., Schmidt, F. L., & Maurer, S. D. (1994, August). The validity of employment interviews: A comprehensive review and meta-analysis. *Journal of Applied Psychology, 79*(4), 599-616.
Harter, J. K., Hayes, T. L., & Schmidt, F. L. (2004). *Meta-analytic predictive validity of Gallup Selection Research Instruments.* Omaha, NE: The Gallup Organization.

12   Gallup Workplace Poll, based on interviews with 1,003 workers, aged 18 and older, conducted October 2003. Based on questions asked of a subsample of employees who make hiring decisions. For results based on the total sample of workers, one can say with 95% confidence that the maximum margin of sampling error is ±3 percentage points.

13   Ibid. Managers rated personality characteristics such as responsibility, ability to take initiative, persistence, open-mindedness, and self confidence as extremely important to their hiring decisions. Yet, only 30% indicated they are more likely to use structured interviews or tests (which are more likely to reliably assess these desired characteristics and predict future performance) than informal interviews to assess candidates. See also Schmidt & Hunter (1998), Schmidt & Rader, (1999), and Harter, Hayes, & Schmidt (2004) for reference to the reliability & validity of structured interviews and tests to assess candidates prior to hiring.

14   Orwell, G. (2005). *Why I write.* New York: Penguin Books.

15   Csikszentmihalyi, M. (1990). *Flow: The psychology of optimal experience*. New York: HarperCollins.

16   Harvey-Jones, J. (1988). *Making it happen: Reflections on leadership*. London: Collins.

17   Clifton, D. O., & Harter, J. K. (2003). Investing in strengths. In K. S. Cameron, J. E. Dutton, & R. E. Quinn (Eds.), *Positive organizational scholarship: Foundations of a new discipline* (pp. 111-121). San Francisco: Berrett-Koehler.

18   Ibid.

19   Krueger, J. (2004, November). How Marriott Vacation Club International engages talent. *Gallup Management Journal*. Retrieved July 18, 2006, from http://gmj.gallup.com/content/default.aspx?ci=13960&pg=1

20   From The Gallup Organization's Employee Engagement Business Impact Database. Based on analysis of top- and bottom-quartile business units on Third Element scores and their profit as a percentage of revenue.

21   Juszkiewicz, P. J., Arora, R., & Harter, J. K. (2004). *Utility analysis of Gallup SRI instruments*. Omaha, NE: The Gallup Organization. Selecting the top 20% of potential manager candidates on their "talents" results in substantial gains in performance.

THE FOURTH ELEMENT:
Recognition and Praise

1   Gallup World Poll, based on interviews in Poland (n=1,000) and throughout the world (N=34,545) with respondents aged 15 and older, conducted in April 2006. For results based on the total sample of respondents, one can say with 95% confidence that the maximum margin of sampling error (per country) is ±3 percentage points.

2   Gallup Workplace Poll, based on interviews with 1,002 workers, aged 18 and older, conducted in October 2005. For results based on the total sample of workers, one can say with 95% confidence that the maximum margin of sampling error is ±3 percentage points.

3   Based on analysis from The Gallup Organization's Employee Engagement Business Impact Database. Comparison of top and bottom quartiles on Fourth Element scores for business units in Gallup's database.

4   From The Gallup Organization's Employee Engagement Business Impact Database. Based on analysis of Fourth Element scores, productivity, and customer engagement across organizations in Gallup's database.

5   This incident was instigated by co-author Wagner twice in his academic career. This appears to be a somewhat common school prank. Author Aubrey C. Daniels relates in *Other people's habits: How to use positive reinforcement to bring out the best in people around you* (New York: McGraw-Hill, 2001), pp. 19-20, how the technique was used on him by an audience at Blue Cross and Blue Shield of Alabama. A guide to the experiment, entitled "Train Your Teacher," was posted on the Web site of the Worsley School in Worsley, Alberta, Canada (http://www.worsleyschool.net/fun/train/yourteacher.html).

6   Koepp, M. J., et al. (1998, May 21). Evidence for striatal dopamine release during a video game. *Nature (393)*, 266-268.

7   The studies are summarized and cited in May, C., et al. (2004). Event-related functional magnetic resonance imaging of reward-related brain circuitry in children and adolescents. *Biological Psychiatry, 55*(4), 359-366.

8   Nash, J. M. (1997, May 5). Addicted: Why do people get hooked? Mounting evidence points to a powerful brain chemical called dopamine. *Time, 149*(18), 68-76.

9   Hamann, S. & Mao, H. (2002, January 21). Positive and negative emotional verbal stimuli elicit activity in the left amygdala. *Neuroreport 13*(1), 15-19.

10 Nash, J. M. (1997, May 5). Addicted: Why do people get hooked? Mounting evidence points to a powerful brain chemical called dopamine. *Time, 149*(18), 68-76.

11 McClure, S. M., York, M. K., & Montague, P. R. (2004). The neural substrates of reward processing in humans: The modern role of fMRI. *Neuroscientist, 10*(3), 260-268.

12 Frank, M. J., Seeberger, L. C., & O'Reilly, R. C. (2004, November 4). By carrot or by stick: Cognitive reinforcement learning in Parkinsonism. *Science Express*, 1-5.

13 Gottman, J. M. (1994). What predicts divorce? The relationship between marital processes and marital outcomes. Hillsdale, N.J.: Lawrence Erlbaum.

14 Losada, M. F., & Heaphy, E. (2004). The role of positivity and connectivity in the performance of business teams: A nonlinear dynamics model. *American Behavioral Scientist, 47*(6), 740-765.

15 McClure, S. M., Berns, G. S., & Montague, P. R. (2003, April 24). Temporal prediction errors in a passive learning task activate human striatum. *Neuron, 38*(2), p. 339-346.

16 Simpson, J. B. (1988). *Simpson's contemporary quotations*. New York: Houghton Mifflin.

17 Kahneman, D., Knetsch, J., & Thaler, R. (1990). Experimental tests of the endowment effect and the Coase theorem. *Journal of Political Economy, 98*(6), 1325-1348.

18 Kahneman, D., & Tversky, A. (Eds.). (2000). *Choices, values, and frames*. Cambridge: Cambridge University Press.

19 A recent example is outlined in Carroll, J., and Newport, F. (2004, September 21). *Reasons why people are voting for Bush or Kerry: Bush voters satisfied with his performance; Kerry voters want Bush's ouster*. Retrieved July 18, 2006, from http://poll.gallup.com/content/default.aspx?ci=13096&pg=1

20 Eastwood, J. D., Smilek, D., & Merikle, P. M. (2001). Differential attentional guidance by unattended faces expressing positive and negative emotion. *Perception & Psychophysics*, *63*(6), 1004-1013. See also Hansen, C. H., & Hansen R.D. (1988). Finding the face in the crowd: An anger superiority effect. *Journal of Personality and Social Psychology*, *54*(6), 917-924.

21 Smith, N. K., Cacioppo, J. T., Larsen, J. T., & Chartrand, T. L. (2003). May I have your attention, please: Electrocortical responses to positive and negative stimuli. *Neuropsychologia*, *41*, 171-183.

22 Gallup Workplace Poll, based on interviews with 1,002 workers, aged 18 and older, conducted in October 2005. For results based on the total sample of workers, one can say with 95% confidence that the maximum margin of sampling error is ±3 percentage points.

23 Seligman, M. E. P., Steen, T. A., Park, N., & Peterson, C. (2005, July-August). Positive psychology progress: Empirical validation of interventions. *American Psychologist*, *60*(5), 410-421.

THE FIFTH ELEMENT:
Someone at Work Cares About Me as a Person

1   Greene, J. D., Sommerville, R. B., Nystrom, L. E., Darley, J. M., & Cohen, J. D. (2001, September 14). An fMRI investigation of emotional engagement in moral judgment. *Science, 293,* 2105-2108.

2   Conniff, R. (2005). *The ape in the corner office: Understanding the workplace beast in all of us.* New York: Crown Business.

3   Milgram, S. (1974). *Obedience to authority.* New York: HarperCollins.

4   Charness, G., & Gneezy, U. (2003, August 16). *What's in a name? Anonymity and social distance in dictator and ultimatum games.* Retrieved July 18, 2006, from http://papers.ssrn.com/sol3/papers.cfm?abstract_id=292857

5   Nagin, D., Rebitzer, J. B., Sanders, S. G., & Taylor, L. J. (2002, September). Monitoring, motivation, and management: The determinants of opportunistic behavior in a field experiment. *American Economic Review, 92*(4), 850-873.

6   Harter, J. K., Schmidt, F. L., Killham, E. A., & Asplund, J. W. (2006). Q^{12} *meta-analysis.* Omaha, NE: The Gallup Organization.

7   Jones, J. R., & Harter, J. K. (2005). Race effects on the employee engagement-turnover intention relationship. *Journal of Leadership and Organizational Studies, 11*(2), 78-88.

8   1 Corinthians 12:25b-26, King James Version.

9   *The Teachings of Buddha.* (2004). Tokyo: Bukkyo Dendo Kyokai.

10 Ridley, M. (1996). *The origins of virtue: human instincts and the evolution of cooperation.* New York: Penguin Books.

11 Laskin, D. (2004). *The children's blizzard.* New York: HarperCollins.

12 Engagement at work is more highly related to company loyalty than is stock ownership. From Gallup Workplace Polls, based on interviews with 1,009 and 1,003 workers, aged 18 and older, conducted in February 2002 and April 2004, respectively. For results based on the total sample of workers, one can say with 95% confidence that the maximum margin of sampling error is ±3 percentage points.

13 Sandberg, J. (2006, February 28). Hiring by school tie happens all the time, but is it a good idea? *The Wall Street Journal,* p. B1.

14 Jones, J. R., & Harter, J. K. (2005). Race effects on the employee engagement-turnover intention relationship. *Journal of Leadership and Organizational Studies, 11*(2), 78-88.

15 Cohen, D., & Prusak, L. (2001). *In good company: How social capital makes organizations work.* Boston: Harvard Business School Press.

THE SIXTH ELEMENT:
Someone at Work Encourages My Development

1   Homer. (1946). *The odyssey* (E. V. Rieu, Trans.). London: Penguin Books.
2   Riley, P. (1994). *Fénelon: Telemachus.* Cambridge: Cambridge University Press. Mentor is a minor character in Homer's *Odyssey*. The fact that Mentor's name became an eponymous term for advisors is largely attributable to François de Salignac de La Mothe-Fénelon's 1699 sequel, *Les Aventures de Télémaque*, the most reprinted book of the 18th century.
3   Blakeslee, S. (2006, January 10). Cells that read minds. *The New York Times*, January 10, 2006, p. F1.
4   Dobbs, D. (2006, April/May). A revealing reflection. *Scientific American Mind, 17*(2), 22-27.
5   Ibid.
6   Blakeslee, S. (2006, January 10). Cells that read minds. *The New York Times*, January 10, 2006, p. F1.
7   Analysis of Gallup Workplace Poll, based on telephone interviews with a nationally representative sample of 1,002 employed adults, aged 18 and older, conducted in October 2005. *For results based on the total sample of employed adults, one can say with 95% confidence that the maximum error attributable to sampling and other random effects is ±3 percentage points.*
8   Nickols, F. (2002). *Mentor, mentors, and mentoring.* Retrieved July 21, 2006, from http://home.att.net/~nickols/mentor.htm
9   Cohen, D., & Prusak, L. (2001). *In good company: How social capital makes organizations work.* Boston: Harvard Business School Press.
10 Jones, D. (2005, June 20). It's not just lonely at the top; it can be "disengaging," too. *USA Today.* Retrieved July 21, 2006, from http://www.usatoday.com/money/companies/management/2005-06-20-bummed-execs_x.htm. As a general pattern, engagement is higher for those with higher status in organizations (for senior management, and middle management). But the gap between management and non-management is substantially narrower on this element.
11 Findings based on a Gallup study of 59 organizations.
12 Allen, T. D., McManus, S. E., & Russell, J. E. A. (1999). Newcomer socialization and stress: Formal peer relationships as a source of support. *Journal of Vocational Behavior, 54*, 453-470.
13 Cohen, D., & Prusak, L. (2001). *In good company: How social capital makes organizations work.* Boston: Harvard Business School Press.
14 Lockwood, P., & Kunda, Z. (1997). Superstars and me: Predicting the impact of role models on the self. *Journal of Personality and Social Psychology, 73*(1), 91-103.
15 Muoio, A. (1998, May). My greatest lesson. *Fast Company*, p. 83. Retrieved July 21, 2006, from http://www.fastcompany.com/magazine/15/one.html?partner=rss
16 Kram, K. E. (1983). Phases of the mentor relationship. *Academy of Management Journal, 26*, 608-625.

The Seventh Element:
My Opinions Seem to Count

1   The Hospital for Sick Children. (2005). *Reasons to believe: The Hospital for Sick Children annual report 2004-2005.* Retrieved June 5, 2006, from http://www.sickkids.ca/annualreport2004_2005/AR0405.pdf

2   Adam, E. E. Jr., and Ebert, R. J. (1989). *Production and operations management: Concepts, models, and behavior* (4th ed.). New York: Prentice Hall.

3   Taylor, F. W. (1911). *The principles of scientific management.* [Electronic version]. New York: Harper Brothers. Retrieved July 19, 2006, from http://www.eldritchpress.org/fwt/ti.html

4   Kanigel, R. (1997). *The one best way: Fredrick Winslow Taylor and the enigma of efficiency.* New York: Penguin Books.

5   Taylor, F. W. (1911). *The principles of scientific management.* [Electronic version]. New York: Harper Brothers. Retrieved July 19, 2006, from http://www.eldritchpress.org/fwt/ti.html

6   Kanigel, R. (1997). *The one best way: Fredrick Winslow Taylor and the enigma of efficiency.* New York: Penguin Books.

7   Taylor, F. W. (1911). *The principles of scientific management.* [Electronic version]. New York: Harper Brothers. Retrieved July 19, 2006, from http://www.eldritchpress.org/fwt/ti.html

8   Kanigel, R. (1997). *The one best way: Fredrick Winslow Taylor and the enigma of efficiency.* New York: Penguin Books.

9   Taylor, F. W. (1911). *The principles of scientific management.* [Electronic version]. New York: Harper Brothers. Retrieved July 19, 2006, from http://www.eldritchpress.org/fwt/ti.html

10   Ibid.

11   Kanigel, R. (1997). *The one best way: Fredrick Winslow Taylor and the enigma of efficiency.* New York: Penguin Books.

12   The incident occurred on Northwest Airlines flight 122 from Minneapolis to Chicago on June 8, 2000. The passenger was co-author Wagner.

13   Northwest Airlines 1999 annual report. Retrieved July 18, 2006, from http://media.corporate-ir.net/media_files/irol/11/111021/reports/Financial_an99.pdf

14   McEwen, W. J., & Fleming, J. H. (2001, October). Stress resistant customer relationships: How smart asset management can boost your stock payoff. *Gallup Management Journal.* Retrieved July 20, 2006, from http://gmj.gallup.com/content/default.aspx?ci=172 See also McEwen, W. J. (2004, May). Skirmish in the skies. *Gallup Management Journal.* Retrieved July 18, 2006, from http://gmj.gallup.com/content/default.asp?ci=11530

15   From The Gallup Organization's Employee Engagement Business Impact Database. Based on analysis of Seventh Element scores and profitability across organizations in Gallup's database.

16   Based on analyses of Gallup Workplace Polls from 2001-2005.

17   Jones, D. C., & Kato, T. (2005, May). *The effects of employee involvement on firm performance: Evidence from an econometric case study* (Working Paper No. 612). Kalamazoo, MI: William Davidson Institute.

18   Ibid.

19   Ibid.

20   Ibid.

THE EIGHTH ELEMENT:
A Connection With the Mission of the Company

1   From The Gallup Organization's Employee Engagement Business Impact Database.
    Based on analysis of Eighth Element scores and business-unit outcomes across
    organizations in Gallup's database.

2   Gallup Workplace Poll, based on interviews with 1,001 workers, aged 18 and older,
    conducted in May 2001. For results based on the total sample of workers, one can say
    with 95% confidence that the maximum margin of sampling error is ±3 percentage
    points.

3   Burrell, B. *The words we live by: The creeds, mottoes, and pledges that have shaped America.*
    New York: Free Press, 1997.

4   Wells' Dairy, Inc. (n.d.). *The big scoop on Blue Bunny.* Retrieved July 19, 2006, from http://
    www.bluebunny.com/About.aspx

5   Lowe's. (n.d.). *Company info: Our heritage.* Retrieved July 19, 2006, from http://
    www.lowes.com/lowes/lkn?action=frameSet&url=lowes.mediaroom.com/index.
    php?s=company_overview

6   Kodak. (n.d.). *About Kodak.* Retrieved July 19, 2006, from http://www.kodak.com/US/
    en/corp/about_Kodak.jhtml?pq-path=2217

7   Kellogg Co. (n.d.). *Our brands.* Retrieved July 19, 2006, from http://www.
    kelloggcompany.com/brands.aspx?id=50&terms=&searchtype=2&fragment=True

8   Siam Commercial Bank. (n.d.). *Legend of SCB.* Retrieved July 19, 2006, from http://www.
    scb.co.th/html/eng/about_legend.shtml

9   Csikszentmihalyi, M. (1990). *Flow: The psychology of optimal experience.* New York:
    HarperCollins.

10 Wrzesniewski, Amy. (2003). Finding positive meaning in work. In K. S. Cameron, J. E.
    Dutton, & R. E. Quinn (Eds.), *Positive organizational scholarship: Foundations of a new
    discipline* (pp. 296-308). San Francisco: Berrett-Koehler.

11 Gallup Poll, based on interviews with a random sample of 1,657 United States residents,
    aged 18 and older, conducted November 15-18, 1990. *For results based on the total sample,
    one can say with 95% confidence that the maximum error attributable to sampling and other
    random effects is ±2 percentage points.*

12 In a Gallup World Poll conducted across 43 countries in Europe, Asia, the Middle
    East, Central and South America, Africa, and North America (n=48,635), 84% said
    they feel their lives have an important purpose or meaning. Those who didn't feel this
    purpose in their lives reported lower well-being and worse health. See also Pratt, M.
    G., and Ashforth, B. E. (2003). Fostering meaningfulness in working and at work. In
    K. S. Cameron, J. E. Dutton, & R. E. Quinn (Eds.), *Positive organizational scholarship:
    Foundations of a new discipline* (pp. 309-327), citing Baumeister, 1991; Dunn, 1996; Ryff &
    Singer, 1998a, 1998b; and Treadgold, 1999.

13 Koerner, M. M. (1994). *Sacredness in service exchanges with medically underserved patients.*
    Paper presented at the annual conference of the American Association for Advances in
    Health Care Research.

14 Ibid.

15 Based on 4.8 million workers studied from 2003 to 2005, including 1.1 million hospital
    workers.

16 Chrismer, B., & Thompson, M. (2005, September/October). Getting plugged in.
    Consulting, 7(5), 38-42.

17 There are three kinds of dirty work typically discussed: that which is 1) physically
    disgusting, 2) a symbol of degradation and 3) morally questionable. Employee
    engagement and inspiration from a company's mission are properly applied only to
    the first two categories, where one can say it's a tough job, but someone has to do it.
    Morally questionable work usually is not an essential function. In this third case, we
    believe society's disapproval is often a sign that the job simply should not exist.

18 Jarman, M. (1998, July 25). Dedicated employees find worth in "dirty" work, study
    shows. *The Dallas Morning News*, p. 1F.

19 Crabtree, S. (1999, March 14). Dirty work. *The Eagle-Tribune* (North Andover, MA), p. F1.

20 Fields, G. (2005, November 2). Bulging jails and tight budgets make job of guard even tougher. *The Wall Street Journal*, p. A1.

21 Pratt, M. G., and Ashforth, B. E. (2003). Fostering meaningfulness in working and at work. In K. S. Cameron, J. E. Dutton, & R. E. Quinn (Eds.), *Positive organizational scholarship: Foundations of a new discipline* (pp. 309-327).

22 Wrzesniewski, Amy. (2003). Finding positive meaning in work. In K. S. Cameron, J. E. Dutton, & R. E. Quinn (Eds.), *Positive organizational scholarship: Foundations of a new discipline* (pp. 296-308). San Francisco: Berrett-Koehler.

23 Ibid.

24 Ibid.

25 Ibid.

26 Badal, S. (2004, December). Cascade effect: The impact of executives and managers on the overall company engagement. Unpublished manuscript, The Gallup Organization, Omaha, NE.

THE NINTH ELEMENT:
Coworkers Committed to Doing Quality Work

1   Ingham, A. G., Levinger, G., Graves, J., & Peckham, V. (1974). The Ringelmann effect: Studies of group size and group performance. *Journal of Experimental Social Psychology*, *10*, 371-384. See also Kravitz, D. A., & Martin, B. (1986). Ringelmann rediscovered: The original article. *Journal of Personality and Social Psychology*, *50*, 936-941.

2   Robbins, S. P. (1996). *Organizational behavior: Concepts, controversies, applications* (7th ed.). Englewood Cliffs, N.J.: Prentice-Hall.

3   McCullough, D. (2005). *1776*. New York: Simon & Schuster.

4   Ibid.

5   Kahan, D. M. (2005). The logic of reciprocity: Trust, collective action, and law. In H. Gintis, S. Bowles, R. Boyd, & E. Fehr (Eds.), *Moral sentiments and material interests: The foundations of cooperation in economic life* (pp. 339-378). Cambridge, Mass.: MIT Press.

6   Ibid.

7   Gallup Workplace Poll, based on interviews with 1,002 workers, aged 18 and older, conducted in October 2005. For results based on the total sample of workers, one can say with 95% confidence that the maximum margin of sampling error is ±3 percentage points.

8   Gallup scientists compared top-quartile to bottom-quartile branch offices on Ninth Element scores.

9   Gallup scientists compared top-quartile to bottom-quartile teams on Ninth Element scores.

10 Fehr, E., & Gächter, S. (2000, September). Cooperation and Punishment in Public Goods Experiments. *The American Economic Review*, *90*(4), 980-994.

11 de Quervain, D. J. F., Fischbacher, U., Treyer, V., Schellhammer, M., Schnyder, U., Buck, A., et al. (2004, August 27). The Neural Basis of Altruistic Punishment. *Science*, *305*, 1254-1258.

12 Fehr, E., & Gächter, S. (2000, September). Cooperation and Punishment in Public Goods Experiments. *The American Economic Review*, *90*(4), 980-994.

13 Ibid.

14 Oakley, B. (n.d.). *It takes two to tango: How "good" students enable problematic behavior in teams*. Retrieved July 19, 2006, from http://72.14.203.104/search?q=cache:zSxA5L-vr6UJ:www2.oakland.edu/users/oakley/Papers/It%2520Takes%2520Two%2520to%2520Tango.doc+%22set+your+limits+early+and+high%22&hl=en&gl=us&ct=clnk&cd=9

15 Kahan, D. M. (2005). The logic of reciprocity: Trust, collective action, and law. In H. Gintis, S. Bowles, R. Boyd, & E. Fehr (Eds.), *Moral sentiments and material interests: The foundations of cooperation in economic life* (pp. 339-378). Cambridge, Mass.: MIT Press.

16 Gallup Workplace Poll, based on interviews with 1,002 workers, aged 18 and older, conducted in October 2005. For results based on the total sample of workers, one can say with 95% confidence that the maximum margin of sampling error is ±3 percentage points.

The Tenth Element:
A Best Friend at Work

1 Joyce, A. (2004, May 9). A workplace without friends is an enemy: Gallup says buddies are a sign of office health. *The Washington Post*, p. F6.

2 Thottam, J. (2005, January 17). Thank God it's Monday! *Time, 165*(3), A58-A61.

3 Buchholz, B. B. (2001, December 26). Friendly reminder: When a coworker or boss is a pal, problems can arise. *Chicago Tribune*, page C1.

4 Glaeser, E. L., Laibson, D., Scheinkman, J. A., & Soutter, C. L. (1999, July). *What is social capital? The determinants of trust and trustworthiness* (Working Paper 7216). Cambridge, MA: National Bureau of Economic Research.

5 Shellenbarger, S. (2000, January 15). Friendships an overlooked toll of job upheavals. *The Ottawa Citizen*, p. I1.

6 From The Gallup Organization's Employee Engagement Business Impact Database. Based on analysis of Tenth Element scores and business-unit outcomes across organizations in Gallup's database.

7 From The Gallup Organization's Employee Engagement Business Impact Database. Comparison of top- and bottom-quartile work units on Tenth Element scores across organizations in Gallup's database.

8 From The Gallup Organization's Employee Engagement Business Impact Database. Based on analysis of Tenth Element scores and business-unit outcomes across organizations in Gallup's database.

9 Putnam, R. D. (2000). *Bowling alone*. New York: Simon & Schuster. Putnam's conclusions are based on his analyses of four major multi-decade studies of social attitudes.

10 McPherson, M., Smith-Lovin, L., & Brashears, M. E. (2006, June). Social isolation in America: Changes in core discussion networks over two decades. *American Sociological Review, 71*, 353-375.

11 Kunstler, J. H. (1993). *The geography of nowhere: The rise and decline of America's man-made landscape*. New York: Simon & Schuster (as cited in Robinson, J. P., & Godbey, G. (1997). *Time for life: The surprising ways Americans use their time*. University Park, PA: Pennsylvania State University Press).

12 Putnam, R. D. (2000). *Bowling alone*. New York: Simon & Schuster.

13 Kanazawa, S. (2002). Bowling with our imaginary friends. *Evolution and Human Behavior, 23*, 167-171.

14 Putnam, R. D. (2000). *Bowling alone*. New York: Simon & Schuster.

15 Poarch, M. T. (1997). *Civic life and work: A qualitative study of changing patterns of sociability and civic engagement in everyday life*. Unpublished doctoral dissertation, Boston University. Cited in Putnam, p. 86.

16 Putnam, R. D. (2000). *Bowling alone*. New York: Simon & Schuster.

17 Ibid.

18 Kahneman, D., Krueger, A. B., Schkade, D. A., Schwarz, N., & Stone, A. A. (2004, December 3). A survey method for characterizing daily life experience: The day reconstruction method. *Science, 306*(5702), 1776-1780.

19 Seashore, S. E. (1954). *Group cohesiveness in the industrial work group*. Ann Arbor: University of Michigan Press (as cited in Jehn, K. A., & Shah, P. P. (1997). Interpersonal relationships and task performance: An examination of mediating processes in friendship and acquaintance groups. *Journal of Personality and Social Psychology 72*(4), 775-790).

20 Argyle, M., & Furnham, A. (1983). Sources of satisfaction and conflict in long-term relationships. *Journal of Marriage and the Family, 45*, 481-493; and Hays, R. B. (1985). A longitudinal study of friendship development. *Journal of Personality and Social Psychology, 48*, 909-924 (as cited in Jehn & Shah, 1997).

21 Gottman, M. T., & Parkhurst, J. T. (1980). A developmental theory of friendship
    and acquaintanceship processes. In W. A. Collins (Ed.), *Minnesota Symposia on Child
    Psychology: Vol. 13. Development of cognition, affect, and social relations* (pp. 197-253).
    Hillsdale, NJ: Lawrence Erlbaum (as cited in Jehn & Shah, 1997).

22 Rawlins, W. K. (1989). A dialectical analysis of the tensions, functions, and strategic
    challenges of communication in young adult friendships. In J. A. Anderson (Ed.),
    Communication yearbook: Vol. 12. (pp. 157-189). Newbury Park, CA: Sage (as cited in
    Jehn & Shah, 1997).

23 Newcomb, A. F., & Brady, J. E. (1982). Mutuality in boys' friendship relations. *Child
    Development, 53,* 392-395; and Whitney, K. (1994). Improving group task performance:
    The role of group goals and group efficacy. *Human Performance, 7,* 55-78 (as cited in
    Jehn & Shah, 1997).

24 Robinson, S., & Weldon, E. (1993). Feedback seeking in groups: A theoretical
    perspective. *British Journal of Social Psychology, 32*(1), 71-86 (as cited in Jehn & Shah,
    1997).

25 The professors found no difference between friend and acquaintance groups on
    planning and monitoring the group's progress, but this may have been due to the simple,
    short-term nature of the experiment.

26 Jehn, K. A., & Shah, P. P. (1997). Interpersonal relationships and task performance: An
    examination of mediating processes in friendship and acquaintance groups. *Journal of
    Personality and Social Psychology 72*(4), 775-790.

The Eleventh Element:
Talking About Progress

1   Performance review as a stream (of consciousness?). (n.d.). Retrieved July 20, 2006, from
    http://blogs.successfactors.com/worst-review-contest/2005/11/performance_review_as_
    a_stream.html

2   Cawley, B. D., Keeping, L. M., & Levy, P. E. (1998). Participation in the performance
    appraisal process and employee reactions: A meta-analytic review of field investigations.
    Journal of Applied Psychology, 83(4), 615-633.

3   Kluger, A. N., & DeNisi, A. (1996). The effects of feedback interventions on
    performance: A historical review, a meta-analysis, and a preliminary feedback
    intervention theory. *Psychological Bulletin, 119*(2), 254-284 (as cited in Kluger, A. N., &
    Van-Dijk, D. (2005, April). *The interactive effect of feedback sign and task type on motivation
    and performance* (Technical Report 1158). Arlington, VA: United States Army Research
    Institute for the Behavioral and Social Sciences).

4   Ittner, C. D., Larcker, D. F., & Meyer, M. W. (2003). Subjectivity and the weighting
    of performance measures: Evidence from a balanced scorecard. *The Accounting Review,
    78*(3), 725-758.

5   Ibid.

6   de Koning, G. M. J. (2004, November). Evaluating employee performance (part 1).
    Gallup Management Journal. Retrieved July 20, 2006, from http://gmj.gallup.com/
    content/default.asp?ci=13891

7   Sandberg, J. (2003, March 14). Self-evaluations prompt professionals' tall
    tales. Retrieved July 20, 2006, from http://www.careerjournal.com/columnists/
    cubicleculture/20030314-cubicle.html

8   Adams, S. (1996). *The Dilbert principle: A cubicle's-eye view of bosses, meetings, management
    fads and other workplace afflictions*. New York: HarperBusiness.

9   Dunning, D., Johnson, K., Ehrlinger, J., & Kruger, J. (2003, June). Why people fail to
    recognize their own incompetence. *Current Directions in Psychological Science, 12*(3), 83-
    87.

10 Ibid.

11 Kruger, J., & Dunning, D. (1999). Unskilled and unaware of it: How difficulties in
    recognizing one's own incompetence lead to inflated self-assessments. *Journal of
    Personality and Social Psychology, 77*(6), 1121-1134.

12 Ehrlinger, J. M., Johnson, K., Banner, M., Dunning, D., & Kruger, J. (2005). *Why the
    unskilled are unaware: Further exploration of (absent) self-insight among the incompetent*.
    Manuscript submitted for publication.

13 Hodges, B., Regehr, G., & Martin, D. (2001, October). Difficulties in recognizing one's
    own incompetence: Novice physicians who are unskilled and unaware of it. *Academic
    Medicine, 76*(10), S87-S89.

14 Haun, D. E., Zeringue, A., Leach, A., & Foley, A. (2000, November). Assessing the
    competence of specimen-processing personnel. *Laboratory Medicine, 31*(11), 633-637.

15 Ehrlinger, J. M., Johnson, K., Banner, M., Dunning, D., & Kruger, J. (2005). *Why the
    unskilled are unaware: Further exploration of (absent) self-insight among the incompetent*.
    Manuscript submitted for publication.

16 Dunning, D., Johnson, K., Ehrlinger, J., & Kruger, J. (2003, June). Why people fail to
    recognize their own incompetence. *Current Directions in Psychological Science, 12*(3), 83-
    87.

17 Ibid.

18 Kluger, A. N., & Van-Dijk, D. (2005, April). *The interactive effect of feedback sign and task
    type on motivation and performance* (Technical Report 1158). Arlington, VA: United States
    Army Research Institute for the Behavioral and Social Sciences.

19 Harter, J. K. (2004, April). *Managing the human difference*. Paper presented at the 2004
    International Positive Psychology Conference, Washington, DC.

20   Gallup Workplace Poll, based on interviews with 1,009 U.S. workers, aged 18 and older, conducted in February 2002. For results based on the total sample of workers, one can say with 95% confidence that the maximum margin of sampling error is ±3 percentage points.

21   Ibid.

22   Gabris, G. T., & Ihrke, D. M. (2001, June). Does performance appraisal contribute to heightened levels of employee burnout? The results of one study. *Public Personnel Management, 30*, 157-172.

23   Gallup Workplace Poll, based on interviews with 1,003 U.S. workers, aged 18 and older, conducted in June 2006. For results based on the total sample of workers, one can say with 95% confidence that the maximum margin of sampling error is ±3 percentage points.

24   From The Gallup Organization's Employee Engagement Business Impact Database. Based on analysis of Eleventh Element scores across organizations in Gallup's database.

25   Cawley, B. D., Keeping, L. M., & Levy, P. E. (1998). Participation in the performance appraisal process and employee reactions: A meta-analytic review of field investigations. *Journal of Applied Psychology, 83*(4), 615-633.

26   Ryan, R. M., & Deci, E. L. (2000, January). Self-determination theory and the facilitation of intrinsic motivation, social development, and well-being. *American Psychologist, 55*(1), 68-78.

27   Ittner, C. D., Larcker, D. F., & Meyer, M. W. (2003). Subjectivity and the weighting of performance measures: Evidence from a balanced scorecard. *The Accounting Review, 78*(3), 725-758.

The Twelfth Element:
Opportunities to Learn and Grow

1   Manuel, D. (1990, March 11). *Oh, the places you'll go!* [Review of the book *Oh, the places you'll go!*]. *The New York Times*, Section 7, p. 29.

2   Shrieves, L. (1990, February 11). A call for the young to explore [Review of the book *Oh, the places you'll go!*]. *Orlando Sentinel*, p. F10.

3   Ibid.

4   Maslow, A. (1943). A theory of human motivation. *Psychological Review, 50*(4), 370-396.

5   Ryan, R. M., & Deci, E. L. (2000, January). Self-determination theory and the facilitation of intrinsic motivation, social development, and well-being. *American Psychologist, 55*(1), 68-78.

6   Spreitzer, G., Sutcliffe, K., Dutton, J., Sonenshein, S., & Grant, A. M. (2005). *Thriving at work.* Manuscript submitted for publication.

7   Fredrickson, B. L., & Losada, M. F. (2005, October). Positive affect and the complex dynamics of human flourishing. *American Psychologist, 60*(7), 678-686.

8   Roberts, L. M., Dutton, J. E., Spreitzer, G. M., Heaphy, E. D., & Quinn, R. E. (2005). Composing the reflected best-self portrait: Building pathways for becoming extraordinary in work organizations. *The Academy of Management Review, 30*(4), 712-736.

9   Career. (n.d.). *MSN Encarta Dictionary.* Retrieved July 21, 2006, from http://encarta.msn.com/dictionary_1861594952/career.html, emphasis added.

10 Gallup Workplace Poll, based on telephone interviews with a nationally representative sample of 1,003 employed adults, aged 18 and older, conducted in June 2006. *For results based on the total sample of employed adults, one can say with 95% confidence that the maximum error attributable to sampling and other random effects is ±3 percentage points.* Similar patterns are observed in surveys of other countries.

11 Ryan, R. M., & Deci, E. L. (2000, January). Self-determination theory and the facilitation of intrinsic motivation, social development, and well-being. *American Psychologist, 55*(1), 68-78.

12 Urry, H. L., Nitschke, J. B., Dolski, I., Jackson, D. C., Dalton, K. M., Mueller, C. J., et al. (2004, June). Making a life worth living: Neural correlates of well-being. *Psychological Science, 15*(6), 367-372.

13 Heath, C., Larrick, R. P., & Wu, G. (1999). Goals as reference points. *Cognitive Psychology, 38*, 79-109.

14 Locke, E. A., & Latham, G. P. (2002, September). Building a practically useful theory of goal setting and task motivation. *American Psychologist, 57*(9), 705-717.

15 Ibid.

16 Seinfeld, J. (Executive Producer). (1998). *Jerry Seinfeld live on Broadway: I'm telling you for the last time.* [DVD]. United States: Columbus 81 Productions (HBO Home Video).

17 Medvec, V. H., Madey, S. F., & Gilovich, T. (1995). When less is more: Counterfactual thinking and satisfaction among Olympic athletes. *Journal of Personality and Social Psychology, 69*(4), 603-610.

18 Tykocinski, O. E. (2001). I never had a chance: Using hindsight tactics to mitigate disappointments. *Personality and Social Psychology Bulletin, 27*, 376-382.

19 Overall, fewer than one in four U.S. workers strongly agrees that their current job brings out their most creative ideas. For those with opportunities to learn and grow, the ratio jumps to more than half. But the Twelfth Element is particularly interactive with the Third and Seventh. For employees who feel they are in the right jobs, whose opinions are valued, and have opportunities to learn and grow, the number of employees who feel their jobs bring out their most creative ideas jumps to nearly two-thirds. Employees with learning and growing opportunities, but absent the Third and Seventh elements, fall back to near the base level of approximately one-fourth on creativity. Learning opportunities without the right fit and open dialogue may represent the difference between mere training and real growth.

20   Wagner, R., & Saad, L. (2000, June 8). Traffic not a major problem for majority of Americans. *The Gallup Poll*. Retrieved July 21, 2006, from http://poll.gallup.com/content/default.aspx?ci=2833

21   Orwell, G. (1954). Why I write. In *A collection of essays by George Orwell*. Garden City, NY: Doubleday.

22   Fredrickson, B. L., & Losada, M. F. (2005, October). Positive affect and the complex dynamics of human flourishing. *American Psychologist, 60*(7), 678-686.

23   Ryan, R. M., & Deci, E. L. (2000, January). Self-determination theory and the facilitation of intrinsic motivation, social development, and well-being. *American Psychologist, 55*(1), 68-78.

24   Ibid.

25   Knowles, M. S., Holton III, E. F., & Swanson, R. A. (1998). *The adult learner* (5th ed.). Woburn, MA: Butterworth-Heinemann.

26   Keyes, C. L. M. (2002). The mental health continuum: From languishing to flourishing in life. *Journal of Health and Social Behavior, 43*, 207-222.

27   Begley, Sharon. "Old Brains Don't Work That Badly After All, Especially Trained Ones" *The Wall Street Journal*; March 3, 2006; page B-1.

28   Harter, J. K., Schmidt, F. L., Killham, E. A., & Asplund, J. W. (2006, March). *Q12 meta-analysis*. Omaha, NE: The Gallup Organization. See also Harter, J. K., Schmidt, F. L., & Killham, E. A. (2003, July). *Employee engagement, satisfaction, and business-unit-level outcomes: a meta-analysis*. Omaha, NE: The Gallup Organization; and Harter, J. K., Hayes, T. L., & Schmidt, F. L. (2004). *Meta-analytic predictive validity of Gallup Selection Research Instruments*. Omaha, NE: The Gallup Organization.
Harter et al 2006, Harter, Schmidt & Killham (2003) Employee Engagement Meta-Analysis, Gallup Technical Paper, Harter et al 2004.

29   *Kingfisher plc Interim Report 2005/06*. (n.d.). Retrieved July 21, 2006, from http://www.kingfisher.com/files/english/downloads/interimreport05.pdf

An Element Unto Itself:
The Problem of Pay

1   Toynbee, P. (2006, April 21). Throw open the books so that we can see what everyone earns. *The Guardian*, p. 33. Retrieved July 21, 2006, from http://www.guardian.co.uk/commentisfree/story/0,,1758105,00.html

2   Guido Fawkes' blog of plots, rumours, & conspiracy. (2006, April 22). Retrieved July 21, 2006, from http://5thnovember.blogspot.com/2006/04/polly-hypocrisy.html

3   Frank, R. H. (1999). *Luxury fever: Why money fails to satisfy in an era of excess*. New York: Free Press (as cited in Van Boven & Gilovich, 2003).

4   Kahneman, D., Krueger, A. B., Schkade, D., Schwarz, N., & Stone, A. A. (2006, June 30). Would you be happier if you were richer? A focusing illusion. *Science, 312*(5782), 1908-1910.

5   Gallup Poll, based on telephone interviews with a nationally representative sample of 564 employed adults, aged 18 and older, conducted August 8-11, 2005. For results based on the total sample of employed adults, one can say with 95% confidence that the maximum error attributable to sampling and other random effects is ±5 percentage points.

6   Sim, V., Bakke, D., Kay, I., & Tulgan, B. (2001, May). What should Hank do about the salary debacle? *Harvard Business Review, 79*(5), 44-49. Bakke, then CEO of AES Corporation, wrote that AES employees were better able to set their own salaries only after they received feedback from colleagues and managers.

7   Morgeson, F. P., Campion, M. A., & Maertz, C. P. (2001, Fall). Understanding pay satisfaction: The limits of a compensation system implementation. *Journal of Business and Psychology, 16*(1), 133-149.

8   Deci, E. L., Koestner, R., & Ryan, R. M. (1999). A meta-analytic review of experiments examining the effects of extrinsic rewards on intrinsic motivation. *Psychological Bulletin, 125*(6), 627-668.

9   Gneezy, U., & Rustichini, A. (2000). Pay enough or don't pay at all. *Quarterly Journal of Economics, 115*, 791-810 (as cited in Sliwka, D. (2003, August). *On the hidden costs of incentive schemes* (IZA Discussion Paper No. 844). Bonn, Germany: Institute for the Study of Labor).

10 Titmuss, R. M. (1971). *The gift relationship: From human blood to social policy*. New York: Pantheon; also presented in Abel-Smith, B., & Titmuss, K. (Eds.). (1987). *The philosophy of welfare: Selected writings by Richard M. Titmuss*. London: Allen & Unwin (as cited in Levitt & Dubner (2005)). See also Upton, W. E. (1973). *Altruism, attribution, and intrinsic motivation in the recruitment of blood donors*. Unpublished doctoral dissertation, Cornell University, Ithaca, NY.

11 Levitt, S. D., & Dubner, S. J. (2005). *Freakonomics: A rogue economist explores the hidden side of everything*. New York: HarperCollins.

12 On average, workers who are paid for the quality and quantity of their work are more highly engaged than those who are not paid for their performance. The key to pay-for-performance strategies is not whether they are used, but how they are managed. From an analysis of a Gallup Workplace Poll, based on interviews with 1,003 U.S. workers, aged 18 and older, conducted in April 2004. For results based on the total sample of workers, one can say with 95% confidence that the maximum margin of sampling error is ±3 percentage points.

13 Sliwka, D. (2003, August). *On the hidden costs of incentive schemes* (IZA Discussion Paper No. 844). Bonn, Germany: Institute for the Study of Labor.

14 McCracken, J. (2006, March 1). Detroit's symbol of dysfunction: Paying employees not to work. *The Wall Street Journal*, p. A1.

15 Solnick, S. J., & Hemenway, D. (1998). Is more always better?: A survey on positional concerns. *Journal of Economic Behavior & Organization, 37*, 373-383.

16   U.S. Securities and Exchange Commission. (n.d.). *Executive compensation: A guide for investors*. Retrieved July 26, 2006, from http://www.sec.gov/investor/pubs/execomp0803. htm#ecfiling

Follow the "named executive officers" link to get the detail on CEO + 4 rule. The key paragraph in the first page is this:

The Summary Compensation Table is the cornerstone of the SEC's required disclosure on executive compensation. The Summary Compensation Table provides, in a single location, a comprehensive overview of a company's executive pay practices. The Summary Compensation Table sets forth the actual compensation paid by the company to each of the named executive officers during the last three completed fiscal years.

17   Norris, F. (2006, June 2). Which bosses really care if shares rise? *The New York Times*, p. C1.
18   Clark, H. (2006, April 20). Whole Foods: Spinning CEO pay. *Forbes*. Retrieved July 21, 2006, from http://www.forbes.com/2006/04/20/john-mackey-pay_cx_hc_06ceo_ 0420wholefoods.html
19   Conniff, R. (2005). *The ape in the corner office: Understanding the workplace beast in all of us*. New York: Crown Business.
20   Adams, S. (2005, October 29). *Dilbert* (comic strip). Distributed by United Features Syndicate.
21   Parade editorial calendar: Special issues (n.d.). *Parade*. Retrieved July 21, 2006, from http://mediakit.parade.com/edit_calendar/cal_specials.html
22   Sandberg, J. (2006, June 20). Why you may regret looking at papers left on the office copier. *The Wall Street Journal*, p. B1.
23   Brosnan, S. F., & de Waal, F. B. M. (2003, September 18). Monkeys reject unequal pay. *Nature, 425*, 297-299.
24   de Waal, F. B. M. (2005, April). How animals do business. *Scientific American, 292*, 72-79.
25   Dulebohn, J. H., & Martocchio, J. J. (1998). Employee perceptions of the fairness of work group incentive pay plans. *Journal of Management, 24*(4), p. 469-488.
26   Case, J. (2001, May 1). When salaries aren't secret. *Harvard Business Review, 79*(5), 37-49.
27   Pfeffer, J. (1998, May-June). Six dangerous myths about pay. *Harvard Business Review, 76*(3), 109-119.
28   Van Boven, L., & Gilovich, T. (2003). To do or to have? That is the question. *Journal of Personality and Social Psychology, 85*(6), 1193-1202.
29   Fehr, E., & Gächter, S. (1997, September). Reciprocity and economics: The economic implications of *homo reciprocans*. Switzerland: University of Zurich Institute for Empirical Economic Research.
30   Camerer, C. F. (2003). *Behavioral game theory: Experiments in strategic interaction*. Princeton, NJ: Princeton University Press.

A Final Note:
The Heart of Great Managing

1   Results of these surveys are based on nationally representative samples of about 1,000 employed adults aged 18 and older. Interviews were conducted by The Gallup Organization by telephone quarterly from October 2000 to October 2002, then semi-annually thereafter. For results based on samples of this size, one can say with 95% confidence that the maximum error attributable to sampling and other random effects is ±3 percentage points. For findings based on subgroups, the sampling error would be greater.

Acknowledgements

A book of this nature requires the dedication of many more people than just its authors. The discoveries behind the 12 Elements and the massive amount of fieldwork that created the employee engagement database are the work product of hundreds of Gallup professionals spanning a decade and a half. We are deeply indebted to them, and privileged to represent their discoveries in this volume.

This book would not have been written without the early and persistent advocacy of Gallup Press Publisher Larry Emond. Geoff Brewer was an insightful and patient editor who helped us separate baby from bathwater, rendering a volume that is more enjoyable to read and more considerate of the readers' time than our original draft. Several of the stories told here first appeared in the *Gallup Management Journal*, and thus benefited greatly from the surgical use of a red pen by Barb Sanford. Mark Stiemann questioned, verified, and improved upon our factual assertions. Paul Petters brought to the task of copy-editing the essential fastidiousness we disregarded in the rush to get ideas on the page.

As the project manager, Rachel Johanowicz ensured that production of the book was always on track and on schedule. Chin-Yee Lai designed the book's powerful cover, and Molly Hardin created the attractive and easy-to-read layout.

The quality of the book would have suffered, or the book would have been published far later, were it not for the work of Heather Totin. Secondary research, travel schedules, interview appointments, manuscript drafts, and early reviewers' comments all intersected at her desk and computer. The assistance of Rachel Brown in the early stages gave the book a solid head start. Jake Sever kept the computers, software, and network running to avoid any Second Element issues in the writing. Many of the interviews for this book were recorded for accuracy by the authors and were meticulously transcribed by Jennie Glass, in our opinion the best transcriber in the world.

Our colleagues Angie Ballinger and Janet Kaiser were crucial in preparing the profile of Nancy Sorrells. The profile of Enio Wetten would not have been possible without the collaboration of Fabricio Drummond, who cheerfully helped a gringo knowing just 25 words of Portuguese get through São Paulo traffic and to Rio Claro, without (although just barely) running out of ethanol. Ken Royal was instrumental in identifying the Stryker and Owens Corning managers profiled in Chapters 3 and 4.

In Kwidzyn, Poland, we handed a reporter's notebook to Aleksander Wawer of the Gallup Warsaw office and witnessed him juggle translations and note-taking like a bilingual journalist with years of experience. In addition to his usual responsibilities putting the draft manuscript to the test and getting it to the presses, Associate Publisher Dr. Piotr Juszkiewicz conducted the initial interview with Elżbieta Górska-Kołodziejczyk in her native language, laying the groundwork for everything that followed. Our colleague Denise McLain helped find Górska within the list of high-scoring managers, and gave us valuable reaction to the draft manuscript.

Debra Manning, Ph.D., instructed Rodd to call her "Dr. Deb," which he took as an invited term of endearment until he found out she prefers that moniker from those she finds most bothersome. Whether for the greater good or just to make us go away, she helped us tremendously with the profiles in Chapters 5 and 8, and also shared her advice on the manuscript.

Steve Ruedisili and Patrick Bogart conducted a number of early interviews with Peter Wamsteeker and his team at Cargill, leading to the moment they approached us and said, "You've got to meet this guy!" Indeed we did. Allyson Cain of the Toronto office was instrumental in bringing to our attention the accomplishments of Susan Jewell at the Hospital for Sick Children.

The story in India was made possible because of the initial fieldwork of our colleague Rajesh Srinivasan, who visited shortly after the turn-around, and the planning of Irfana Khan from the Bangalore office. We also wish to thank Leo Mobi, our indefatigable guide in India.

Leslie Rowlands of the London office helped make arrangements for us to interview and visit Philippe Lescornez's team in Brussels and Simon Gaier's store in Wrexham, but failed to remind us that everyone in England and Wales drives on the left side of the road.

The manuscript benefited tremendously from the insights and encouragement of many patient confidantes who reviewed the initial draft, among them Lee Broadston, Bette Curd, Jim Clifton, Bob Dean, Dr. John Dykes, Sherry and Eldin Ehrlich, Robert E. Gordon Sr., Steve Grizzell, Elyse Harris, Denise McLain, Greg Murray, Connie Rath, Tom Rath, and Jessica Tyler. We also deeply appreciate the readers of the *Gallup Management Journal* who took the time to read a partial manuscript and give us their unvarnished assessments, many of which led to substantial improvements in the text. We thank David Osborne for his leadership in gathering this important feedback.

We have been honored to work with a team of some of the most insightful scientists in the world. Among them, we particularly thank Jim Asplund, Raksha Arora, Dr. Sangeeta Badal, James Court-Smith, Dee Drozd, Dr. John Fleming, Julie Hawkins, Dr. Ted Hayes, Jon Hughes, Emily Killham, Dr. Deb Manning, Dr. Gale Muller, Sujatha Mukandan, Marco Nink, Eric Olesen, Dr. Glenn Phelps, John Reimnitz, Dr. Frank Schmidt, Dr. Steve Schulz, Dr. Steve Sireci, Dr. Joseph Streur, and Yongwei Yang. All made discoveries that have influenced our thinking.

We thank our colleagues who have built the largest and most unique database of workplace opinion in the world: Dr. Sangeeta Badal, Chad Davis, Steph Davis, Brian Dawson Dan Hale, Kerri Janzen, Doug Little, Glenda Nelson, Chad Piening, Stephanie Plowman, Gary Simpson,

Ryan Steeves, and Mandy Unterbrink. Tim Dean and the Gallup team of interviewers have managed the fielding of numerous workplace polls over the years, the source of many insights.

The history of the 12 Elements discovery dates back many decades. A team of intelligent and determined colleagues spent countless hours setting the historical record straight: Tom Bender, Jim Boudreau, Mary Kay Brown, Frank Conley, Dr. David Day Michael Dever, Craig Elson, Susan Ferrare, Molly Hanford, Coleen Jones, Dr. Tim Judge, Joe Kwiatkowski, Brian McCormick, Steve O'Brien, Sheila Owens, Evan Perkins, Reggie Poole, Shari Schneider, Arthur Schwab, Danielle Siciliano, Marguerite Walsh, and Paul Weiner.

In memory, we thank Dr. Donald O. Clifton, whose theory and discoveries continue to inspire our curiosity and passion about the importance of the workplace. Jim is deeply grateful to him for his 17 years of mentorship. Rachel Penrod was indispensable to Jim's work on this book, managing his schedule, organizing his work life, and providing a positive atmosphere at work every day. Given Jim's profession, his wife, RaLinda, may endure more test questions than any of Gallup's millions of respondents. She has been infinitely patient with his frequent travel and his lack of attentiveness to immediate surroundings when he is thinking about research. Jeri and Rick Price, Ken and Dorothy Harter, and Sandy and Bob Dean were, true to form, especially supportive and encouraging during the researching and writing of the book.

Rodd is indebted to Dr. Gale Muller for helping to clear a path through consulting responsibilities to allow the completion of the book. He would also like to thank James E. Shelledy, former editor of *The Salt Lake Tribune*; and Angus H. Twombly, former vice president of marketing for the *Portland Press Herald* and the *Maine Sunday Telegram*; for epitomizing the principles described in this book to an impressionable future author. Rodd's wife, Nora, and their children Noelle, Parks, and Charlie Wagner were incredibly understanding and, with time, vigilant. No family should have to spend a Minnesota winter warning each other "Don't go in there! He's writing!" but they bore up well under the pressure.

Most of all, we wish to thank the many managers and employees, named and unnamed, who submitted to what must have seemed interminable questions, who hesitated to speak openly about some of the most challenging times in their lives, but did so in the hope that what they learned would help readers of this book create better places to work.

About the Authors

Rodd Wagner is a principal of The Gallup Organization. Upon joining the company in 1999, he gravitated toward the study of high-performing managers and how human nature affects business strategy. At Gallup, Wagner interprets employee engagement and business performance data for numerous Fortune 500 companies. Wagner was formerly the research director for the *Portland Press Herald* and *Maine Sunday Telegram*; a reporter and news editor for *The Salt Lake Tribune*; and a radio talk show host. He holds an M.B.A. from the University of Utah Graduate School of Business. Wagner, his wife, Nora, and their three children live near Minneapolis, Minnesota.

James K. Harter, Ph.D., is chief scientist for The Gallup Organization's international workplace management practice. He has authored or co-authored more than 1,000 research studies for profit and non-profit organizations. Some of this research has been popularized in the business bestsellers *First, Break All the Rules*, and *How Full is Your Bucket?*, and in academic articles, book chapters, and publications such as *USA Today*, *The Wall Street Journal* and *The New York Times*. He is co-author of "Manage Your Human Sigma," published in the *Harvard Business Review*. Harter has worked for The Gallup Organization since 1985, and lives in Omaha, Nebraska, with his wife, RaLinda, and their two sons.

Learn More

To stay up-to-date on the latest research and insights into the 12 Elements of Great Managing, visit the *Gallup Management Journal* at http://gmj.Gallup.com, where Rodd Wagner, Jim Harter, Ph.D., and other management experts regularly contribute articles and manager profiles.

Readers of *12* can receive a six-month trial subscription to the *Gallup Management Journal*. Simply go to:

http://commerce.gallup.com/ma/code/,
then follow these instructions:

- If you already have a Gallup membership, enter your username and password, then click "Log In."

- If you do not have a Gallup membership, click "Create an Account" and enter the required information. Click "Submit Registration," then log in to continue. Enter your username and password, then click "Log In."

- Enter the six-month promotional code **12GreatManager**, then click "Continue."

- Review your order and click "Submit Order" if the information is correct.

For questions or assistance, e-mail galluphelp@gallup.com

Gallup Press exists to educate and inform the people who govern, manage, teach, and lead the world's six billion citizens. Each book meets The Gallup Organization's requirements of integrity, trust, and independence and is based on Gallup-approved science and research.